A Lender's Guide To

ENVIRONMENTAL LIABILITY MANAGEMENT

THOMAS M. MISSIMER

Missimer International, Inc.

LEWIS PUBLISHERS

Boca Raton New York London Tokyo

Acquiring Editor:	Ken McCombs
Project Editor:	Les Kaplan
Marketing Manager:	Greg Daurelle
Direct Marketing Manager:	Arline Massey
Cover Design:	Dawn Boyd
PrePress:	Greg Cuciak
Manufacturing:	Sherri Schwartz

Library of Congress Cataloging-in-Publication Data

Missimer, T. M.
A lender's guide to environmental liability management / Thomas M. Missimer.
p. cm.
Includes bibliographical references and index.
ISBN 0-87371-994-8
1. Liability for environmental damages—United States. 2. Lender liability—United States. I. Title.
KF1298.M57 1996
346.73′073—dc20
[347.30673] 95-53806
CIP

International Standard Book Number 0-87371-994-8
Library of Congress Card Number 95-53806
Printed in the United States of America 1 2 3 4 5 6 7 8 9 0
Printed on acid-free paper

To the memory of my grandmother,
Mary Catherine Missimer
(1902–1995)

PREFACE

Environmental issues in America emerged as a national priority in the 1960s and early 1970s. With the founding of the U.S. Environmental Protection Agency as an independent agency on December 2, 1970, and with the discovery of numerous environmental problems, ranging from air pollution to fouled waters to the disappearance of many common species of plants and animals, the American people demanded that more attention be focused on cleaning up our environment. The demands of the people and a series of well-publicized national environmental disasters led to the passage of federal laws with serious consequences to environmental polluters and to the business community.

Perhaps the most draconian laws creating environmental liabilities to the business community were the Comprehensive Environmental Response, Compensation, and Liability Act (1980) and the Superfund Amendment and Reauthorization Act (1986). From a pragmatic viewpoint, these laws shifted the responsibility for the enforcement of environmental laws, particularly in the area of contamination with toxic and hazardous substances, from the federal and state enforcement agencies to bankers and various other financial institutions. One might ask why the enforcement burden and financial responsibility were placed on lending institutions. The answer is quite simple and is best stated by the infamous bank robber Willie Sutton. When asked why he robbed only banks, Sutton stated, "because that's where the money is."

It is very important for the modern financial institution and its employees to understand fully the environmental liabilities facing the lender each day. These liabilities can be managed, allowing the institution to operate without unnecessary exposure to financial losses; at the same time, opportunities for new areas of lending can be opened. This text is written primarily for the lender and those professionals who deal regularly with lenders, such as realtors, investors, and environmental consultants. The text is intended to increase the understanding of all professionals involved in the process; therefore, the use of technical jargon is minimized. No equations are used in the text, therefore, assuming that the theories of groundwater flow and contamination transport can be explained to all professionals without the use of detailed mathematics.

Thomas M. Missimer
Fort Myers, Florida
October, 1995

ACKNOWLEDGMENTS

Many lenders, attorneys, scientists, and engineers contributed either directly or indirectly to the contents of this book. The entire manuscript was reviewed for technical content and editorial correction by Richard L. Holzinger, executive vice-president and chief financial officer of Missimer International, Inc. Technical reviews of the entire manuscript were provided by Trey Beeson, vice-president of environmental services, Missimer International, Inc. and Douglas Widmer, environmental consultant (former administrator of environmental site assessments with ViroGroup, Inc.). Technical reviews of Chapters 5, 6, and 7 were provided by Robert Maliva, Ph.D., senior scientist with Missimer International, Inc. Chapter 8 was reviewed by Richard W. Workman, president of Coastplan, Inc. Chapters 2, 6, and 7 were reviewed by Terry Lewis, Esquire of Lewis, Longman & Walker of West Palm Beach, Florida. Terri Jacobsen, Esquire of Morgan, Lewis & Bockius, Miami, Florida provided literature and assistance on some legal issues. James L. Kammert, Esquire, director of Credit Policy, Environmental Legal Officer, and Administration, Barnett Banks, Inc., contributed literature and various concepts and ideas. Joe Swiger, radon consultant, provided information on current radon gas assessment practices.

The manuscript was read for editorial correctness and word processed by Linda Kraczon with Missimer International, Inc. Certain photographs in Chapter 5 were taken by Jerry Bedan with Missimer International, Inc.

THE AUTHOR

Thomas M. Missimer is president and principal hydrogeologist of Missimer International, Inc., a groundwater and environmental consulting firm. Mr. Missimer received a B.A. degree in geology from Franklin & Marshall College in 1972 and a M.S. degree in geology from Florida State University in 1973. He is completing his Ph.D. in marine geology and geophysics at the Rosenstiel School of Marine and Atmospheric Science, University of Miami.

For nearly 20 years, Mr. Missimer has worked as an environmental consultant and as a consultant to many different lending institutions, assisting them in the management of environmental liability problems. He served on the national steering committee on environmental site assessments for the Association of Ground Water Scientists and Engineers. He has published over a hundred papers in journals, guidebooks, and proceedings of various conferences. In addition he has published another book, entitled *Water Supply Development for Membrane Water Treatment Facilities* (1995, Lewis Publishers).

Mr. Missimer serves on a number of advisory and governmental committees. He was appointed by Florida Governor Lawton Chiles and confirmed by the Florida Senate to a 3-year term as a member of the Florida Board of Professional Geologists, on which he served as vice-chairman and chairman. He also serves as vice-chairman of the Technical Advisory Committee to the Governor's Commission for a Sustainable South Florida. He has been elected chairman of the geology and hydrology section of the Florida Academy of Sciences for the years 1976, 1977, and 1995.

Mr. Missimer is a groundwater professional, certified by the Association of Ground Water Scientists and Engineers, a hydrogeologist, certified by the American Institute of Hydrology, and a certified geologist by the American Institute of Geologists. He is licensed as a professional geologist in several states and is a member of numerous scientific organizations, including the Geological Society of America and the American Water Works Association.

TABLE OF CONTENTS

Chapter 7

Chapter 8

Appendices

LIST OF TABLES

LIST OF FIGURES

1 AN INTRODUCTION TO ENVIRONMENTAL LIABILITIES AND HOW TO USE THIS BOOK

For centuries lending institutions have operated under the basic precepts of common law and with common sense. Historically, the basic function of the lending institution, being a place in which to save and from which to borrow money, was the primary business until the mid-nineteenth century, when it began to pursue other areas of business. The evolution of the industry changed its exposure to environmental liability from the basic risk involving the inability of a borrower to repay a loan to a quagmire of liabilities going far beyond simple loan exposure.

Despite the passage of federal, state, and local legislation creating these environmental liabilities, federal bank regulators followed the ingenious policy of generally ignoring the exposure problem until 1993. It is interesting to note that many well-managed lending institutions developed environmental liability policies long before they were required to do so. On February 25, 1993, the Director of the Federal Deposit Insurance Corporation, Stanley J. Poling, transmitted a letter with an attachment entitled "Guidelines for an Environmental Risk Program" (see Table 4.2) to the chief executive officers of member banks in the United States. The text of this letter reads as follows:

> A lending institution should have in place appropriate safeguards and controls to limit exposure to potential environmental liability associated with real property held as collateral. The attached guidelines contain information and recommendations about implementing an environmental risk program, that can be tailored to the needs of the lending institution. Examiners will review the institutions's compliance with its own environmental risk program as part of the examination of the lending and investment activities.

The curious wording of this letter clearly suggests that an environmental risk program should be adopted, but it avoids the words *must* or *required* or any other term that actually mandates that a program be implemented. One could interpret the letter to suggest that if an institution does not have a policy, then it must be in full compliance with its own policy. The point here is that the federal government is not about to protect a lending institution from environmental liability. In fact, rather than protect a lending institution, the U.S. Environmental Protection Agency would just as soon extract as many assets as possible from an institution in order to help clean up contamination problems. Protection of lending institutions from environmental liabilities is the sole responsibility of the owners and management of the institution. Control of exposure to environmental liabilities is simply good business practice.

WHAT ARE THE TYPES OF ENVIRONMENTAL LIABILITIES?

The general history of environmental legislation with regard to pollution control and correction followed a course related to the easy observation, detection, or reaction to irritation caused by the problem. The first concern to generate a public outcry was air pollution, because it was readily apparent and it tended to smell bad. The next area of public attention was surface-water pollution, because again it was directly observable and caused problems with drinking water and recreational use of surface-water bodies. The last area of public attention was the pollution of groundwater, which was ignored for many years, simply because it was not directly observable and was not apparent until the problem entered a source of drinking water supply. Although groundwater pollution was the last problem to gain public attention, it is the problem that has caused the lender the largest number of headaches and expenses.

The acquisition of property containing contaminated soil or groundwater is the primary issue covered in this text. There are a number of ways that a lending institution can become responsible for soil and/or groundwater cleanup costs in addition to the potential loss of asset value or collateral. The issue of contamination can extend beyond simply the cost of the cleanup. If the contamination causes either real or perceived damage to a third party, a lender may face additional financial liabilities and, in certain cases, potential criminal penalties. The lender usually does not have fee simple title to a property, but has a security interest, normally limiting the liabilities solely to the value of the loan. However, the lender can be exposed to the full liability for contamination cleanup by becoming the owner/operator of a site, as in the case of accepting administration of a trust or as a result of foreclosure. Also, there has been a court ruling that a lender can become responsible for contamination if the lender exerts direct influence on the decision-making process of a business (Fleet Factors case, see Chapter 2). Exposure to the cleanup of contamination can be minimized without unduly interfering in the management of an operating company.

Lenders face other environmental liabilities in addition to those arising from soil and groundwater contamination. The issue of wetlands protection and sovereign lands (use of tidal wetlands) can significantly affect the use and value of real property. The occurrence of endangered species and unique or endangered habitat also influences property values and utilization potential. Within existing structures, the use of toxic or hazardous building materials, such as asbestos or urea fiberboard, can create indirect liability to a lender or, in the case of institution-owned structures, it can cause direct liability for public exposure. Additional liabilities can be created by the occurrence of radon gas and other indoor air quality problems within existing structures, thereby exposing a lender to indirect, direct, and/or third party liabilities. Because of recent public attention, the environmental liabilities associated with human exposure to electromagnetic fields (electric power lines) have also become an issue for lenders to assess and understand. All of these issues are discussed in some detail in this text. Each environmental issue must be evaluated by the lender in terms of the perceptions and realities of the associated liabilities.

HOW TO USE THIS BOOK

All lenders and professionals dealing with lenders need to be knowledgeable with regard to the realities of environmental liabilities. Many lenders fear the environmental liabilities associated with particular transactions and tend to avoid the deals. The purpose of this book is to help the lender confront the issues with the knowledge necessary to make informed decisions that would benefit borrowers and improve the profits of the institution. This book was written to serve both as an educational tool and as a desktop reference to find either an answer to a specific problem or a suggestion for a general procedure. Often the most important question facing the lender is what thought process is necessary to make a decision on whether to proceed with or decline a financial deal. The informed lender has more options available to save deals plagued with some environmental problem as compared to the uninformed lender, who may prematurely reject a potentially profitable deal.

This book is organized into an introduction, seven text chapters, and an appendix. Chapters 2 and 3 are included for informational purposes and general education. Chapter 2 covers the environmental liabilities created by the passage of major federal legislation that directly or indirectly affects lending institutions. There is a clear explanation of how the lender can become entangled in these environmental liabilities. Chapter 3 gives an introduction to the subject of soil and groundwater contamination. It includes an explanation of how to recognize contamination in terms of definitions and practicalities. There is an explanation of how groundwater flows and transports contamination. The chapter ends with a general discussion of contamination containment and cleanup methods. Chapter 4 addresses the subject of environmental policy for lending institutions. It includes the key elements that should be included in the policy and how to construct an environmental policy manual. Chapter 5 is a detailed explanation of "due diligence" and the methods used to minimize lending institution exposure to environmental liabilities. This includes a discussion about types of transactions that should require environmental "due diligence" investigation and the level of effort and expense necessary to minimize environmental liability exposure. The transaction screening process (TSP) and phase I environmental site assessment methodologies are explained in detail. Chapter 6 is perhaps the most important part of the text for all lenders to read. This chapter gives some suggested procedures to deal with a contamination problem once it is discovered. Chapter 7 offers some warnings on how lenders can become entangled with environmental liabilities by simply managing a trust or exerting influence over management of an operating company. Chapter 8 covers a variety of environmental issues that may or may not be investigated during a phase I environmental site assessment. These issues include wetlands, sovereign lands, asbestos and clean indoor air, radon gas, endangered species and unique habitat, and electromagnetic fields. Finally, the appendix provides a table listing some common soil and groundwater pollutants with the associated business or manufacturing type. This table may be very useful to lenders making loans to industries with which they have little experience or knowledge. The remaining appendices consist of some sample lending agreements and contracts.

All of the chapters in this book are broken down into third order (or fourth order in Chapter 4) subheadings to facilitate the reader's ability to readily locate the subject of interest. There are a series of references and a list of additional published materials at the end of each chapter to allow readers to obtain additional information if they so desire. The index of the book is rather detailed, again to allow the easy location of a particular subject.

2 ENVIRONMENTAL LAW AND THE LENDER

Environmental awareness in the United States inspired the passage by Congress of an entire series of environmental laws during the 1970s and 1980s. These laws were designed to reduce and regulate pollution, to maintain or improve the environment, and to save certain unique environmental features. All of these laws affect the lender to some degree by jeopardizing the ability of a borrower to repay the principal on a loan, by jeopardizing the collateral equity, or possibly by creating direct and unexpected liability for the lender. All lenders should be aware of the types of liabilities that are created by each law and how to best manage these potential liabilities. Environmental liabilities affect virtually all real property transactions, the acceptance and management of trusts, acquisitions by the lending institution, and even loans made to businesses by lending institutions.

The discussions of the laws and court decisions in this chapter are not legal opinions and are based on current analyses of legal scholars and authors. These analyses are presented to help the lender understand the basic concepts of the laws and how the courts are interpreting them. If a lender requires a legal opinion regarding any of the laws or court cases discussed, the opinion should be obtained from a qualified environmental attorney.

LIABILITY FOR SOIL AND GROUNDWATER CONTAMINATION

Perhaps the most ominous set of laws affecting lending institutions are those related to soil and groundwater contamination. All real estate transactions involve some level of exposure to the environmental liabilities created under these laws. This exposure is not limited to a standard sale or purchase, but goes far beyond simple transactions to include the management of trusts, leases, and asset and stock purchases. The presence of contamination on or beneath a property represents an enormous financial burden for the land owner, whether the owner is a corporation, an individual, or a lending institution. The laws place the burden primarily on the polluter, but any entity in the chain of title could become responsible for some or all of the cleanup costs. As an example of the potential financial burden, the current cost of investigating a Superfund contamination site prior to initiation of any cleanup activities commonly ranges above $10 million per site. Costs to assess and clean up other more common contamination problems, such as those associated with leaking underground fuel storage tanks, currently are averaging over $200,000 per site.

The primary federal laws that form the legal basis for liabilities arising from soil and groundwater contamination include

- the Comprehensive Environmental Response, Compensation and Liability Act of 1980 (known as "CERCLA" or "Superfund"), as amended by the Superfund Amendments and Reauthorization Act of 1986 ("SARA"), which is in 42 U.S.C., Section 9601
- the Resource Conservation and Recovery Act of 1976 (known as "RCRA"), which is found in 42 U.S.C., Section 6901
- the Underground Storage Tank Program, RCRA Subtitle I, found in U.S.C., Section 6991

These federal laws were adopted by many states in their current form, but individual states have passed additional laws covering the same issues, with some being stricter than the federal laws. Some local government programs have also passed laws and ordinances that provide an additional layer of liability. The jurisdiction for enforcement of these laws has been delegated to some states under primacy agreements, and some states have delegated the lead responsibility to local governments. All levels of government may be involved to some degree in complex contamination problems.

Regulation of Contamination Under CERCLA

The Comprehensive Environmental Response, Compensation, and Liability Act (CERCLA) has been described by many legal analysts as one of the most "draconian" laws ever passed by Congress. The clear objective of Congress was to clean up the soil and groundwater contamination problems in the United States by placing responsibility on owners or operators of a facility (including land) from which a hazardous substance is released and on certain prior owners or generators or transporters of hazardous substances. Any financially viable entity involved in ownership or operation of the polluted site faces potential cleanup liability. Liability under CERCLA is joint and several, which means that any party with involvement in the property as an owner or operator may be held responsible for all or part of the cleanup costs. The liability is strict liability, without regard to fault, and the liability is retroactive, which means that any person having fee simple title to a property at any point in time when pollution occurred is exposed to the full burden of cleanup costs, even if that person had no involvement in the creation of the contamination problem. Some of the information used in this discussion was taken from Pettigrew (1993) and Pettigrew and Jacobsen (1992).

Joint and several liability assigns cleanup and cost reimbursement at a Superfund site to the responsible parties where there is no proof that the costs are clearly divisible. Potentially Responsible Parties (PRPs) are defined under CERCLA as

1. Generators of hazardous or toxic substances
2. Transporters of toxic or hazardous substances
3. Owners and operators, including current owners of contaminated property, even if they did not own the property at the time that disposal or discharge occurred and parties that owned the property at the time of the disposal or discharge, whether or not they had knowledge of the disposal
4. Lenders who acquire title to a contaminated property through foreclosure
5. A lender or creditor that is deeded to have participated in the management of the property

Under this legal concept, the government can recover the full response costs from all parties or any single party. This harsh provision of CERCLA has been upheld in numerous federal court challenges on constitutional and other legal grounds.

A significant court decision supporting joint and several liability under CERCLA occurred in the *U.S. v. R.W. Meyer, Inc.* (1991) (see References), in which the court ruled that the liability is joint and several if the harm cannot be divided. The issue of the volume of hazardous or toxic waste contributed to a site versus joint and several liability has been the subject of considerable litigation. Joint and several liability has been maintained, despite facts showing defendants sent minimal amounts of waste to a site, because there was no proof of divisibility (*American Cyanamid Company v. O'Neil*, 1990). A technical difficulty in proving that liability is clearly divisible lies in determining the volume of released contamination versus the total volume of waste stored at a site. For example, assume that a million drums of some toxic substance were placed in a landfill. Subsequently, about 50 drums leaked and contaminated the groundwater, costing millions of dollars for investigation and cleanup expenses. If a company were responsible for contributing only 50 drums out of the million drums, were those 50 drums the ones that leaked, or did they remain intact? There is no practical or absolute method of dividing the responsibility in this example. The issue of divisibility can become even more complex, as in the cases of contamination caused by multiple substances at waste disposal sites, contamination occurring at temporary waste storage sites, or contamination at incinerator sites where air toxics may have been discharged over a large area.

The issue of divisibility has been investigated further by the courts in a recent decision in *U.S. v. Alcan Aluminum Corporation* (1992). In this case, the Circuit Court of Appeals reversed a District court decision that the sole nonsettling Potentially Responsible Party (PRP) was jointly and severally responsible for the remaining response costs. The court ruled that if Alcan could prove that its product contained hazardous constituents below naturally occurring background levels, the harm would be considered to be divisible with regard to Alcan. Some legal scholars believe that this ruling could be "the beginning of the end for joint and several liability under Superfund," and that it "brings causation back into the equation as an affirmative defense" (Pettigrew, 1993). The issue of joint and several liability under CERCLA is still in a legal state of flux, but the lender should still consider this aspect of liability when exercising due diligence to manage risk.

The concept of strict liability without fault was reaffirmed in *U.S. v. Cannons Engineering Corporation* (1990). Strict liability means that a party can be held liable regardless of intent or negligence. Although this has been the consistent interpretation of the courts in the past, in *U.S. v. Alcan Aluminum Corporation* (1992) the courts held that equitable facts required that a party be given the opportunity to prove no fault and thereby relieve itself of CERCLA liability. Since adoption of the SARA amendments in 1986, the government is required to demonstrate "a release or threatened release of a hazardous substance by a potentially responsible party causing the government or private party to incur response costs." Some cases that have affirmed this concept are *Kaiser Aluminum & Chemical Corporation v. Catellus Development Corporation* (1992) and *Dedham Water Company v. Cumberland Farms Dairy, Inc.* (1991). Under CERCLA, "hazardous substances" also include toxic or hazardous substances defined under other environmental statutes designated by the U.S. Environmental Protection Agency, including the Clean Water Act, the Resource Conservation and Recovery Act, and the Toxic Substances Control Act.

The concept that a property owner has liability for all cleanup and other response costs, regardless of fault, has some basis in logic and science. A sophisticated purchaser, owner, or operator that is not responsible for release of a toxic or hazardous substance should nevertheless have obtained knowledge of the problem through due diligence investigation prior to acquisition. If the contamination problem remained on the site during any term of ownership, releases of the toxic or hazardous substance(s) into the soil and/or groundwater may have continued during all or part of the term of ownership. Therefore, although the owner or operator may not have had knowledge of the original improper disposal, the process of contamination continued during the term of ownership; thus, any owner in the chain of title after the original disposal occurred is considered to be a Potentially Responsible Party (PRP). This is an example of the logic used by federal, state, and local environmental agencies to find a pocket deep enough to bear the financial burden of cleanup costs.

There are few viable defenses to CERCLA liability for landowners or operators of facilities. In Section 107(b), the three limited defenses to liability are listed as (1) an act of God, (2) an act of war, and (3) an act or omission of a third party. The use of the act of God defense is not as straightforward as it appears. For example, if an earthquake occurs and causes a release of a hazardous or toxic substance, this would seem to be an act of God. However, if the facility were located in a region where earthquakes are known to occur, then the owner or operator should have designed the facility to withstand earthquake damage, and the act of God defense would not apply. An example of an act of God that would apply may be the impact of a meteorite on a facility, resulting in a discharge. The act of war defense applies to a very limited number of situations. The final defense involves an act of a third party that has no legal or business relationship with the property owner or operator. An example is the accidental discharge of a hazardous or toxic substance on a property by a third party, such as a chemical spill along a highway caused by an accident. The owner of the property upon which the spill occurred is not liable under CERCLA, unless the owner takes no action to contain the problem. (The 1986 SARA amendment expanded third party defense to include "innocent purchasers.") These defenses are impractical or invalid in most real world cases.

There are few exemptions from CERCLA liabilities once an action is taken. Secured creditors are exempt, but with certain restrictions based on several court decisions (see the discussion of the *Fleet Factors* case). Trustees, including bankruptcy trustees, are not exempt from CERCLA actions. Most successor corporations are not exempt from CERCLA liabilities. A parent corporation may be held liable under CERCLA as an operator, particularly when day-to-day management activities are involved. Corporation officers, directors, shareholders, and employees may be subject to CERCLA liabilities if they are actively involved in management of a CERCLA facility. Absentee landlords, estates, and in some specific cases, real estate agents may be subject to CERCLA liabilities if they are operators or involved in property management. Penalties may even be extracted from estates of deceased parties, if the properties are subject to CERCLA liabilities.

By statute, secured creditors are not directly liable for CERCLA costs. Lending institutions become exposed to CERCLA liabilities by becoming owners or operators, by participating in the management of the property, or by having the "capacity" to control a CERCLA facility, even if the power is not exercised. The most commonly cited court case that defined the liability of a lender in a CERCLA site was the *U.S. v. Maryland Bank and Trust* (1986). In this case Maryland Bank and Trust "purchased" a property at a foreclosure sale to recover equity on a mortgage held by the institution on the property. When the institution became the owner, the court held the bank liable for the cleanup costs of hazardous substances on the property, despite the fact that the discharge occurred on the site prior to bank ownership. This is a prime example of strict liability without regard to fault. In *U.S. v. Mirabile* (1985), the courts held that a secured creditor who participates in the day-to-day operations of a facility may be held liable for response costs under CERCLA (Smallwood, 1990). This is an example of the creditor becoming an "operator." Perhaps the most difficult court case to interpret by a lender was the *U.S. v. Fleet Factors* (1989). The court ruled that any secured creditor with the capacity to control a CERCLA facility, even if the power was not exercised, would be held liable. This ruling conflicted with other court rulings regarding the definition of "power" or "influence" over management of a facility affected by a CERCLA action (Bergsoe Metal Corporation case, 1990). Might the very act of monitoring a loan be defined as "influence" over facility operation? How might this affect the number of other controls used by lending institutions to maintain financial scrutiny over various types of loans secured by property and/or other assets?

In the SARA amendments of 1986, lenders were relieved of some liabilities created by CERCLA under the Innocent Landowner Defense (CERCLA 9607

Section 107(b)(3)). This provision of the law required that a landowner, including a foreclosing lending institution, must have made "all appropriate inquiry" into the previous ownership and uses of the property consistent with "good commercial and customary practice." This inquiry was termed a "due diligence" investigation. However, in the SARA amendments there was no definition of the scope of a "due diligence" investigation or "all appropriate inquiry." In the late 1980s, legislation was introduced in Congress by Representative Curt Weldon of Pennsylvania to specifically define the scope of the "due diligence" investigation. The text was as follows:

(I) Recorded chain of title documents regarding the property, including all deeds, leases, restrictions, and covenants. The chain of title shall be of sufficient length of time to account for previous ownership and uses of the property which are likely to have an adverse environmental impact on the property but in no case for less than 30 years.

(II) Commercially available aerial photographs of the property which may reflect prior uses of the property.

(III) Determination of the existence of federal, state and local environmental clean up liens against the property.

(IV) Reasonably obtainable federal, state, and local records of existing and potentially contaminated sites, including site investigation reports for such contaminated sites; reasonably obtainable federal, state and local environmental records of activities likely to have an adverse impact on the property (including records of environmental problem sites, landfill and other disposal site records, underground storage tank records and known hazardous waste handler and generator records); and such other reasonably obtainable federal, state and local environmental records which report incidents or sources of contamination on the property.

(V) A visual site inspection of the property and all facilities and improvements on the property, a.k.a. a visual inspection of immediately adjacent properties from the subject property, to determine or discover the obviousness of the presence or likely presence of contamination on the property (including chemical use, storage, treatment and disposal practices, past or present).

The Weldon amendment was opposed by many in the U.S. Environmental Protection Agency and failed to obtain congressional approval.

After the Weldon "due diligence" definition failed to pass Congress and after the great distress within the lending industry created by the Fleet Factors decision, the U.S. Environmental Protection Agency was directed to promulgate a rule to define lender liability in the context of CERCLA. EPA issued the CERCLA Lender Liability Rule to clarify "safe harbor" provisions for secured creditors under CERCLA. This rule gave lenders the ability to exercise certain management functions without incurring CERCLA liability. There were six primary provisions of the rule:

1. An environmental assessment of the collateral is not required to maintain the security interest exemption.
2. Lenders can freely enforce and monitor borrower environmental cleanups as loan conditions or terms.
3. Lenders can work freely with troubled borrowers on financial and administrative matters.
4. Lenders can freely renegotiate, restructure, or otherwise resolve loans in default.
5. Lenders generally may foreclose on and operate collateral property without voiding the exemption, as long as the property is properly marketed for sale and no firm, fair offer is refused.
6. Institutional trustees or fiduciaries who act as property managers are not protected by the rule (23 FR 9999, May 15, 1992).

After great effort by lenders and the EPA to resolve the uncertainties created by the Fleet Factors decision, the CERCLA Lender Liability Rule was adopted and promptly challenged with litigation. The Chemical Manufacturers Association and the State of Michigan challenged the rule in the U.S. Court of Appeals in Washington, D.C. The court ruled on February 4, 1994 that the EPA Rule was an improper "extensive quasi-legislative effort" to exempt lenders from liability provisions of CERCLA (*Kelly v. U.S.E.P.A.*).

Despite the fact that the CERCLA Lender Liability Rule was struck down, there have been some court decisions favorable to lenders in other federal court districts (Fleet Factors occurred in the Second District) with regard to CERCLA liabilities. A lender who owned a site under a sale/leaseback agreement during the release of hazardous substances was protected in *Waterville Industries, Inc. v. Finance Authority of Maine* (1993). In this case, the lender first paid under a loan guaranty, then took title by deed in lieu of foreclosure and leased the site back to the defaulted borrower with an option to purchase. The court ruled against the purchaser, who argued that the lender was not exempt from CERCLA. The court noted that the decision was not based on the EPA Lender Liability Rule, which was not in effect at that time. The First Circuit Court ruled that a lender was not liable under CERCLA for contamination on a site that it acquired through foreclosure in *U.S. v. McLamb* (1993). The justification the court used was that the lender tried to sell the site "almost immediately," did not contribute to prior contamination, and sold the site to "the first available buyer." This logic was very similar to that contained in the EPA rule. The court concluded that the lender acted as a secured creditor (Kammert, 1994). In a rather interesting case, the First Circuit Court ruled in favor of a CERCLA exemption for a lending institution that discovered that a site was contaminated but did not disclose that fact to the purchaser (*Northeast Doran v. Key Bank of Maine,* 1994). The court held that the lender was neither an owner nor operator of the site under CERCLA, and the failure to disclose did not give rise to a CERCLA cause of action. Despite this court ruling, a lender with material knowledge with regard to damage on a property who does not disclose the problem to a purchaser could be subject to litigation on other legal grounds. At the current time the only protection that a lender has with regard to CERCLA liabilities is to require or perform a "due diligence" investigation of a property prior to financing or foreclosure. With the rule invalidated, current EPA guidance is that lender liability is determined on a case-by-case basis, generally using the rule criteria as the analytical framework. The due diligence investigation is defined as a phase I environmental site assessment or other investigation defined by the institution environmental policy (see Chapters 4 and 5).

It is important to note that federal laws did create some exemptions for lenders as well as the due diligence test for the "innocent land purchaser" defense. However, when many states adopted the federal laws under primacy agreements, they did not adopt some of the exemptions. In fact, some state and local governments have adopted more restrictive interpretations of the CERCLA liabilities. Some of these governmental groups have adopted the "super lien" concept that funnels all funds earned on the sale of a property that was formerly contaminated to reimburse the government for response costs. Legal challenges to these more restrictive laws generally have been denied, even by federal courts.

Groundwater contamination liabilities may trigger liabilities other than those contained within CERCLA. Common law issues may arise from site problems, such as third party actions brought against owners or operators under "toxic tort" claims. Some common law theories that may be used in third party action suits include negligence, nuisance, trespass, strict or absolute liability, and products liability. Some of these actions may be very serious, especially when contaminated water causes health damage. Parties with knowledge of a contamination problem, especially owners or operators who take no action to contain, clean up, or alleviate the problem may be subject to criminal prosecution.

In certain cases, a lending institution may be able to recover costs of a CERCLA cleanup. If a cost recovery action is a real possibility, the assessment and cleanup procedures must follow very specific guidelines contained in the National Oil and Hazardous Substance Pollution Contingency Plan (40 CFR 300), commonly termed the National Contingency Plan (NCP). This option is legally complex, adds considerable cost to assessment and remediation, and may be ambiguous, especially if litigation is involved.

Resource Conservation and Recovery Act Liabilities

The Resource Conservation and Recovery Act of 1976 (42 U.S.C., Section 6901, known as "RCRA") provides regulations for past, ongoing, and future generation, transportation, treatment, storage, and disposal of hazardous wastes. There are some similarities between CERCLA and RCRA liabilities, because the RCRA strict liabilities for soil and groundwater contamination extend to parties with a remote connection to the site. RCRA permits are required for all facilities handling or storing hazardous wastes, and the permittees are strictly liable for contamination of soil and groundwater.

Virtually all manufacturers and many other types of businesses come under the jurisdiction of RCRA as generators of hazardous wastes. The type and number of RCRA permits required depend on the volume of waste generated, the type of waste, and the length of time that the waste is stored on the site.

Lenders are exposed to RCRA liabilities if ownership of a RCRA-regulated treatment, storage, and disposal (TSD) facility is taken by foreclosure. The liabilities can be extensive if the site requires a TSD closure. Lenders are also exposed to RCRA liabilities due to generator's liability related to disposal of wastes from the borrower's site. Based on an analysis presented in Kammert (1994), there are five RCRA liability issues that merit lender attention, including (1) TSD closure liability, (2) assessment without closure, (3) EPA approved nonclosure per RCRA, (4) EPA approval before lender takes title, and (5) generator liability. When sites are known to be contaminated with solid wastes, a determination should be made prior to foreclosure if the site is classified as a TSD and will be subjected to cleanup under a RCRA closure. Contamination cleanup under this action is very complicated and commonly costs many times more than a conventional cleanup, especially when nonpetroleum contamination is involved. The EPA commonly uses a more lenient policy that allows persons who are not owners or operators of a TSD site to remediate it without facing RCRA liabilities. Therefore, any lender facing a potential TSD foreclosure should obtain authorization in writing to proceed with assessment without involving TSD closure. Whether or not a state agency takes the lead authority in a site cleanup oversight, the EPA must confirm that the site may be cleaned up without exposure to RCRA regulation. Prior to taking title to the property, a lender should obtain a variance or exemption from TSD procedures to conduct the assessment and to complete the remediation. When the lender must dispose of hazardous waste generated by a borrower, as in the case of a foreclosure or workout, the lender should rely on consultants to analyze and manifest the waste. The lender may append an exhibit to the manifest, stating that the lender did not generate the waste, is relying on a consultant to ascertain the contents, and is disposing of the waste to protect a security interest. This procedure may protect the lender from future liabilities at waste disposal facilities.

RCRA is an extraordinarily complex law. Decisions by lenders on any site involving potential RCRA liabilities should be evaluated carefully with the help of experienced legal and environmental consultants. One of the first options that should be evaluated is the possibility of cost recovery actions, if the party causing the contamination problem can be clearly identified and has the resources available to compensate the institution.

OTHER ENVIRONMENTAL LIABILITIES

Clean Water Act

The 1977 amendments to the Federal Water Pollution Control Act of 1948 are commonly termed the *Clean Water Act*. Section 404 of the Clean Water Act and the existing authorization in the Rivers and Harbors Act of 1899 initiated modern regulation of wetlands in the United States. The Act extends regulatory jurisdiction over *all* waters of the United States, including associated wetlands. Current federal policy is to prevent any net loss of wetlands to the extent possible. Wetland regulations can greatly affect the value and overall utilization potential of a property. Permits are required from the U.S. Army Corps of Engineers to dredge, fill, or alter wetlands in any way. Lenders must be concerned about jeopardized security interest caused by property value loss or extensive permitting delays in potential use of properties containing wetlands.

Endangered Species Act

The Endangered Species Act of 1973 created special protection for animal and plant species considered to be in danger of becoming extinct or threatened. Protection of endangered species and the habitats containing them can significantly affect the value of property or the utilization of the property. If a proposed activity that requires a federal permit jeopardizes an endangered or threatened species, that permit cannot be issued. Lenders must consider the effect of this act on the potential loss of security interest or loss of value of properties utilized as collateral.

Clean Air Act

The Clean Air Act of 1970, with the amendments of 1977 and 1990, set the standards for air discharges of particulate materials and air toxics. Any financial institution lending to a business having air discharges should be sure that the proper permits have been obtained. The issue of air emissions is more complex within areas designated as "air attainment areas." Lenders must be aware of the potential liabilities pertaining to air quality that could impair the repayment of loans. Financial losses caused by fines and/or the purchase of upgraded pollution control equipment may be substantial.

Occupational Safety and Health Act

The Occupational Safety and Health Act was passed in 1970 to regulate occupational exposure to toxic and hazardous substances. In operating facilities, employee exposure to toxic and hazardous substances can bring considerable financial liability to any owner or operator, including lending institutions. This issue should be assessed in all institution-owned facilities and in facilities operated under trust agreements.

THE FUTURE OF FEDERAL ENVIRONMENTAL LAWS

All environmental laws are currently in a state of flux because of new, more conservative political views in Congress. Perhaps the most significant changes in environmental laws involve air regulation. Also, it is anticipated that a large number of changes will occur in the revision of CERCLA and in the Endangered Species Act. Wetlands regulation rooted in the Clean Water Act may also be changed. Perhaps the most significant changes directly affecting lending institution policies and activities will occur in the proposed CERCLA revisions.

Reform of CERCLA

At this time, Congress is considering a number of major revisions to CERCLA. The 103rd Congress considered a Superfund reform bill (S. 1834, H.R. 4916) but did not act on the legislation. Coglianese (1994) reported that elimination of retroactive liability is the current theme of the revision, with remedy selection reforms included. The emphasis of remedy reforms is on risk assessment, including adoption of realistic exposure scenarios and mandated cost-benefit analyses for expensive cleanups. The EPA has taken an aggressive position against the bill, with EPA Administrator Carol Browner accusing various witnesses of providing "misinformation" to congressional committees. She has advised a congressman that the proposed reforms will pose human health problems. Congress is also considering a $1 billion cut in the funding for cleanup of Superfund sites. The recovery of "natural resources" damages is also under attack. It is likely that some revisions will be enacted by Congress within the next few years, although many observers of Congress believe that removal of the "retroactive liability" provision within CERCLA is not likely in the near future.

Other Environmental Legislation

The anti-environmental attitude of many in Congress will probably cause revision of many environmental laws. Perhaps the prime candidate for revision is the Endangered Species Act. There is a widespread national belief that several environmental groups have taken advantage of the Act as a cover to promote their agenda. It is likely that Congress will provide some relief to landowners with regard to the limitation of land use. Another law that may be revised is the Clean Water Act. A great deal of controversy has arisen over wetlands use and the definition of wetland areas. The revision to this Act may be a part of some "landowner rights" bill, which would limit the restrictions that government may invoke on a property without purchasing it. This type of legislation could trigger a barrage of "taking" suits against federal, state, and local governments that use environmental laws to limit land use.

REFERENCES FOR FURTHER READING

Coglienese, M. P., Solid waste, CERCLA, and RCRA update, in Annual Environmental and Land Use Law Update, August 17–19, 1995, Lecture Outlines, The Florida Bar, 1995, 6.3.

Kammert, J. L., Lender liability/environmental contractual provisions in real estate transactions, in Environmental and Land Use Law Update, The Florida Bar, 1994, 11.1.

Pettigrew, R. A., Groundwater contamination and business transactions: financial risks and legal liabilities, in Seventh Annual Environmental Permitting Summer School Manual, The Florida Chamber of Commerce, Tallahassee, FL, 1993, 725.

Pettigrew, R. A. and Jacobsen, T., Groundwater contamination and business transactions: financial risks and legal liabilities, in Sixth Annual Environmental Permitting Summer School Manual, The Florida Chamber of Commerce, Tallahassee, FL, 1992, 947.

Smallwood, M. F., Environmental liabilities under Superfund, in Solid and Hazardous Waste Management: Short-Course Manual, The Florida Chamber of Commerce, Tallahassee, FL, 1990, 187.

Court Case Citations

American Cyanamid Co. v. O'Neil, 493 U.S. 1071 (1980).
Bergsoe Metal Corp. 910 F. 2d 668 (9th Cir. 1990).
Dedham, Water Co. v. Cumberland Farms Dairy, Inc., 770 F. Supp. 41 (D. Mass. 1991).
Kaiser Aluminum & Chemical Corporation v. Catellus Development Corporation, 976 F. 2d 1338 (9th Cir. 1992).
Kelly v. EPA, 15 F. 3d 1100 (CA DC 1994).
Northeast Doran v. Key Bank of Maine, 1994 WL 13835 (CA1 1994).
U.S. v. Alcan Aluminum Corp., No. 91-5481 (3d Cir. 1992).
U.S. v. Cannons Engineering Corp., 899 F. 2d 79 (1st Cir. 1990).
U.S. v. Fleet Factors, 901 F. 2d 1150 (11th Cir. 1990).
U.S. v. Maryland Bank & Trust Co., 632 F. Supp. 573(D. Md. 1986).
U.S. v. McLamb, 5F 3d. 69 (CA4 1993).
U.S. v. Mirabile, 15 ELR 20994 (E.D. Pa. 1985).
U.S. v. R. W. Meyer, Inc., 932 F. 2d 568 (6th Cir. 1991).
Waterville Industries, Inc. v. Finance Authority of Maine, 984 F. 2d 549 (CA1 1993).

3 A PRIMER ON SOIL AND GROUNDWATER CONTAMINATION

WHAT IS CONTAMINATION?

Contamination may be defined as "to make impure by contact or mixture." This typical dictionary definition implies that some measure or standard exists, yet offers no clues concerning what contamination might mean in the context of the law or in the plethora of laws, rules, and regulations formulated by federal, state, and local agencies.

Natural processes, as well as the activities of man, cause contamination. The determination that soil or groundwater is contaminated is based on some set of concentrations for various substances that are determined to be the standard. This standard is based on health and safety considerations, such as those applying to drinking water, for example, and other concerns, such as general environmental effects or conditions.

Processes Causing Natural Contamination

Natural contamination occurs as a result of the normal processes that affect the surface or subsurface of the earth, such as the occurrence of rainfall or the movement of groundwater. When it rains, the runoff can cause erosion of soils and transport of the eroded soils and other materials into streams. In this case, particulate soil is a contaminant of the streams. Rainfall also infiltrates the soil and becomes part of groundwater flow. When the groundwater comes in contact with naturally occurring substances, such as coal seams or metallic ore deposits, the water can dissolve some of these substances. If the groundwater contains acid or high concentrations of metals and discharges into a stream, the stream becomes contaminated with the metals or acid. The concept here is that contamination is a concentration of some substance above the naturally occurring conditions or a concentration that tends to adversely affect life. In nature, an ecosystem adapts to the concentrations of naturally occurring substances in and around it. Thus, for all practical purposes, even high concentrations of metals or acidic water may not represent an adverse condition at a given location. On the other hand, when a natural disaster occurs producing a major change to the natural system, the ecosystem is suddenly altered, and a loss of life and change in the system may occur. Examples would be volcanic eruptions or the passage of a hurricane. In most cases, the ecosystem or environment recovers from the temporary episode of contamination, but in some cases the change is permanent.

Man-Caused Contamination

Man-caused contamination can be similar to either the natural slow leak of dissolved metals into a stream or to the catastrophic explosion of a volcano. An example of slow but devastating contamination of the environment is a leak of a dry cleaning fluid, such as perchloroethelene, into the groundwater. Although the leak may be unobserved for many years and its movement is very slow through the groundwater, one day it may begin to drain into a stream or into a well, causing either the death of organisms or human sickness. The Valdez oil spill is an example of massive environmental contamination, which occurred suddenly and caused extensive environmental destruction. Man-caused contamination should be cleaned up, because in most cases ecosystems will recover from the damage inflicted on them when the sources of the contamination are removed.

There are many types of contaminants that are of concern to property owners, the business community, and lenders. In 1984, the U.S. Congress requested that the Office of Technology Assessment assemble a list of the most common substances that become contaminants to the soil and/or groundwater. This list appears in Appendix A. The list is long, and many of the chemicals are not commonly known to the public. However, the substances on the list can be grouped into the most common types of contaminants, which are hydrocarbons, solvents, metals, pesticides, fertilizers, salts, domestic wastewater components, and others. This information is important to assist property buyers and lenders to understand clearly the sources of these groups of contaminants, the uses of lands that contain the contaminants, the types of industries involved, and the relative costs of cleaning up the problems caused by the discharge of these substances.

Legal and Statutory Definitions of Contamination

When defining contamination within the context of laws, rules, and regulations, there are specific maximum contaminant levels (MCLs) or guidance concentrations defined in various federal, state, and local water quality and other standards. In terms of legal liability and consequential financial responsibility, there is no contamination unless the concentration of a regulated substance exceeds a maximum contaminant level in the soil or the groundwater. These concentrations or MCLs are measured in soils using the Toxicity Characteristic Leaching Potential method (TCLP). This method provides an assessment of the potential for the leaching of the contaminant from the soil into the groundwater and is a laboratory standard method. Concentrations of dissolved contaminants in the surface water or groundwater are measured in water samples sent to laboratories. A more detailed discussion of sampling and quality control issues will occur later in the text. Upon measurement of the potential contaminant concentrations, a comparison is made between the regulatory standards (or maximum contaminant levels) and the concentrations in the samples. If the concentration in a sample or multiple samples exceeds the standard(s), there may be a contamination problem. The reason that the word *may* is used is because a single sample cannot and should not be used to define contamination, and in many cases the regulations are not applied in a uniform or absolute manner.

The principal federal statutes that provide definitions for the maximum contaminant levels in water are the Safe Drinking Water Act (1972) and the Resource Conservation and Recovery Act (1968). The primary and secondary drinking water standards are published in the Code of Federal Regulations, Chapter 40. If the site in question is defined as a storage or depository area for hazardous waste, then the Resource Conservation and Recovery Act action levels are used to determine whether contamination is present. Definition of soil contamination is truly problematic because currently there are no promulgated federal standards with regard to soil contamination, and each state or local government treats the issue in a different and sometimes convoluted manner. There are a variety of guidance standards, such as the Resource Conservation and Recovery Act action levels and the Superfund proposed soil screening levels. Some specific contaminants are treated individually with specific standards, such as polychlorinated biphenyls (PCBs).

Usually, the task of defining contamination should not be undertaken unless the lender is a specialist in environmental law. Deciding which regulation applies and how it applies to a particular situation can be most difficult, and sometimes numerous choices are possible. In order to place the contamination definition problem in context, only the federal regulations and statutes have been used in this text. The problem is considerably more complex when all the various state and local government program regulations are considered. The best approach for determining whether contamination is present on a site and whether cleanup will be required is to obtain opinions from specialists with the proper credentials. Because of the complexity in interpretation of the laws and rules, it is common to obtain a second opinion. A general guide to cleanup criteria for soil and groundwater for federal and state regulations is provided by the American Society for Testing & Materials (Buonicore, 1995). This guide is updated each year and is a helpful tool in making a determination regarding potential problems.

THE HYDROLOGIC CYCLE AND THE FLOW OF GROUNDWATER AND SURFACE WATERS

The Hydrologic Cycle

The surface of the earth is quite dynamic, and water is constantly being recycled between the oceans, the land surface, and the ground. This cycling of water is commonly termed the hydrologic cycle (Figure 3.1). Movement of water through the hydrologic system is the principal reason that soil and groundwater

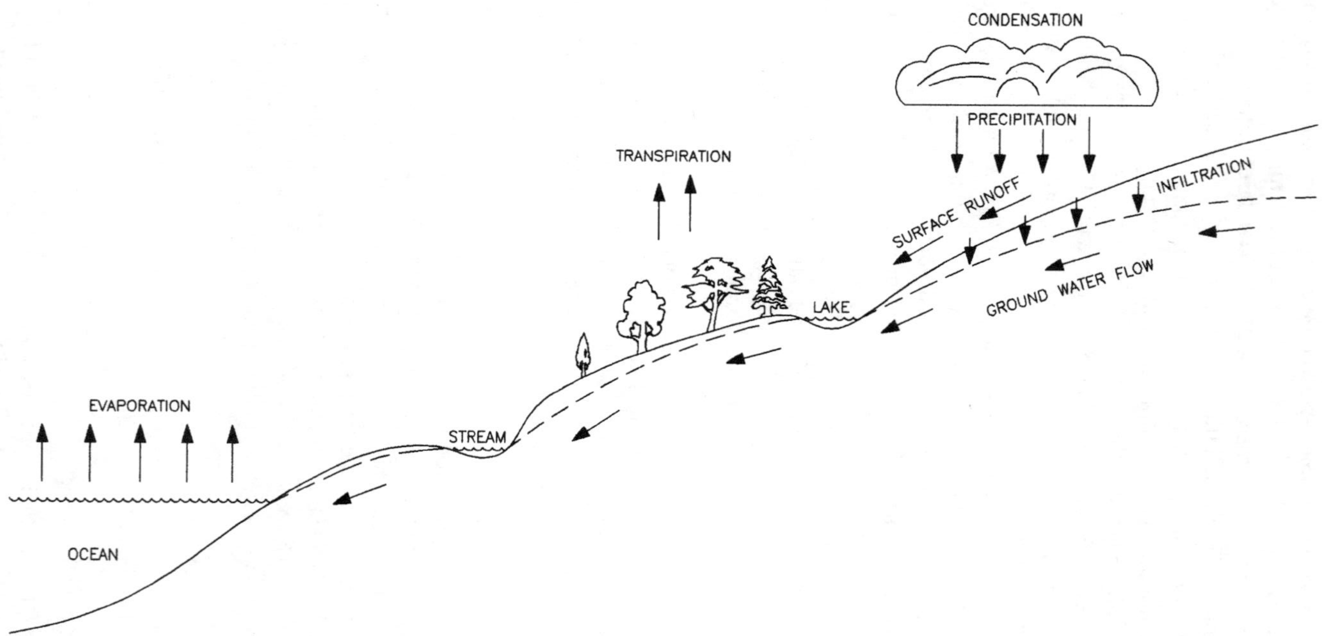

Figure 3.1 Movement of water through the hydrologic cycle. Water is recycled from the oceans and surface water back into the atmosphere. Rainfall enters the groundwater system and streams, which flow back to the sea, and the process begins anew. (From Missimer, T. M. and Boggess, D. H., Fluctuations of the Water-Table in Lee County, Florida, 1969–1973, Open-File Report 74019, U. S. Geological Survey, 1973.)

contamination are serious problems. Water is the universal solvent and is the principal transporter of dissolved substances in ground

The engine that powers the hydrologic cycle is the sun, which provides heat to evaporate water from the giant ocean reservoirs, lakes, streams, and the surface of the land. As water becomes vapor and rises into the atmosphere, it is transported by the winds and eventually begins to condense, first forming clouds and then rainfall. Rainfall or precipitation falls upon the land surface or into lakes or streams. Some of the water runs off the land surface to feed the streams or lakes, and the remaining water infiltrates the ground and percolates downward to add to groundwater stored beneath the land surface.

Groundwater Flow

Groundwater tends to flow downhill as the result of gravity. Eventually, the groundwater flows through the subsurface and enters streams, lakes, or the sea. Most of the groundwater added to the streams flows downhill and discharges into the oceans, and the cycle begins anew. Some of the groundwater never returns to the sea but is recycled directly back to the atmosphere by *evaporation* or indirectly by the process of loss through living plants, called *transpiration*. The processes involved in the hydrologic cycle are affected by the local climatic regime and the local geologic and hydrologic conditions. While the principles of water movement are common to all hydrologic systems, the rates and quantities of groundwater and surface water flows vary greatly from region to region. This natural variation causes fundamental differences in the susceptibility of given geographic regions to contamination.

Flow of groundwater is controlled by the permeability, or hydraulic conductivity, of the soil or the aquifer through which the water flows (Figure 3.2), the porosity of the geologic framework (Figure 3.3), and the slope of the water table, or what is termed the *potentiometric surface*. Water flows through the pores between grains in the rock or soil (Figure 3.2) or through fractures or cracks in the rock. Since water actually flows through the rock, groundwater flow is much slower than surface water flow. In most cases it moves at rates between a few feet per day to a few feet per year. The flow of groundwater does not follow a straight line as it moves from pore to pore or fracture to fracture, but follows a meandering or tortuous pathway.

There is a tendency for groundwater flow to be more rapid when the geologic materials have high permeabilities. For example, coarse sands generally have high permeability and clays have low permeability. The highest permeabilities tend to occur in limestones or dolomites, in which caverns can form and entire rivers can flow beneath the ground. These systems are relatively rare, and most groundwater flow is the simple, slow movement between pores. Another major factor controlling the flow of groundwater is the slope of the water table, particularly in unconfined shallow aquifers. Gravity is the principal force controlling flow, which tends to be downhill. One might ask why the weasel word *tend* is used instead of just stating that groundwater flows downhill. There are other factors controlling groundwater flow, such as heat or temperature changes and

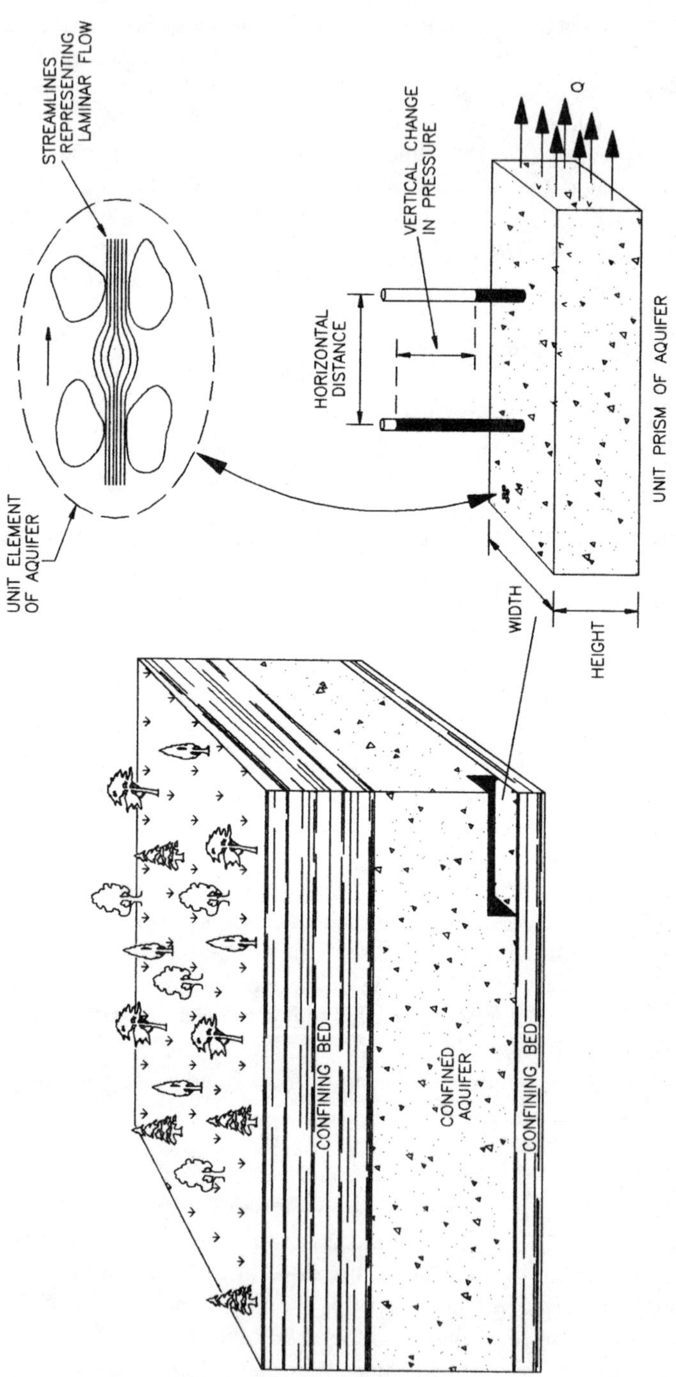

Figure 3.2 Flow of groundwater. Water flows through the connected pores between grains or in cracks and fissures (*upper right*). Groundwater flows through an aquifer in response to changes in pressure, normally from high pressure to low pressure (*lower right*). An aquifer is permeable and saturated with water. (From Heath, R. C., Basic Ground-Water Hydrology, Water Supply Paper 2220, U. S. Geological Survey, 1984.)

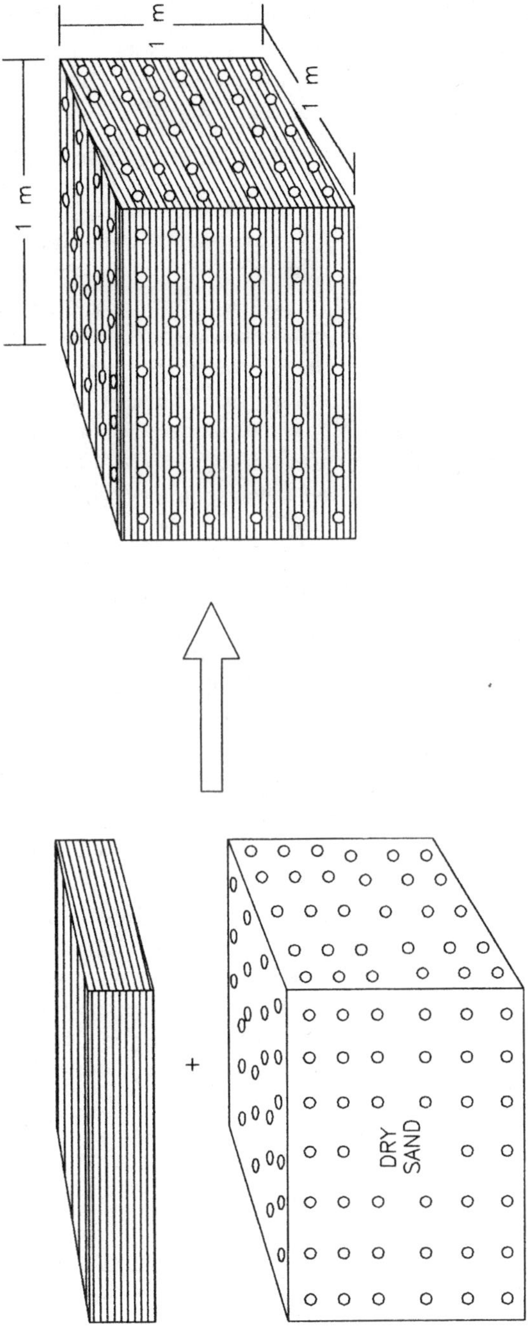

Figure 3.3 Concept of porosity. The framework of an aquifer consists of sediment or rock. When the rock is dry, the pores are filled with air (lower left). When water enters the ground, the pores are filled with water (right, straight lines illustrate water). If the water that fills the pores is removed, it would represent the volume of the porosity for a given volume of an aquifer (upper left). The porosity of an aquifer ranges from a few percent to 40 percent of the total volume. The larger the porosity, the more water stored. (From Heath, R. C., Basic Ground-Water Hydrology, Water Supply Paper 2220, U. S. Geological Survey, 1984.)

variations in aquifer structure, that can divert flow or cause abrupt changes in flow direction. However, in most cases the flow of water moves from high areas to low areas; a land owner or lender, when viewing the land, can use the direction of the land surface slope as a general indicator of groundwater flow direction. In flat areas, the most common groundwater flow direction is toward the nearest surface drainage feature, such as a stream or ditch.

Aquifer Types

The geologic materials through which groundwater flows are termed *aquifers*. An aquifer is formally defined as porous material having sufficient permeability and thickness to yield water to wells at an economical rate. A determination of what *economical* means is more a question for lenders than hydrologists. There are several different types of aquifers, based on the types of geologic materials that form their skeletal framework. The shallowest aquifer type is termed an *unconfined aquifer*, which means there is no low permeability material between the surface of the land and the base of the aquifer (Figure 3.4). This type of aquifer is most susceptible to contamination, because it has no natural protection from substances entering it. The second type of aquifer is a *semi-unconfined aquifer*, which contains some low permeability material between land surface and the base of the aquifer. While the vertical flow of water is somewhat inhibited, the aquifer still functions in a manner similar to an unconfined aquifer and is quite susceptible to contamination. A *semi-confined aquifer* contains a low permeability material both above and below it. In order for water to enter the aquifer, it must either flow into it from some uphill location where there is no confinement or it must flow through the confining beds. In many cases the flow of water through the confining beds must be artificially induced by pumping the aquifer. This aquifer type has some natural protection from contamination because of the confinement. The last aquifer type, and the rarest, is the *confined aquifer*. In this case, the aquifer is bounded by impervious material both above and below it. This aquifer type is only susceptible to contamination at its uphill recharge area or through improperly constructed water or oil wells. Examples of the flow through an unconfined and a confined aquifer are shown in Figure 3.5. The position of the water table generally follows land surface topography, but is altered by surface drainage features, such as rivers, streams, and ditches. The position of the potentiometric surface of the confined aquifer follows the general slope of the land surface, but is not greatly affected by small altitude changes.

Discussion

This general explanation of groundwater flow does not contain all the detailed physics governing flow and the various mechanisms, including the equations, that are used to calculate flow velocities under various physical conditions. If the reader is interested in additional information on groundwater hydrology or hydrogeology, there are a number of textbooks available with varying degrees of technical content (Domenico and Schwartz, 1990; Fetter, 1988; Freeze and

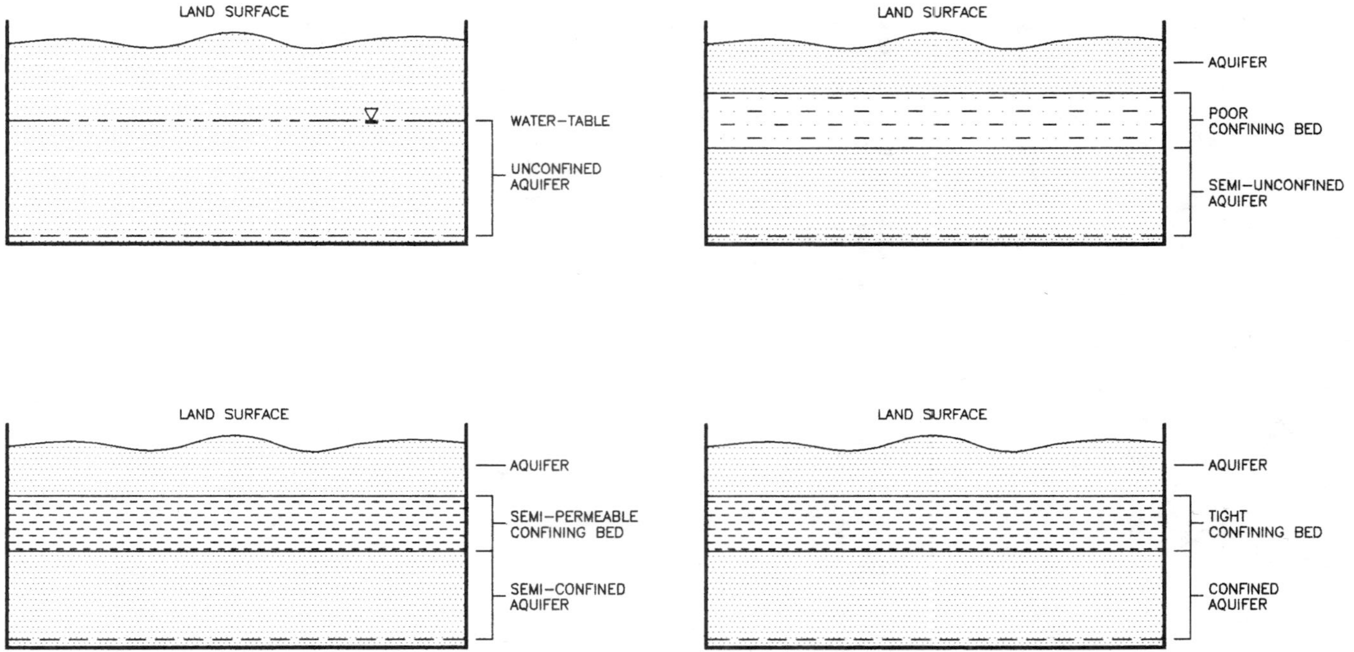

Figure 3.4 Types of aquifers. An unconfined aquifer contains no material of low permeability between land surface and the bottom of the aquifer (*upper left*). A "semi-unconfined" aquifer contains some material that has a somewhat lower permeability than the aquifer as a whole; this material occurs between land surface and the base of the aquifer (*upper right*). A semi-confined aquifer contains material of low permeability both above and below the aquifer, but when a semi-confined aquifer is pumped, water moves through the confining materials into it (*lower left*). A confined aquifer contains materials of very low permeability both above and below it; and almost no water enters it vertically (*lower right*). (Based on Kruseman, G. P. and De Ridder, N. A., Analysis and Evaluation of Pumping Test Data, International Institute for Land Reclamation and Improvement, Wageningen, The Netherlands, 1991.)

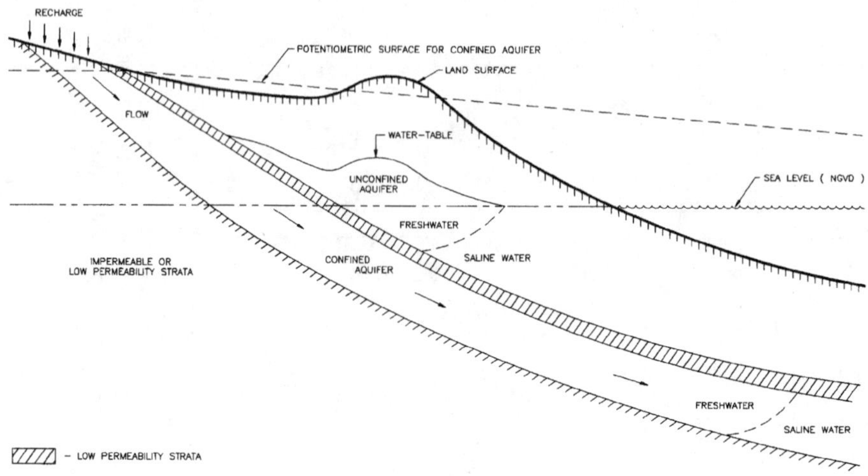

Figure 3.5 Groundwater generally flows downhill from areas where recharge occurs, toward the sea or streams. The water table in an unconfined aquifer closely follows the contours of land surface. In a confined aquifer, flow is governed by pressure changes that may occur independent of what occurs at land surface.

Cherry, 1979; Todd, 1980). A good general text on the subject of groundwater hydrology was published by the U.S. Geological Survey (Heath, 1984).

HOW DOES CONTAMINATION MOVE?

Basic Principles Governing Movement

Movement of contamination is probably the most important factor influencing the cost of cleanup. As contamination spreads, the general cost of cleanup can expand geometrically. The purpose of this discussion is to explain the basic principles of contamination transport. There are several modes of contamination movement.

Once the contamination enters the soil, it can remain inert in the soil, can become dissolved in rainfall and enter the unsaturated zone or the aquifer system, can give off volatiles or gases that can migrate in the soil or beneath parking lots or buildings, can sink into the aquifer as a free product and continue to dissolve for periods of time as long as centuries, or can be moved across land surface by the wind or surface-water runoff. Some contamination can enter surface water directly and move rapidly downstream in the current. Sometimes undiscovered contamination can be moved inadvertently around by the activities of man, such as excavation or land surface clearing.

Contamination Movement in Groundwater

The most common mode of contamination transport is via groundwater flow, either in the unsaturated zone or within the aquifer. The unsaturated zone is the region from land surface to the top of the water table. This area contains a mixture

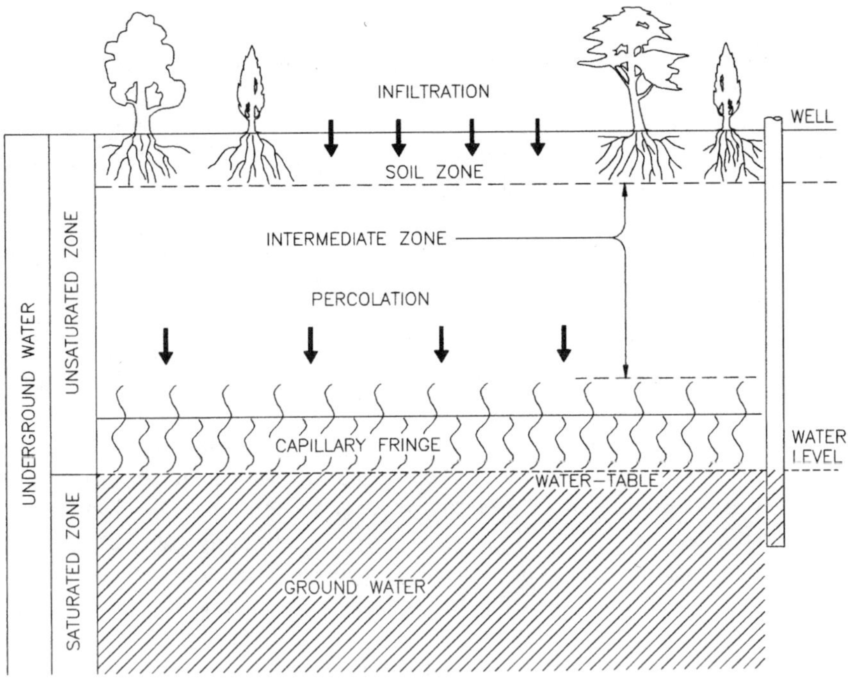

Figure 3.6 Structure of a shallow aquifer. An aquifer begins at the top of the water table, which marks the zone of saturation. The area above the water table is called the unsaturated zone. When rain falls on the land surface, it infiltrates and then percolates through the soil to the water table. When the water table rises to land surface, no more water can enter the system.

of air and water in various proportions, depending on the types of sediment or rock of which it is composed and the proximity to the top of the water table or the saturated zone (Figure 3.6). The first movement of a contaminant is downward through the unsaturated zone to the top of the aquifer, which is commonly termed the *water table*.

This downward movement is not a straight line, but follows a tortuous pathway, either as a liquid waste or in a dissolved state in rainwater. As the contaminant moves downward, it spreads out because of the processes of diffusion and dispersion. What initially may begin as a small circle at the point of entry at land surface becomes a much larger circle with some irregularities at the water table. The circle tends to become larger with depth, especially if the depth to the water table is large. The vertical spread of the contamination appears analogous to an inverted cone.

Effects of Chemical Properties on the Movement of Contaminants

Once a contaminant enters the aquifer, its movement is governed not only by the flow of water through the aquifer but also by the physical and chemical properties of the contaminant itself. Some contaminants with a density lower than water float on the water table. Others are heavier than water and sink to the base of the aquifer. Gasoline and other petroleum products are examples of floating contaminants. More dense contaminants that sink include the chlorinated solvents, such as perchloroethelene (dry cleaning fluid) and tetrachloroethylene (common solvent). Movement of a contaminant is a two-fold process involving movement of the free product and movement of the dissolved or aqueous phase. The term *free product* refers to the pure polluting liquid.

Contaminants, both free products and those in the dissolved or aqueous phase, tend to move slower than the actual velocity of natural groundwater flow. Hydrologists use the terms *Darcy flow* or *advective flow* for the flow of groundwater. Contaminants do not usually flow at the same rate as the groundwater because of the tortuous path of flow and the fact that molecules of the contaminant tend to adhere to the aquifer materials to some degree; also the molecules may be bigger than the water molecules and travel slower. The difference in the transport velocities of naturally flowing groundwater and the rate of contaminant movement is commonly called the *retardation factor*. The primary technical terms for the processes of contaminant migration in groundwater are *advection* (normal groundwater flow at average flow rate), *dispersion* (mixing process caused by localized changes in groundwater velocity), *diffusion* (movement of contaminants caused by their concentrations and chemical properties), and *reactivity* (chemical reactions of the contaminant to water, to the geologic framework of the aquifer, to itself, as in the case of breakdown into other substances, and to other contaminants).

Contaminants that tend to stay in place with little migration tend to be much easier to clean up than very soluble contaminants that migrate readily with the flow of groundwater. For example, DDT is a commonly known and banned pesticide, which is a common contaminant on agricultural properties throughout the United States. DDT is a rather large molecule that has a low solubility in water; therefore, it normally does not migrate far from its point of origin. Why is the word *normally* used? There are always exceptions or cases in which hydrogeologic or chemical conditions can allow even the most inert or large-sized molecular contaminants to migrate. One example is the sudden formation of a sinkhole that drops the contaminant directly into the aquifer system, allowing it to disperse very quickly. Another example is when a contaminant mixes with another chemical substance, enabling it to "piggyback" through the groundwater system. An example is the mixing of pesticides with some highly soluble solvents, such as acetone or alcohol.

Contamination Plumes

Fortunately, contaminants normally do not move very quickly through the groundwater system, but they continue to move day and night until the contaminant (1) is restricted by a natural geologic barrier, (2) becomes so dilute in concentration that it cannot be detected, or (3) is cleaned up. The rate of contaminant movement is controlled by the hydrogeologic conditions on and near the site, the chemical nature of the contaminant, and the volume of the contaminant that has entered or is entering the ground. The configuration of the contamination in the groundwater system is termed a "plume." Some examples of certain types of contamination sources and plumes are shown in Figure 3.7.

Chemical Properties of Contaminants

The chemical nature of the contaminants is significant to every aspect of movement and to the ultimate cleanup strategies used. Some contaminants are chemically stable and travel unaltered through the groundwater in a more or less steady manner. These types of contaminants are relatively soluble in water and travel continuously with the flow of water. Some examples are benzene and acetone. Other contaminants move only when there is some change within the groundwater system to initiate movement. Contamination from heavy metals, such as lead or chromium, does not move in a steady manner. Commonly, when heavy metals enter the groundwater system from sites such as landfills or plating facilities, the dissolved metals move some distance from the source and then stop moving as they are adsorbed to the aquifer materials. They do not chemically react to the geologic materials but are temporarily "stuck" in place. The metals tend to migrate again in response to a change in the chemistry of the groundwater. This change can be a minor variation in pH (acidity) caused by common events, such as a rainfall or a more drastic change, such as a release of low pH water from a surface source (e.g., runoff from a landfill, a sulfur pile, or a coal pile). Contaminants that migrate in an unsteady manner are difficult to assess, because water samples collected from any given location in the aquifer tend to yield inconsistent results.

All organic contaminants tend to break down into simpler compounds with time. This can be good or bad, depending upon the nature of the new organic compound formed. Naturally occurring bacteria and chemical interactions are the agents most responsible for the breakdown of organic contaminants. The most complete breakdown would occur if the original contaminant were to be reduced to carbon dioxide and water, along with a few inert, nonreactive compounds. This will eventually occur, but the issue is one of time, coupled with the rate of migration of the contaminant. The rate of contaminant breakdown can range from a few hours or days, as is the case with most modern pesticides, to decades or centuries, as is the case with certain persistent and banned pesticides such as DDT. Certain compounds, such as perchloroethelene, have intermediate decay components, such as vinyl chloride, which may be more toxic than the original contaminant. The key lesson to be learned from this discussion is that if organic compound contamination is contained and cleaned up to some concentration, then natural agents will eliminate the remaining contamination, given enough time.

Surface Water Contamination

Most of the discussion in this section has centered around groundwater contamination, because it is typically the most difficult and expensive problem

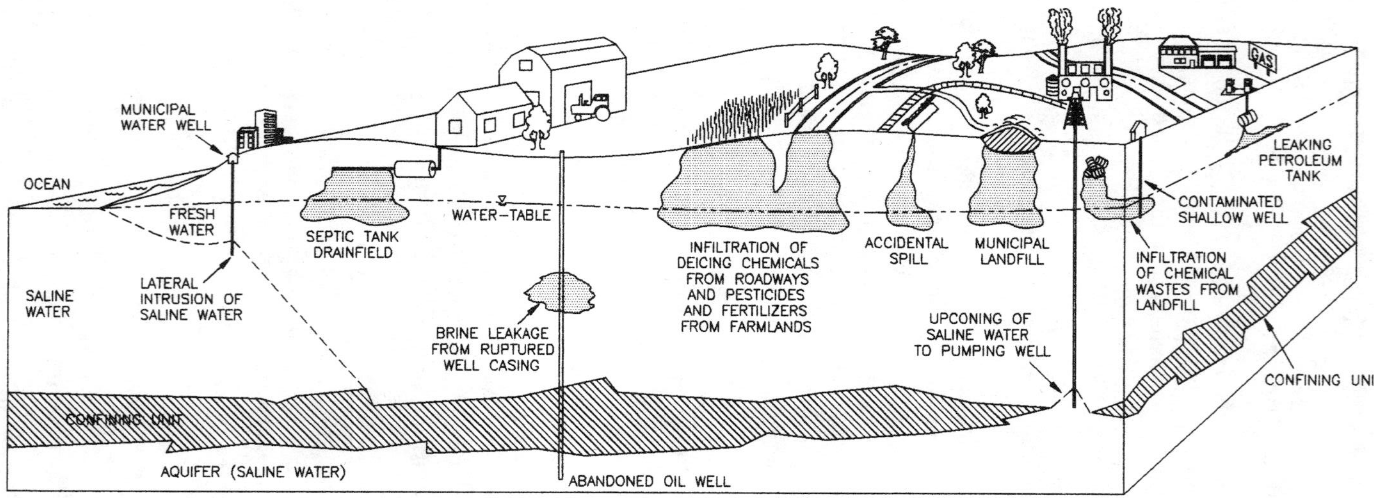

Figure 3.7 Examples of groundwater contamination and plume formation. (From Fetter, C. W., *Contaminant Hydrogeology,* Macmillan, New York, 1992. With permission.)

encountered by lenders, particularly for real estate lending. However, the other contaminant transport agents may also create substantial liabilities.

Contamination of surface waters is a particularly significant issue that can have disastrous and immediate consequences. There are two basic types of surface water contamination, the sudden catastrophic discharge and the slow leak. Examples of sudden discharges include the rupture of a petroleum storage tank along a river, such as the Ashland Oil discharge into the Ohio River, or the sudden collapse of a waste impoundment, such as the Cities Service phosphate "slime" pond discharge into the Peace River, Florida. Slow leaks or discharges can occur from operating activities, such as industrial wastewater disposal facilities; they also occur in the form of contaminated groundwater entering a stream or untreated urban runoff. If the contaminant floats on the water, it may be visible, and technology is readily available to clean it from the system. However, when the contaminant is spread by current, wind, and tides, it can become a major environmental disaster with severe financial consequences. Slow leaks of contaminants, such as heavy metals, solvents, or pesticides, may go undetected for years because the problem cannot be observed directly and concentrations of the contaminants in the water may not be high enough to trigger regulatory action. However, the slow build-up of contamination in the sediments of the stream, lake, or sea bottom may create a severe long-term problem and significant liability. Filter-feeding organisms in the water column or organisms feeding on bottom sediments may uptake the contaminant and "bio-magnify" it by spreading it up the food chain.

Contaminants in streams can move rapidly away from the source in the current. The dissolved component of the contaminant tends to become diluted rapidly and may not become a major environmental issue. If there is an undiluted free product component that floats, it will be transported quickly and coat the stream shorelines while creating a direct and immediate threat to downstream water supplies. The biggest long-term problem occurs when the free product or the dissolved component is deposited in the sediments. In this case, the contaminant can become remobilized as a result of sediment transport caused by floods, ice movement, or other natural processes. Cleanup of streams, lake sediments, or nearshore marine environments may not be possible.

Wind-Blown Contamination

A less common agent of contamination transport is the wind. Particulate waste placed outdoors is subject to wind transport, which can create surface-water or groundwater contamination problems. This particular problem is more relevant to the operation of facilities, such as cement plants, coal storage piles, and others, in which particulate control is an issue.

Further Reading on Contamination Transport

Those readers interested in exploring the technical aspects of contamination can obtain more in-depth information from several textbooks, which provide any degree of scientific explanation desired. The textbooks by Fetter (1988) and Domenico and Schwartz (1990) cover all aspects of the technical nature of groundwater contamination, from the mechanisms to the mathematics. There are a number of other technical textbooks and monographs addressing the problem of groundwater contamination, including Fried (1975) and others. All of these publications are highly technical and require the reader to be reasonably knowledgeable in hydrogeology, engineering, and mathematics.

CLEANUP OF CONTAMINATION

Fundamental Cleanup Principles

There are two fundamental technical principles governing contamination cleanup. First, the contamination should be contained as soon as possible or practical. Second, the source of the contamination should be eliminated as soon as possible to minimize the problem. These principles seem simple in concept, but unfortunately we are not dealing with a world that responds solely to technical considerations. The practical, regulatory, legal, political, and financial considerations of dealing with a contamination problem are far more complex and costly than the contamination cleanup. This section deals primarily with the technical aspects of the cleanup processes and the general legal procedures used by regulatory agencies to assure compliance.

Assessment/Cleanup Protocols

There are a series of protocols used in the assessment and cleanup of hazardous or toxic waste problems, depending on the laws and rules that are applied to the problem. If the site is a Superfund location, a CERCLIS site, or a site where an attempt will be made to obtain reimbursement from other responsible parties, then the procedure described in the National Contingency Plan must be followed (U.S. Environmental Protection Agency, 1988). The exact procedure to be followed must be researched by attorneys and consultants specializing in this type of problem. It is extremely unwise to begin any work on a cleanup without first following the proper legal protocols. Use of an improper procedure could cause the individual lender and/or the institution to suddenly inherit all of the liability and perhaps even some criminal sanctions. This subject will not be explored any further at this point, because the purpose of this section is to describe the possible cleanup methods for various types of sites and the strategies that lead to the choice of cleanup methods.

Contamination Assessment

Once it is established that a contamination problem exists and before any strategy can be applied or a cost estimate formulated, the extent and nature of the problem must be assessed. This procedure is commonly termed *contamination assessment*. During an assessment, the contamination problem is assessed in terms of the hydrogeology, the contaminant chemistry, the possible interactions between contaminants, the location of the contamination both areally and with depth in the soil and the aquifer, and the concentrations of the contamination within the plume. In the case of a simple problem, such as the discharge of 5 gallons of waste oil into low permeability soil, the assessment may involve the collection of a few soil samples, the collection of a water sample from the water-table aquifer, and the production of a certified report. This type of assessment may be completed in a few days or weeks, depending on how fast the laboratory results can be obtained and a report produced. Contamination problems that are more difficult to assess, such as the discharge of perchloroethelene from a dry cleaner into the ground for 20 years, may take several phases of study conducted over several months or even years. The complexity of the assessment is based on the local hydrogeology, the types of contaminants involved, the volume of the contaminant discharged, and the age of the site.

Contamination Containment Strategies

Once the contamination assessment is completed, it is time to formulate a strategy for cleanup of the problem, if the contaminants can be cleaned up. If the contaminants have entered the groundwater and are moving away from the source, it is very important to contain the plume before it migrates across a property boundary or enters a stream, building basement, or well. There are a series of methods that can be used to slow or curtail the migration of a contamination plume. The most common method of plume containment is to use a temporary or permanent slurry wall or a similar structure (Figure 3.8). When the water-table aquifer lies close to the land surface and the aquifer is relatively thin, the use of a containment method is quite feasible and cost effective. When the aquifer is thick (perhaps over 50 ft) and the plume is extensive, the only method of containment may be to pump a sufficient quantity of water from the aquifer to reverse the flow direction. This method creates a wastewater that must be treated to remove the contaminant before the water can be discharged or returned to the aquifer. These methods are considered to be only stop-gap measures until the final cleanup strategy is formulated. It is critical to decide upon a containment method and implement it as quickly as possible in order to keep cleanup costs and liabilities to a minimum.

Contamination Cleanup Strategies

There are a limited number of realistic strategies that can be employed to clean up contamination (Table 3.1). Depending on the type of contamination present, the most common methods are (1) excavate, remove, and dispose; (2) pump and treat; (3) treat in place; and (4) contain and abandon. The first strategy applies mostly to soil contamination that cannot be treated to eliminate the toxicity, such as heavy metals or some pesticides. In many cases, soils that are contaminated with metals must be disposed of in an approved hazardous waste landfill. The second strategy can involve soil or groundwater contamination,

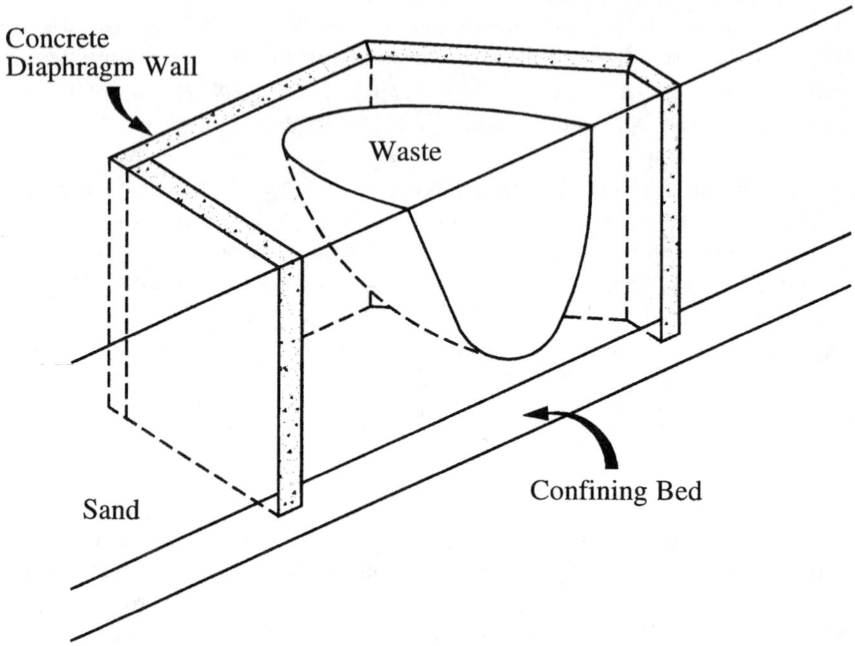

Figure 3.8 Containment of contamination using slurry wall. Full containment of a contamination problem can be achieved by constructing a wall from land surface into the lower confining bed. (From Mitchell, J. K. and Brandon, T. L., Containment Barriers for Land Disposal Solvent-Bearing Hazardous Wastes, Open-File Report, Environmental Institute for Waste Management, University of Alabama, 1985.)

particularly when the contamination is a liquid waste, such as petroleum or an organic solvent. This strategy involves the design and construction of a collection system, using either wells or galleries connected by pumps to an on-site treatment plant (Figure 3.9). The treatment system can be quite simple, as in the case of a stripping tower used to remove volatile organic compounds, or very complex, as in the case of an industrial wastewater plant needed to remove arsenic. The third option includes various bioremediation methods and some physical methods, such as thermal treatment and air sparging. It is relatively rare that cleanup can be accomplished by using an in-place treatment method without using one of the other methods along with it. The fourth strategy is becoming a more common method of dealing with sites where cleanup may not be feasible within the framework of practicality or cost considerations. This method essentially includes the full containment of the contamination using slurry walls or the incorporation of the contamination into an inert material such as cement or glass. A risk assessment is normally required to assure that there is no potential harm to off-site areas containing water supply wells or streams. The use of this strategy may preclude certain future land uses on the site and may lead to future liabilities. Therefore, it must be carefully evaluated before being implemented. A new strategy being tested by the U.S. Environmental Protection Agency for inter-city,

TABLE 3.1 Contamination Remediation Methods

1. Physical Extraction
   Removal of soils
   Landfilling
   Incineration
   Removal of liquids by
   excavation or pumping
   Treatment to reduce volume
   Incineration
   Separation and disposal
   Vacuum extraction
2. Pump and Treat
   Use of wells or galleries to
   intercept contaminants
   Air stripping
   Wastewater plant treatment
3. In-Place Treatment
   Thermal treatment
   Vacuum extraction
   Bioremediation
   Air sparging
4. Contain and Abandon
   Sheet piling
   Slurry walls
   Vaults
   Monitoring

heavily contaminated sites is the "Brownfields" program, which allows much of the contamination to remain in place where the site will be redeveloped with heavy industry (Smary and Donohue, 1994).

Further Reading on Cleanup Methods and Strategies

The preceding discussion provides a basic overview on the subject of toxic and hazardous waste cleanup and is not a comprehensive technical treatment of the subject. More complete references on the subject of contamination assessment and remediation strategies are available. Three comprehensive technical references on assessment procedures and contamination fate and transport are Knox, Sabatini, and Canter (1993), the U.S. Environmental Protection Agency (1988), and Canter and Knox (1985), a technical text on remediation methods, which contains a rather comprehensive annotated bibliography. The U.S. Environmental Protection Agency has published a series of technical reports on remediation methods and procedures, operating methods, and remedial cost estimation (U.S.E.P.A., 1982; 1986; 1987; 1988a; 1988b; 1992). Also, there are a number of journals that are published on a quarterly or monthly basis that contain papers solely on the subject of contamination. In order to obtain information on the very latest technology, it is suggested that the researcher consult journals via an information search service. These references should be reviewed in order to assess cleanup options. It should be noted that most of these references are written at a technical level that assumes expertise in engineering, hydrology, and chemistry.

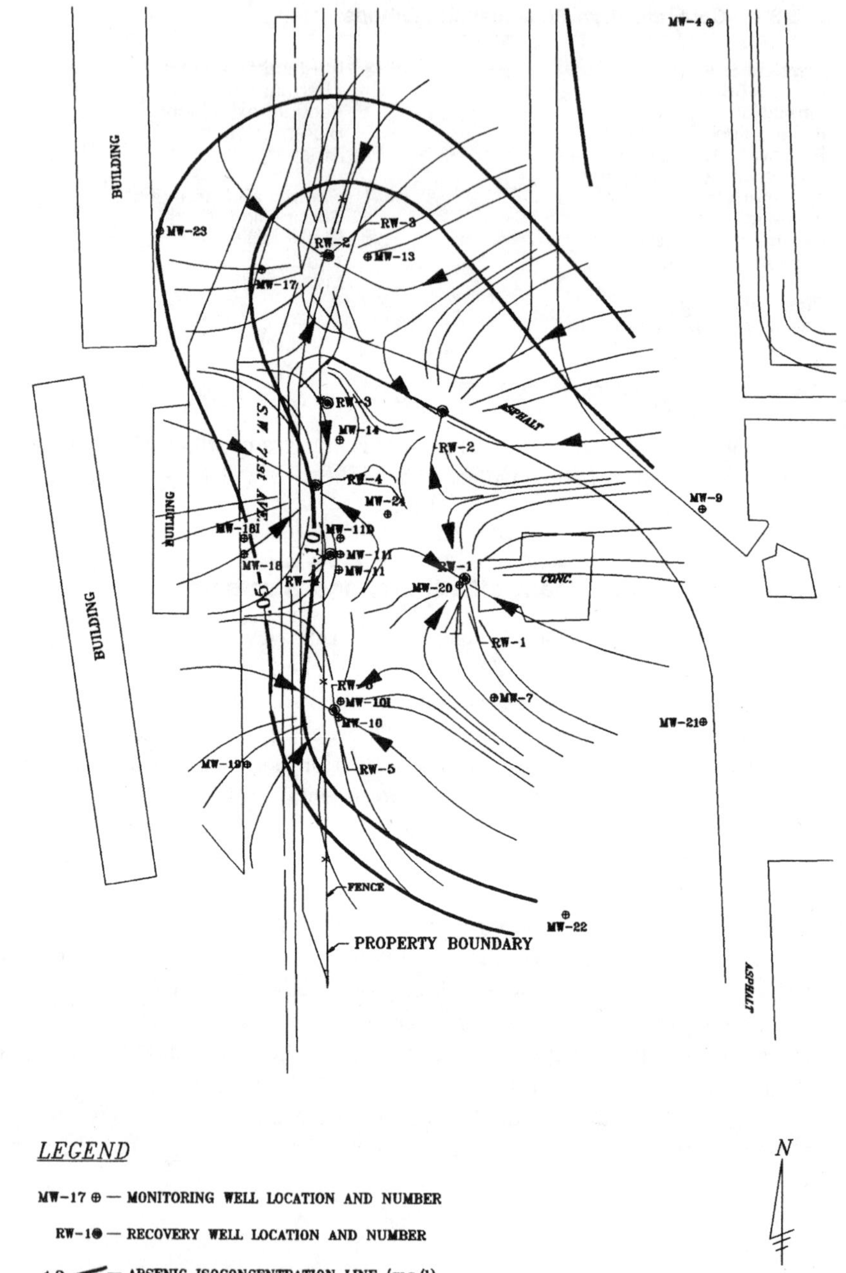

Figure 3.9 Pump and treat contamination cleanup strategy. An arsenic contamination problem is to be eliminated using a series of collection wells. The plume is being captured in wells and the water transmitted to a water treatment facility.

REFERENCES FOR FURTHER READING

Buonicore, A. J., Ed., Cleanup Criteria for Contaminated Soil and Groundwater, ASTM D564, American Society for Testing & Materials, West Conshohocken, PA, 1995, 326 pp.

Canter, L. W. and Knox, R. C., *Groundwater Pollution Control,* Lewis Publishers, Boca Raton, FL, 1985, 526 pp.

Domenico, P. A. and Schwartz, F. W., *Physical and Chemical Hydrogeology,* John Wiley & Sons, New York, 1990, 824 pp.

Fetter, C. W., *Applied Hydrogeology,* 2nd ed., Merrill, Columbus, OH, 1988, 592 pp.

Fetter, C. W., *Contaminant Hydrogeology,* Macmillan, New York, 1992, 458 pp.

Freeze, R. A. and Cherry, J. A., *Groundwater,* Prentice-Hall, Englewood Cliffs, NJ, 1979, 604 pp.

Heath, R. C., Basic Ground-Water Hydrology, Water Supply Paper 2220, U.S. Geological Survey, 1984, 84 pp.

Knox, R. C., Sabatini, D. A., and Canter, L. W., *Subsurface Transport and Fate Processes,* Lewis Publishers, Boca Raton, FL, 1993, 430 pp.

Kruseman, G. P. and DeRidder, N. A., Analysis and Evaluation of Pumping Test Data, International Institute for Land Reclamation and Improvement, Wageningen, The Netherlands, 1991, 377 pp.

Missimer, T. M. and Boggess, D. H., Fluctuations of the Water-Table in Lee County, Florida, 1969–73, Open-File Report 74019, U.S. Geological Survey, 1973, 23 pp.

Mitchell, J. K. and Brandon, T. L., Containment Barriers for Land Disposal Solvent-Bearing Hazardous Wastes, Open-File Report, Environmental Institute for Waste Management, University of Alabama, 1985, 74 pp.

Office of Technology Assessment, Protecting the Nation's Groundwater from Pollution, OTA 0-276, The Author, U.S. Congress, Washington, D.C., 1984, 2 vol.

Smary, E. E. and Donohue, D. J., The "Brownfield-Greenfield" debate: addressing CERCLA and MERA-based impediments to industrial reuse and redevelopment, *Mich. Environ. Law J.,* 13, 4, 1994.

Todd, D. K., *Groundwater Hydrology,* 2nd ed., John Wiley & Sons, New York, 1980, 535 pp.

U. S. Environmental Protection Agency, Handbook for Remedial Action at Waste Disposal Sites, EPA-625/6-82-006, The Author, Washington, D.C., 1982, 497 pp.

U. S. Environmental Protection Agency, Handbook for Stabilization/Solidification of Hazardous Waste, EPA/540/2-86/001, NTIS PB87-116745, The Author, Washington, D.C., 1986.

U. S. Environmental Protection Agency, Remedial Action Costing Procedures Manual, EPA/600/8-87/049, NTIS PB88-113691, The Author, Washington, D.C., 1987.

U. S. Environmental Protection Agency, Guidance for Conducting Remedial Investigations and Feasibility Studies Under CERCLA, EPA/540/G-89/004, OSWER Directive-93553-01, NTIS PB89-184626, The Author, Washington, D.C., 1988a.

U. S. Environmental Protection Agency, Technology Screening Guide for Treatment of CERCLA Soils and Sludges, EPA/540/2-88/004, NTIS PB89-13267, The Author, Washington, D.C., 1988b, 127 pp.

U. S. Environmental Protection Agency, General Methods for Remedial Operational Performance Evaluations, EPA/600/R-92/002, NTIS PB92-166842, The Author, Washington, D.C., 1992, 37 pp.

4 THE LENDING INSTITUTION ENVIRONMENTAL POLICY

All U.S. commercial and savings banks should have a written environmental risk policy. If an institution has not yet implemented such a policy, it may be in violation of Federal Deposit Insurance Corporation policies or other federal banking regulations, policies, and guidelines.

An environmental policy is not just another shelf document to be used as a paperweight; it must be a living, breathing document that is consulted daily by those responsible for the management of the loan portfolio, the trust department, the institution-owned facilities, and the officers involved in commercial lending. This includes the marketing department and those ambitious lenders who aggressively bring new credit extension into the loan portfolio. In a competitive world where performance is preeminent, it is easy to overlook certain policies that may complicate a credit extension or create an illusion of noncompetitiveness. If aggressive lenders clearly understand the environmental policy, they can actually use the policy to their advantage in sales involving sophisticated clients. Borrowers who wish to circumvent the institution's environmental policy are probably not the most desirable clients; they may even add additional risks to the institution's loan portfolio.

For an environmental policy to be successful, it must be a readily usable document. The institution must endorse the policy at the Board level and communicate that endorsement to each officer and employee. The institution must enforce the policy so that any officers who do not cooperate are disciplined accordingly or are terminated. The officers and all involved employees of the institution must be thoroughly trained in the use of the policy and its ramifications. They should be aware of the fact that the policy protects not only the institution but also the employees. A central officer in the institution should be designated as the environmental policy officer or manager. This person must be available to answer questions regarding the policy and the situations that may arise from the policy that may not be specifically addressed. Continuous monitoring for compliance to the policy is extremely important. Periodically or at least annually, the policy should be revised to reflect the passage of any new federal and state regulations that could increase or decrease liability. Perhaps the most important business concept that must be held sacred within the policy is that it must be reasonable and not overly protective. An institution that goes beyond the reasonable management of environmental risk may soon join the growing ranks of merged or consolidated institutions resulting from decreased profitability.

CREATION OF AN ENVIRONMENTAL RISK MANUAL

The document that records an environmental risk policy is commonly termed the *environmental risk manual*. Preparation of the environmental risk manual should be a team effort, led by the designated environmental officer, to recommend the policy for adoption by the institution's board of directors. The internal team should include but not be limited to the environmental policy officer and representatives from each of the major departments in the institution affected by environmental issues. These might include individuals responsible for real estate acquisitions and maintenance, commercial loan portfolio management, institutional acquisitions, trust management, and legal issues. External members of the team usually should include a specialist in environmental law, one or more environmental consultants with special expertise, and perhaps a facilitator to bring the ideas together into a working document. Ultimately, the Board of Directors is responsible for determination of the level of risk that is palatable for the organization.

A high quality environmental risk policy and its manual typically require about a year to complete, depending to a large degree on the complexity of the institution. The policy and manual of a small institution with a residential portfolio will be far less complex than that of a multinational institution or an insurance company.

CONTENTS OF AN ENVIRONMENTAL RISK MANUAL

There are a number of very important reasons to develop and implement an environmental risk manual. As discussed in Chapter 2, there are many liability issues that currently confront lending institutions, particularly the liabilities arising from the Comprehensive Environmental Response, Compensation, and Liability Act. The amendments to this act state that "all appropriate inquiry" is the standard in the due diligence process for buyers of property. All lending institutions should be concerned about avoiding CERCLA liabilities arising from uninformed decisions. The variety of economic issues involved includes potential loss of collateral or security interest and the potential exposure to third-party legal actions. The Federal Deposit Loan Corporation requires development and compliance with a written environmental policy. Similarly, federal regulations require the institution to maintain proper documentation and monitoring of transactions, using personnel who are trained regarding the contents and administration of the policy.

The environmental risk manual must be a comprehensive, well-organized document containing all of the institution's environmental policies. The manual should be indexed for key words, with major section headings that provide all users with easy access to the desired information. A typical table of contents for an environmental risk manual is given in Table 4.1. The major headings include

- background information,
- policy statements,
- consultants/ information systems,
- evaluation steps,
- documentation/specific industries,
- problem assets/other real estate owned,
- glossary,
- index.

Table 4.1 Outline for a typical lending institution environmental risk manual

Background Information on Risks and Rewards: FDIC Environmental Guidelines	
	Criminal Sentences and Civil Penalties
	Indirect Customer Harm
	Direct Institution Harm
	Environmental Rewards/New Business Opportunities
Background Information on Due Diligence	
	Historical Overview
	Delegation Process
	Future Trends
	Investigation Requirements
	EPA Safe Harbors Rule
	The Basic Principle
Policy Statements	
	Introduction
	Environmental Due Diligence Methods Definitions
	Policies
	Policy Revisions
Consultants	
	In-House Experts
	Consultant Qualification Process
	Institution-Hired Consultants
	Customer-Hired Consultants
	Institution-Hired Attorneys
Evaluation Steps	
	Introduction
	Checklist Method Guidance
	Transactional Screen Process Guidance
	Phase I Environmental Site Assessments Guidance
	Environmental Audits Guidance
Documentation/Specific Industries	
	Environmental Agreements
	Monitoring of Facilities Guidance
Problem Assets	
	Managing Problem Assets
	Selling/Leasing Problem Assets
	Glossary

The major headings should provide all the information that a user needs to understand fully the philosophy upon which the institution's policy is based, the federal regulations, and the practical impacts of the liability. The following discussion, which is organized under major topic headings, could be used as the basis for the development of an actual environmental risk manual. Of course, each institution must make many decisions that will tailor the manual to the operating policies and business philosophy of that institution. This text uses some emphatic language, influenced by a conservative approach, which may be modified to reflect the character of the institution or to reflect changes in environmental laws.

Background Information on Risks and Rewards: FDIC Environmental Guidelines

Improper management of environmental risks may cause liability or financial losses to affiliated banks, the trust company, or customers of the institution. These liabilities and financial losses could significantly weaken the loan portfolio and could threaten the financial standing of the institution. On February 23, 1993, the Federal Deposit Insurance Corporation sent a letter to all member institutions containing "Guidelines for an Environmental Risk Program" (Table 4.2). The current version of this manual stresses the points that are included in the suggested guidelines. However, this manual also includes guidelines to monitor credits after initial underwriting for any adverse changes in the institution degree of risk brought on by new borrower activities or newly adopted environmental rules and regulations.

Criminal Sentences and Civil Penalties

There are many business managers and executives currently serving prison sentences for violating the nation's environmental laws. Hundreds of others have paid fines or have served suspended sentences that involved community service or home confinement. Federal Minimum Sentence Guidelines require judges to take into account the existence or nonexistence of environmental policies, evidence of efforts undertaken throughout an organization to implement those policies, and related compliance programs when determining the severity of sentences and/or fines for any individual or corporation. Although no lenders, bankers, or trust officers are known to have served time for environmental crimes, financial institution officers have been threatened with individual liability actions in connection with Superfund litigation. They have been required to produce personal financial statements and individual tax returns in addition to corporate records to determine potential settlement amounts from their personal assets and/or corporate assets. These records are the basis for joint and several liability.

Indirect Customer Harm

Customer harm impacts the lender in three fundamental ways: opportunity loss, disrupted cash flow/bankruptcy, and/or impaired collateral value and liability for upkeep costs. The impact can be substantial, especially when cumulative or "trickle-down" impacts are considered, such as a business loan failure causing the default of another mortgage held by the same institution.

When loan or trust business cannot be concluded quickly or becomes impossible because of environmental issues, opportunity loss is incurred by the institution or the trust company unit. Staff time is expended for business development, when business calls and visits with potential customers are made, when credit and other information is compiled, and when credit analyses and underwriting credits are completed. Environmental problems or issues, including the need to clean up contaminated sites or to obtain agency approvals, can delay, prevent, or change the economic viability of existing businesses, contemplated projects, or other activities.

Environmental problems encountered by businesses or individuals who have received loans can lead to financial troubles for the borrower. Costs may increase for environmental compliance measures, cleanup of hazardous or toxic substance leaks or spills, petroleum product leaks or spills, upgrades of environmental control equipment and preventive systems, health and safety violations, or payments to third parties for environmental damages. These added costs reduce cash flow and affect the borrower's ability to meet payment schedules, which may ultimately lead to bankruptcy. The size of a business does not protect it from becoming a victim of such environmental damages; firms ranging in size from mom-and-pop operations to multibillion dollar conglomerates have been financially impaired or bankrupted. Thus, a borrower or lender must consider the possibility of interrupted cash flow, inability to meet loan repayments, and complete write-downs of loans as potential consequences when dealing with environmental issues. Soil and/or groundwater contamination can also impair or completely devalue the real property used as loan collateral, which is the planned secondary source of loan repayment. When cleanup costs exceed property value, the lender may be forced to abandon the collateral property.

Direct Institution Harm

There are many ways that environmental problems may directly affect a lending institution adversely, including increased loan loss reserve requirements, charged-off loans, loss of lien priority, direct environmental liability, necessity to obtain environmental permits directly, and third-party liability actions.

Environmental problems causing decreased cash flow, impaired collateral, or a weakening of customers in other ways lead to credit downgrades. In these cases, the institution or the federal bank examiners may require increased loss reserves for these loans, which leads directly to increased expenses and lower profits.

When both the primary and secondary means of credit collection fail, the institution may have no other choice than to write-down problem loans. There are cases in which the tenants of income-producing properties have contaminated the borrower's property, which also served as collateral for a loan. This problem impairs the collateral, sometimes to the point where foreclosure is not an economical alternative.

In some bankruptcy cases, environmental cleanup and agency administrative costs are deleted from the proceeds available to creditors. In a number of states

Table 4.2 Federal Deposit Insurance Corporation Guidelines for an Environmental Risk Program (February 25, 1993)

BACKGROUND

The potential adverse effect of environmental contamination on the value of real property and the potential for liability under various environmental laws have become important factors in evaluating real estate transactions and making loans secured by real estate. Environmental contamination, and liability associated with environmental contamination, may have a significant adverse effect on the value of real estate collateral, which may in certain circumstances cause an insured institution to abandon its right to the collateral. It is also possible for an institution to be held directly liable for the environmental cleanup of real property collateral acquired by the institution. The cost of such a cleanup may exceed by many times the amount of the loan made to the borrower. A loan also may be affected adversely by potential environmental liability even where real property is not taken as collateral. For example, a borrower's capacity to make payments on a loan may be threatened by environmental liability to the borrower for the cost of a hazardous contamination cleanup on property unrelated to the loan with the institution.

The potential for environmental liability may arise from a variety of federal and state environmental laws and from common law tort liability. The most significant environmental law establishing liability for the cost of cleaning up hazardous contamination on real property is the Comprehensive Environmental Response, Compensation and Liability Act (also known as "CERCLA" and "Superfund"). CERCLA establishes a broad legal framework that creates potential liability for the cleanup costs of hazardous contamination. Entities that may be potentially liable for these cleanup costs are the current and past owners of the contaminated property, the current and past operations of business on the property, entities that disposed of hazardous substances at the property, and entities that transported hazardous substances for disposal to property selected by the transporter. CERCLA provides a secured creditor exemption from liability for banks and other lenders that do not participate in the management of the property. The United States Environmental Protection Agency has issued a rule interpreting the secured creditor exemption under CERCLA, 57 Fed. Reg. 18344 (April 29, 1992). In addition to the federal Superfund law, most states have enacted legislation that establishes similar liability under state law for hazardous contamination cleanup costs.

The other primary federal environmental law relating to hazardous contamination liability is the Resource Conservation and Recovery Act (also known as "RCRA"). RCRA establishes a comprehensive statutory and regulatory framework that governs the generation, transportation, storage, discharge and disposal of solid and hazardous wastes, and, when necessary, the cleanup of hazardous contamination. RCRA also establishes regulations governing the prevention, detection and cleanup of releases from underground storage tanks containing certain hazardous substances or petroleum. Under authorization by Congress, many states establish and administer RCRA programs as part of each state's environmental laws.

Other federal environmental laws that establish environmental liability include, among others, the Clean Water Act, the Clean Air Act and the Toxic Substance Control Act. The states, including the local jurisdictions within each state, have also enacted many other environmental laws and regulations. In addition to federal and state environmental laws, potential environmental liability may result under common law tort suits based on hazardous contamination.

Institutions need to implement an environmental risk program in order to evaluate the potential adverse effect of environmental contamination on the value of real property and the potential environmental liability associated with the real property. The failure of an institution to evaluate potential environmental risks associated with real property may contribute to an institution's inability to collect on its loans and affect the institution's financial condition.

ENVIRONMENTAL RISK PROGRAM

As part of the institution's overall decision-making process, the environmental risk program should establish procedures for identifying and evaluating potential environmental concerns associated with lending practices and other actions relating to real property. The board of directors should review and approve the program and designate a senior officer knowledgeable in environmental matters responsible for program implementation. The environmental risk program should be tailored to the needs of the lending institution. That is, institutions that have a heavier concentration of loans to higher risk industries or localities

Table 4.2 Federal Deposit Insurance Corporation Guidelines for an Environmental Risk Program (February 25, 1993) (Continued)

of known contamination may require a more elaborate and sophisticated environmental risk program than institutions that lend more to lower risk industries or localities. For example, loans collateralized by 1- to 4-family residences normally have less exposure to environmental liability than loans to finance industrial properties. The environmental risk program should provide for staff training, set environmental policy guidelines and procedures, require an environmental review or analysis during the application process, include loan documentation standards, and establish appropriate environmental risk assessment safeguards in loan workout situations and foreclosures.

Training The environmental risk program should incorporate training sufficient to ensure that the environmental risk program is implemented and followed within the institution and the appropriate personnel have the knowledge and experience to determine and evaluate potential environmental concerns that might affect the institution. Whenever the complexity of the environmental issue is beyond the expertise of the institution's staff, the institution should consult legal counsel, environmental consultants and other qualified experts.

Policies When appropriate, loan policies, manuals and written procedures should address environmental issues pertinent to the institution's specific lending activities. For example, the lending manual might identify the types of environmental risks associated with industries and real estate in the institution's trade area, provide guidelines for conducting an analysis of potential environmental liability and describe procedures for the resolution of potential environmental concerns. Procedures for the resolution of environmental concerns might also be developed for credit monitoring, loan workout situations and foreclosures.

Environmental Risk Analysis Prior to making a loan, an initial environmental risk analysis needs to be conducted during the application process. An appropriate analysis may allow the institution to avoid loans that result in substantial losses or liability and provide the institution with information to minimize potential environmental liability on loans that are made. Much of the needed information may be gathered by the account officer when interviewing the loan applicant concerning his or her business activities. In addition, the loan application might be designed to request relevant environmental information, such as the present and past uses of the property and the occurrence of any contacts by federal, state, or local governmental agencies about environmental matters. The loan officer or other representative of an institution might visit the site to evaluate whether there is obvious visual evidence of environmental concerns.

Structured Environmental Risk Assessment Whenever the application, interview, or visitation indicates a possible environmental concern, a more detailed structured investigation by a qualified individual might be appropriate. This assessment might include surveying past ownership and uses of the property, inspecting the site and contiguous parcels of property and reviewing company records for past use or disposal of hazardous materials. A review of public records might include contact with federal and state environmental protection agencies to determine whether the borrower has been cited for violations concerning environmental laws and a review of federal and state lists identifying real property with significant environmental contamination.

Loan Documentation Loan documents should include language to safeguard the institution against potential environmental losses and liabilities. Such language might require that the borrower comply with environmental laws, disclose information about the environmental status of the real property collateral, and grant the institution the right to acquire additional information about potential hazardous contamination by inspecting the collateral for environmental concerns. The loan documents might also provide that the institution has the right to call the loan, refuse to extend funds under a line of credit, or foreclose if the hazardous contamination is discovered in the real property collateral. The loan documents might also call for an indemnity of the institution by the borrower and guarantors for environmental liability associated with the real property collateral.

Monitoring The environmental risk assessment should continue during the life of the loan by monitoring the borrower and the real property collateral for potential environmental concerns. The institution should be aware of changes in the business activities of the borrower that result in a significant increased risk of environmental liability associated with the real property collateral. If there is a potential for the environmental contamination to adversely affect the value of the collateral, the institution might exercise its rights under the loan to require the borrower to resolve the environmental condition and take those actions that are reasonably necessary to protect the value of the real property.

Table 4.2 Federal Deposit Insurance Corporation Guidelines for an Environmental Risk Program (February 25, 1993) (Continued)

Involvement in the Borrower's Operations Under the federal Superfund law, CERCLA, the institution may have an exemption from environmental liability as the holder of a security interest in the real property collateral. In monitoring a loan for potential environmental concerns, and resolving those environmental situations as necessary, the institution should evaluate whether its actions may constitute "participating in the management" of the business located on the real property collateral within the meaning of CERCLA. If the actions are considered to be participating in the management, the institution may lose its exemption from liability under CERCLA.

Foreclosue A lender's exposure to environmental liability may increase significantly if it takes title to real property held as collateral. The institution should evaluate the potential environmental costs and the potential for environmental liability in conjunction with an assessment of the value of the collateral in reaching a decision to take title to the property by foreclosure or other means.

SUPERVISORY POLICY

Examiners will review an institution's environmental risk program as part of the examination of its lending and investment activities. When analyzing individual credits, examiners will review the institution's compliance with its own environmental risk program. Failure to establish or comply with an appropriate environmental program will be criticized and corrective action required.

and counties (for example, Dade County, Florida), local laws or ordinances elevate the estimated cost for environmental cleanup to a parity with tax liens and ahead of other creditors. This loss of lien priority creates additional write-downs of real properties.

A lending institution can incur direct environmental liabilities if the institution (1) is deemed by a regulatory agency or court to be "an operator" of a borrower's business that has environmental problems, (2) takes title to a contaminated property in attempting to collect on its collateral, or (3) owns facilities that have released hazardous or toxic substances, even if the problems were caused by a prior owner (see Chapter 2). Action by federal, state, and local agencies, as well as citizen action, can be brought against the lending institution, which is perceived as a "deep pocket." Liability is not limited to cleanup costs but may also include administrative costs, fines, and damages to natural resources, depending on the circumstances and the agency direction. Insurance may not cover all or even most of these situations. Therefore, it is critical that preloan environmental investigations be conducted to reduce risk.

There are cases in which an institution might otherwise be able to foreclose on collateral but may not be able to use the property, operate a business on the property, or sell the property to others because of a lack of one or more environmental permits. The necessary permits can cover many areas, including air emissions, dredging and filling of wetlands, surface-water management, water use, and a host of others. The presence of an eagle's nest or some other endangered animal or plant species may render a property nearly useless for economic activity. If the appropriate permit or permits cannot be obtained, the property cannot be used, resulting in a substantial or total loss.

Perhaps the most feared potential loss from an environmental problem is the threat of a third-party action brought against the institution. If a contamination problem migrates away from a foreclosed property, the lending institution could be sued under various common law theories for strict liability, nuisance, negligence, and trespass. Even if the institution wins in a court proceeding, the trial costs alone are often substantial.

Environmental Rewards/New Business Opportunities

Based on the experience of learning either to avoid or properly manage environmental risks, a lender may discover opportunities for new or increased business that others in the industry might neglect due to fear or ignorance. In many cases, high risk businesses that effectively manage their environmental risk may be highly desirable as lending customers when compared to relatively simple operations where the business owners or managers are ignorant or careless in handling environmental matters.

Background Information on Due Diligence

Historical Overview

Any environmental risk manual should clearly explain the legal aspects of the liabilities associated with environmental problems and the concept of "due diligence." The manual should repeat the basic concepts, supported with numerous examples, to emphasize the importance of understanding both institutional and individual exposure problems. A detailed discussion of the historical development of environmental laws and regulations is included in Chapter 2 of this book. The key concepts from the federal law, incorporated in state and local laws, are

1. Owners or operators of businesses are strictly liable for contamination.
2. Contamination liability is joint and several regardless of fault (In other words, if there is any association with a contaminated property, any past or current owner or operator can be assessed the entire cost of cleanup.).
3. Liability is retroactive.

The environmental liabilities created under the CERCLA and RCRA laws are draconian in nature and are perhaps the most punitive of all federal civil laws.

Delegation Process

State and local governments have continued to expand their regulatory roles with regard to environmental enforcement. The main reason for this expansion is the pattern set by federal legislation of granting the states control over the environmental regulatory process, provided that the standards are equal to or more stringent than federal regulations. State and local governments have also benefited from the income obtained from fines. This delegation of authority to states and localities has led to the passage of numerous new state and local laws, leading to a morass of new regulations. This process has greatly complicated the overall environmental compliance strategy used by businesses, because local government regulations are commonly more restrictive than state regulations and, in some cases, conflict with higher government regulations. Unfortunately, compliance with the local government regulations does not necessarily remove a business from reviews by either state and/or federal agencies. In the delegation process, the highest governing agency, in many cases the U.S. Environmental Protection Agency, may overrule the state or local government on any matter rooted in an original federal statute.

Future Trends

Many states have developed very detailed procedures to deal with the environmental issues involved in the transfer of real property. An example of this general trend is the New Jersey Industrial Site Recovery Act (ISRA). This act, pertaining to industrial property transfers, is a general model for this type of regulatory approach. According to the New Jersey Department of Environmental Protection and Energy (DEPE), the purpose of the ISRA approach to environmental regulation is to encourage proper environmental practices, detect environmental problems early, prevent abandonment of hazardous waste sites, identify and remediate environmental problems with private funds by responsible parties, and protect buyers. ISRA requires the owners of industrial property to obtain from DEPE either a declaration that the property is not contaminated and poses no potential threat to human health or the environment or approval for a cleanup plan if the property is contaminated. This includes property used for generation, handling, transportation, treatment, storage and/or disposal of hazardous substances. Provisions of ISRA apply at the time an industrial business is closing, terminating, or transferring operations.

This type of legislation has been discussed on the federal level and by various states over the past decade. However, the current conservative trend toward government regulation does not bode well for the development of this type of procedure on a widespread basis. This legislation would encourage industrial property owners and their lenders to be certain that environmental problems are identified and corrected on a timely basis.

Investigation Requirements

Based on CERCLA and the cases that interpret it, a current property owner can be held liable for cleanup of contamination. This liability for cleanup costs holds, even if the owner, such as a lending institution that took the property back through a foreclosure or through a deed in lieu of foreclosure, did not cause the environmental problem. In 1986, the Superfund Amendments and Reauthorization Act gave lending institutions some minor relief regarding CERCLA liabilities by creating the "innocent landowner defense." To use this defense, in addition to other requirements, the purchaser of a property

> must have undertaken, at the time of acquisition, all appropriate inquiry into the previous ownership and uses of the property consistent with good commercial

> or customary practice in an effort to minimize liability. For purposes of the preceding sentence the court shall take into account any specialized knowledge or experience on the part of the (purchaser), the relationship of the purchase price to the value of the property if uncontaminated, commonly known or reasonably ascertainable information about the property, the obviousness of the presence or likely presence of contamination at the property, and the ability (emphasis above added) (42 USC Section 9601 (35)).

The U.S. Environmental Protection Agency made a public interpretation of the "innocent landowner" defense in the form of a document, entitled "Guidance on Landowner Liability under Section 107 (a) (1) of CERCLA, De Minimis Settlements under Section 122 (g) (1) (B) of CERCLA and Settlements with Prospective Purchasers of Contaminated Property." This document did not precisely address the definition of "all appropriate inquiry" or what should be covered by the environmental investigation.

It is very important to note that the "innocent landowner" defense may provide some protection against federal actions under CERCLA, but this defense does not necessarily carry over into state and local jurisdictions. In fact, the "innocent landowner" defense was not adopted by many states having primacy over contamination cleanup issues.

Potential buyers and lenders handling real property have attempted to define properly the meaning of "all appropriate inquiry" by developing a type of environmental investigation for a property, originally termed an *environmental audit* and later called an *environmental site assessment* (see Chapter 5). The scope of these environmental investigations varied widely, based on the requirements of the lending institution and the methods employed by the consultants performing the investigations. There were no uniform standards on which to base a comparison of these investigations. The first organization to adopt a uniform methodology for environmental site assessments was the Association of Groundwater Scientists and Engineers (1992), although this method was not widely adopted. About a year later, the American Society for Testing and Materials published two documents to standardize what was termed a *phase I environmental site assessment* and the *transaction screening process*, with the respective standard numbers 1527 and 1528. Copies of these standards should be purchased from ASTM and should be made available in the environmental risk policy manual.

Although the "all appropriate inquiry" investigation created by the CERCLA/SARA federal laws has been the motivating force in defining due diligence investigations of properties, the problems found are rarely covered by these federal laws. Some issues involving the on-site disposal of hazardous wastes are covered by the federal Resource Conservation and Recovery Act (RCRA) or other federal statutes. However, the vast majority of contamination problems are covered under a variety of state environmental laws and rules that do not require direct federal involvement. As discussed in Chapter 3, it is very important to understand clearly the meaning of "contamination" within the framework of both state and local laws.

EPA Safe Harbors Rule

On April 29, 1992, the U.S. Environmental Protection Agency published a rule on lender liability under CERCLA. This rule provided that a party holding indicia of ownership in property "primarily to protect a security interest" (in general, a secured creditor) should not be held liable by EPA under CERCLA for cleaning up environmental contamination. This rule was overturned by the courts on February 4, 1994. Although this rule granted some temporary relief to lending institutions, it applied only to the activities of a second creditor as an "owner and operator" and not as a "generator or transporter" of hazardous substances, which did not exempt the creditor from liabilities within the Resource Conservation and Recovery Act and from lawsuits initiated by third parties, such as individuals or other state or federal agencies.

The short-lived EPA rule was implemented because of the reaction by lenders to *U.S. v. Fleet Factors* and other court decisions (see Chapters 2 and 7). The Fleet Factors decision suggested that a secured creditor could be held liable under CERCLA for participation in management of a facility, even though the degree of participation was far less than an involvement in the day-to-day operations. This court decision meant that an individual or institution might be environmentally liable for merely having the ability to influence decisions about environmental matters, even if such influence was not exercised. This decision still applies to the Eleventh Circuit, covering Florida, Georgia, and Alabama.

Despite the fact that the EPA rule provided for certain permitted activities or "safe harbors," environmental due diligence was still necessary, because accurate estimates of environmental cleanup costs were difficult, as was the resale of the property, even after cleanup was completed, due to market factors and the "environmental stigma" associated with the cleanup. The basic bottom line came down to the fact that to take a property that had a value less than the cost of cleanup did not make good business sense.

Although the EPA rule was short-lived, the basic philosophy of the rule is important because attempts may be made in the future to revive it. The rule focused on two aspects of the borrower/secured creditor relationship to determine if there was "participation in management" (see Chapter 7). The first test was whether the secured creditor had "undertaken responsibility for the borrower's hazardous substance handling or disposal practices." The second test of the rule was whether the secured creditor exercised day-to-day management control over environmental compliance or over all substantial operations (as opposed to only financial or administrative aspects of the business). If the relationship failed either test, then the security interest exemption was lost. The rule also contained specific permitted activities or "safe harbors" that were not constructed to be improper participation in management. Those provisions of particular interest involved the "policing" of a loan or security interest, workout activities, actions tied to foreclosure, or actions taken to protect a security interest. Activities permitted in the policing of a loan or security interest included the following

- Requiring the borrower to clean up the facility during the term of the security interest
- Requiring the borrower to comply or come into compliance with applicable federal, state, and local environmental and other laws, rules, and regulations during the term of the security interest
- Obtaining or exercising authority to monitor or inspect the facility (including on-site inspections) in which indicia of ownership are maintained or to monitor the borrower's business and financial condition during the term of the security interest
- Taking other actions to adequately police the loan or security interest (such as requiring a borrower to comply with warranties, covenants, conditions, representations, or promises from the borrower)

Activities permitted in a workout were

- Restructuring or renegotiating the terms of the security interest
- Requiring the payment of additional rent or interest
- Exercising forbearance
- Requiring or exercising rights pursuant to an assignment of accounts or other amounts owing to an obligor
- Requiring or exercising rights pursuant to an escrow agreement pertaining to amounts owing to an obligor
- Providing specific, general financial or other advice, suggestions, counseling, or guidance
- Exercising any right or remedy the holder is entitled to by law or under any warranties, covenants, conditions, representations, or promises from the borrower

Activities permitted under foreclosure were

- Purchase at foreclosure sale
- Acquisition or assignment of title in lieu of foreclosure, termination of a lease or other repossession
- Acquisition of a right to title or possession
- An agreement in satisfaction of the obligation, or any other formal or informal manner (whether pursuant to law or under warranties, covenants, conditions, representations, or promises from the borrower) by which the holder acquires title to or possession of the secured property

The EPA rule also contained specific guidelines with regard to post-foreclosure activities that might be conducted and still maintain the security exemption. As long as the secured creditor did not participate in management prior to foreclosure, it could sell, re-lease property held pursuant to a lease financing transaction (whether by a new lease financing transaction or a substitution of the lessee), liquidate, maintain business activities, wind up operations, undertake any response actions under Section 107(d) (1) of CERCLA or under the direction of an on-site coordinator, and take measures to preserve, protect, or prepare the secured asset prior to sale or other disposition.

Another important provision of the EPA rule was that the secured creditor had to dispose of the property in a "reasonably expeditious manner" or must have followed the "safe harbor" of advertising the property for resale within 12 months after the foreclosure was completed and title acquired. If a written, bona fide offer of fair consideration was received after 6 months from foreclosure, the secured creditor was required to respond in writing within 90 days. If a written response was not given, then the secured creditor was deemed to have rejected the bona fide offer, resulting in a loss of the security interest exemption. As long as the secured creditor continued its efforts to market the property in conformity with the EPA rule, the security interest exemption was maintained.

Soon after adoption of the EPA rule, the courts ruled that EPA did not have the statutory authority to promulgate its Lender Liability Rule, although there is a possibility that Congress will amend CERCLA in the future to clarify the secured lender exemption. There have been cases in which the courts have protected lenders from owner/operator liability under CERCLA without citing the Lender Liability Rule. Therefore, if the lender must take title to land in order to protect its security interest, it should follow due diligence and management practices similar to those cited in the now defunct EPA rule.

The Basic Principle

Based on the discussion in this section, the importance of "due diligence" in the form of an environmental investigation that satisfies the "all appropriate inquiry" rule should be clear. Environmental investigations of specific nature should be conducted before a loan is consummated and before the decision is made to foreclose or take title to a property. In all cases, it is necessary to perform the due diligence environmental site investigation prior to a foreclosure, even if a similar investigation was made prior to the purchase of the same property. Properties taken in foreclosure must be sold to maintain CERCLA exemption, even if the bank takes title in compliance with applicable laws and regulations. If the cost of cleanup exceeds the value of the property, then obviously there is no advantage in obtaining title, even though the bank may be protected from liability under an EPA CERCLA exemption or some other limited state exemption.

A reasonable financial cushion should be added to the estimated environmental cleanup costs, since these costs are very difficult to estimate accurately. If possible, cleanup activities should be completed before the institution takes title to the property. The procedures dealing with problem assets are discussed in more detail later in this manual (see Chapters 6 and 7).

Policy Statements

A series of policies must be developed to define the degree of due diligence or investigation required by the institution for given types and sizes of credit extensions. These policies must be crafted carefully to incorporate protection from environmental liabilities in consideration of competition. The corporate philosophy of the institution and its appetite for risk will influence the wording of these policies, so no specific recommendations can be made. The degree of risk taken by each institution depends on how aggressively the institution's management decides to pursue the market, the geographic location of the institution, and the institution's loss experience. Environmental risks tend to be greater in the industrialized parts of the United States and lesser in rural areas. Certain state and local laws can increase environmental liabilities, which may cause institutional policies to vary in those geographic areas. These policies affect the potential for losses and influence competitive forces. A balance must be developed between environmental due diligence, the level of risk the institution finds acceptable, and the need to maintain a competitive structure. These decisions should be made by upper management, with input and recommendations from support staff. The policies must then be followed strictly by all of the institution's employees.

Environmental Due Diligence Methods Definitions

It is necessary to define the basic due diligence methods that are employed in the policy statements presented. In most institution environmental policies, the only due diligence method performed by nontechnical, in-house employees is the checklist. All other environmental investigations, including the transaction screen process, phase I environmental site assessments, additional phases of environmental site assessments, and environmental audits, are performed by trained environmental professionals. If no such professionals are employed by the institution, then qualified environmental consultants must be retained.

All defined due diligence methods should follow a phased approach, in order to meet the objective of limiting liability while conserving capital. When potential or real problems are encountered, further investigation is then required prior to extending credit, establishing a trust relationship, or taking title to real estate. Usually, defining an environmental problem is a process, beginning with the discovery of the problem during either a transaction screen process, or a phase I environmental site assessment (see Chapter 5). The process then leads to additional verification of the problem and ultimately to remediation, when necessary (see Chapter 6). The institution's personnel should not draw conclusions concerning the possible impacts of an environmental problem until the entire process is completed so the cost to clean up the problem may be quantified. In certain instances, a number of investigations are conducted simultaneously to expedite a solution.

A similar investigative process is employed when real estate is used to secure a loan with the proceeds to be used for another purpose. An investigation of environmental issues may also be required prior to the extension of credit for working capital to manufacturing companies or small businesses that use, store, or transport hazardous or toxic substances. Outside consultants may be required to assist the institution in assessing environmental liabilities, especially when extending credit to high-risk businesses or in large amounts.

The first step in environmental due diligence involves the completion of an internal checklist by trained institution personnel, who gather information from interviews with the site owner and/or operator and from a site visit. Additional information on the development and use of this checklist is provided under the subheading "Evaluation." Some institutions may forgo development of the checklist and use the other methods described.

The next and more comprehensive step in the due diligence investigation involves the use of the transaction screen process (see Chapter 5). This method is defined in ASTM Practice E 1528 and involves the completion of a questionnaire by the site owner or operator, the site tenants, and an environmental professional. Qualified, outside environmental professionals should perform these investigations unless there are highly trained environmental professionals employed by the institution. Also, the institution should address liability issues that may arise from using internal personnel to perform these due diligence investigations. Institutions should use in-house personnel only when assessing institution-owned real estate. The scope of a transaction screen process can be modified to include other environmental issues when it is deemed necessary. Any outside consultants used to perform these investigations should be prequalified according to the policy manual's statement on consultants (see subheading, "Consultants").

A phase I environmental site assessment should be required on many types and sizes of transactions. This due diligence method is defined in ASTM Practice E 1527 (see Chapter 5). Institution customers normally retain preapproved environmental professionals to perform these investigations for real estate credit extensions or trust conveyances. The institution should retain approved consultants to perform these investigations on problem loans where foreclosure is contemplated.

Additional phases of environmental investigation normally involve the sampling and testing of soil and/or groundwater when contamination is suspected. There are other types of due diligence investigations that can be required to assess specific environmental issues, such as air emissions problems, wetland delineation, or a host of others (see Chapter 8). These additional phases of investigation are structured to either confirm or deny the presence of a problem, then to assess the extent of the problem, and finally to recommend some remedial action. The final phase would be to complete the cleanup of contamination, work usually done by qualified environmental consultants and contractors.

An environmental audit (or environmental compliance audit) is an assessment of the site activities and operations with respect to compliance with various environmental laws and regulations, including an assessment of waste disposal practices. The environmental audit process is an exceptionally complex investigation that requires a team of specialized environmental consultants. Both institutional customers and the institution itself should hire qualified specialists when the need arises to perform this type of investigation.

Policies

Policies must be formulated that consider all the business areas in which the institution has potential environmental liability exposure. Each institution is unique both in terms of structure and of the types of financial services offered. Therefore, the number and types of environmental policies necessary will be unique for each institution. About seven different policy types will meet the needs of a moderate-sized lending institution.

An affiliate bank business lending policy applies to all associated banks owned by a single institution. The text of this policy should include a statement with regard to the specific scope of due diligence investigation to be used for various size and risk category loans. For example, the policy may state that all credit extensions on real property or secured by real property must be analyzed for environmental risk by trained institution personnel using the checklist method. If the loan is in excess of some capital amount, a transaction screen process must be used. Many lending institutions require a TSP for all commercial or industrial property transaction values ranging from $100,000 to $500,000. If the credit extension is for a high-risk property or the value of the transaction is high, then a phase I ESA is required. For example, many lending institutions require a phase I ESA for any credit extension above $1 million. If the credit extension is being considered for an operating business that uses, stores, or transports significant quantities of hazardous or toxic substances, then an environmental audit should also be required. Because of the considerable cost of an environmental audit, it is necessary to determine which types of businesses would require that level of due diligence. For example, businesses that have had past records of poor environmental management (environmental violations found in public records) or businesses that are significant generators of hazardous waste under RCRA (as opposed to a small-quantity generator) would require an environmental audit. As part of the policy, the lending institution may require as part of the credit extension conditions that the borrower sign an environmental agreement (see Appendix B).

A critical part of the environmental policy is a risk matrix. It is not appropriate to give a real example of an institution risk matrix, because these documents are highly confidential, due to the competitive issues that are involved. Most risk matrix documents begin with a series of property or business types, categorized by SIC codes from highest to lowest risk. The property or land uses are listed along the left side of the document. A series of additional factors are listed across the top of the document, such as number of environmental violations, age of operation, last time pollution control equipment was purchased, quantity of hazardous waste generated, sophistication of owner or operator, value of transaction, and any past payment problems. In many cases, over ten risk categories are listed. A numerical rating is placed in the appropriate box on the form, and the figures are tabulated to yield a risk factor. The level of due diligence investigation is set from the ranges of numerical risk values listed in the policy. A lending institution may include policy restrictions on certain types of transactions or require increasing levels of sign-off for transactions above certain risk levels.

Another very important part of the risk policy is a method to resolve internal conflicts, such as when there is a question over whether or not to make a credit extension and whether an exemption to the policy may be warranted. Special circumstances can arise that may require an exemption for all or specific aspects of the policy. As an example of such extenuating circumstances, a major institution customer in good financial standing might request a credit extension on a newly purchased facility that falls within the highest risk level category. The institution must decide if the value of the customer's business merits taking higher than normal risks. The policy must include a conflict resolution procedure that specifies who will make the final decision, what information must be made available to the decision maker, and how the process might be expedited. The board of directors of a large lending institution probably will not make the final decision, since this is an operating matter. The decision is usually made by the chief executive officer or chief operating officer. The environmental policy officer may be designated to make the final decision on conflicts with lesser financial impact or may present a recommendation to the final decision maker.

Other policies also should be developed to define specific due diligence requirements. A dealer financial services lending policy or other named policies may apply to a variety of financial services provided, such as asset-based lending. An emergency situations policy applies to sudden or unexpected environmental situations that occur at a facility having a credit extension from the institution or a credit extension used to clean up a spill of a hazardous substance. Also, the policy may cover situations in which an institution customer exhibits some irresponsible environmental management practices that may merit a withdrawal of credit. A number of issues should be addressed in this policy. As an institution acquires experience in an environmental risk management program, emergency situations that arise will lead to revisions in this policy that will assist in the resolution of future similar problems.

A real estate services division policy should be developed that covers real estate owned and/or managed by the lending institution. In many cases lending institutions have carefully limited their exposure to environmental liabilities in the lending process but have ignored similar issues in the acquisition of other institution properties to be used as primary or branch locations. Also, the day-to-day operations of institution-owned facilities must be managed with due consideration given to environmental issues. Depending on the internal structure of a given institution, the division involved in acquisitions should be given specific policy guidance in the level of due diligence required to assess environmental liabilities involving properties to be acquired. This should include buildings, equipment, and the portfolio of credit extensions to be inherited. This policy may be quite complex, depending on the size, complexity, and aggressiveness of the institution.

A residential mortgage lending policy should be developed to address the environmental concerns covered in a series of standard publications. The policy should incorporate the Fannie Mae special appraisal considerations, an appraiser clause about environmental conditions (standard appraisal document), and the Fannie Mae environmental hazard assessment. Normally, there are few environmental risks associated with single-family, residential lending. However, there are some exceptions that have caused adverse financial consequences. The use of either underground or above-ground fuel storage tanks, as a heating fuel source, is common in many single-family dwellings. The existence of asbestos insulation or roof tiles has also created problems. Residential condominiums in high-rise structures can present the same risk exposures as in any commercial building. Therefore, it is necessary for a lending institution to have or create an environmental policy that covers residential properties.

Every lending institution encounters problem loans and must face the issue of foreclosure in order to maintain the security interest. The policy covering these issues is commonly termed the "Special Assets/Other Real Estate Owned Policy." Exposure to environmental liabilities caused by "influence" on management of an operating facility is an unresolved legal issue, covered in more detail in Chapter 7. The issue of foreclosure requires detailed analysis and specific policy language (see Chapter 6). The policy should include a description of the methods to be employed to monitor problem credit extensions. Specific attention should be given to how lenders work with customers to resolve environmental issues without becoming involved as an "operator" under CERCLA (see Chapter 7). The due diligence policy on foreclosure should include both a definition of the due diligence investigation method and the scope that is mandated for various types of properties and values of assets. This foreclosure policy also must include guidance regarding properties that will require post-foreclosure management to maintain the security interest.

Under CERCLA, a trustee may be defined as an owner and/or an operator, depending on the specific circumstances involved. Each lending institution should have a trust policy to manage environmental liability. The environmental liabilities of a trustee may include the lending institution and the individual employee listed as the trustee. Liabilities for environmental responses under CERCLA can extend beyond the asset value of the trust, depending on the management activities and control of the property exerted by the trustee. The trust policy should contain specific guidance on the levels of due diligence required to accept properties or businesses into a trust. This guidance must include not only an assessment of the risk assumed through ownership but also must address the contingency that the institution may be required to operate a facility that would create exposure to all of the same environmental issues that any operator faces (e.g., operational health and safety issues, toxic torts). The trust policy would probably use the same risk matrix as the affiliate bank business lending policy, with the exception of adding the risk from the operating component. Trusts present risk assessment and monitoring difficulties far beyond the normal credit extension process because of the widespread geographic locations of these assets. While an institution does business in only a small geographic region of the country, a trust may contain properties in every state. The differences in state and local government regulations compared with the federal regulations can create additional compliance issues and liability that must be managed within the context of the policy.

Policy Revisions

Environmental policies must be reviewed regularly because of changes in laws and rules at the federal, state, and local government levels. At best, the policies should be reviewed annually, or the institution should retain legal counsel to monitor changes in the law to warn the institution when policy modifications are necessary. In recent years, the lending industry has taken a proactive stance to revise specific portions of CERCLA, especially in light of court decisions defining the influence a lender may exert on a business (see Fleet Factors in Chapters 2 and 7) and the liability of trustees (see *City of Phoenix v. Garbage Services Company* in Chapter 7). Revision of CERCLA will require some modifications of environmental policies. A disturbing trend that has arisen is the propensity of certain state and local governments to enact laws that are even more restrictive than CERCLA. The use of the Super Lien against contaminated properties can place a regulatory agency in first position to recover response costs for contamination cleanup. These issues must be reviewed within the context of the environmental policies of each institution when expanding into a new geographic area, acquiring another institution, or entering into trust agreements with properties spread over a wide geographic area.

Consultants

In-House Experts

Special environmental expertise is required regularly by either the officers or employees of the institution or its clientele. Commonly, there is a simple need to answer a question regarding the scope of an environmental investigation or to obtain an interpretation of some element of the environmental policy. Many of these questions can be answered by the institution environmental policy officer or a designated in-house expert. Whereas larger institutions may employ an in-house environmental attorney and a small staff of environmental professionals to manage environmental liabilities, most institutions will have only a few trained officers who are able to answer general questions. Beyond that point, they will recommend the use of outside consultants. Care should be taken by in-house experts when advising customers regarding complex environmental issues because an error in advice could lead to personal or institution liability. Additionally, to avoid the implication of impropriety, it is usually best to retain an independent third party with no vested interest in the transaction. When such a complex issue arises, the institution employee should first consult the designated environmental officer, and that person should suggest that the client obtain a second opinion from an outside consultant or should simply recommend that the customer seek outside counsel for advice.

Consultant Qualification Process

Since environmental attorneys, consultants, and contractors will be needed by the institution and its customers on a regular basis, it is important that all the environmental professionals be qualified to perform the services offered. Unfortunately, the large growth of the environmental industry has led to a proliferation of unqualified persons entering the field, which can create additional liability for the uninformed clients who use the services provided by these persons.

All environmental consultants retained by lending institutions should be prequalified, and a list of these professionals should be maintained for internal use. Each year or two, the institution might solicit qualified consultants by distributing a qualifications form, which must be completed by those who wish to perform services. This form should require, at a minimum, the following information

- The name of the company and the addresses of all operating locations, the type of corporation, the year of establishment, the types of environmental services offered (such as full-service, wetlands evaluation, endangered species evaluation, environmental site assessments, asbestos inspection, environmental contracting for disposal)
- A profile of the work force
- A listing of all duly licensed personnel (such as engineers and geologists) and their years of environmental consulting experience
- A summary of expert witness experience
- A financial profile including the name of the company accountant
- Insurance coverages, including worker's compensation, general liability, professional liability, contractor's liability, and pollution liability (Note: Copies of the professional liability and pollution liability policies and any exceptions to these policies should be required.)
- A summary of any legal actions brought against the company or insurance claims settled
- A summary of quality control measures used by the firm and a copy of any generic quality assurance plan
- A summary of laboratory services offered, if any
- A list of laboratories that are used by the firm and what methods are used to select them
- A summary of the expertise of the firm in the use of ASTM standards for conducting environmental site assessments
- A summary of past work for the institution
- A list of client references
- A certification that the information provided is accurate

After reviewing the qualifications, about five or six consultants should be selected for use for the next 1- to 2-year period. This list should include a sufficient number of consultants with all of the required expertise. It is rare that one firm has personnel qualified in all of the fields of expertise, so it is important to have a mix of the larger firms and smaller ones offering high-quality, special expertise.

Institution-Hired Consultants

All institutional consulting requirements should be approved centrally, through the institution environmental policy officer, and only those consultants on the list should be used unless there is some special requirement or availability issue. This policy should be applied to the primary institution as well as to any affiliated banks, trusts, and associated parts of the business. A typical contract to retain an environmental consultant for a phase I ESA is given in Appendix C.

Customer-Hired Consultants

The qualification method used by an institution to select its own environmental consultants should also be used to assist customers in obtaining qualified environmental consultants. The same solicitation used by the institution could be used to prequalify consultants for customers. A list of qualified consultants could be maintained in a central institution file and provided to customers. All institution employees should be advised to provide environmental consultant names only from the list prequalified by the institution. Loan officers who assist customers by actually soliciting consultants to bid on the work may be assuming liability exposure for the institution and themselves if an error is made by the environmental consultant.

If customers use an environmental consultant other than one on the approved list, the institution may reject the consultant's report and require a new report, request that the consultant fill out the prequalification form, or require a review of the work by an outside institution-approved consultant. There may be occasions when the report provided by the customer consultant does not meet the standards contained in the institution environmental policy and must be rejected. This decision should be made by the institution environmental policy officer or another qualified in-house expert. The report commissioned by the customer may sometimes meet all of the policy standards, so all that is necessary for acceptance is some additional information on the consultant. At the time of the initial customer contact, the environmental policy should be discussed to avoid any misunderstandings or unnecessary expense in the environmental liability assessment process. The officer should communicate effectively the policy's protection features that help the customer minimize liability and manage risk in transactions.

Institution-Hired Attorneys

Legal expertise is required to assess many different types of situations involving environmental liability. Not all law firms have environmental law experience or expertise. The institution should solicit law firms in a manner similar to that used to obtain other qualified environmental consultants. The process of solicitation can be guided by recommendations from knowledgeable persons or corporations known to the institution that have used this type of service in the past. There are logistical and cost issues when using a specialty law firm. The location of the law firm usually should be convenient for the institution's environmental policy officer. When a difficult situation arises, an institution should also seek a second opinion, particularly on matters where some type of CERCLA action is involved.

Evaluation Steps

Properties and businesses applying for credit must be evaluated carefully with regard to environmental liability that could adversely affect the institution. This evaluation program applies to all transactions involving real property, trusts, acquisitions, and credit extensions to high-risk businesses. The outlined approach is tailored to apply the most intensive due diligence investigation to the properties that bring the highest exposure or risk to the institution. There are some transaction types that will always pose a very high risk, so the overall policy of the institution may preclude credit extension to these facility types. This policy determination can be accomplished using combined SIC codes.

The following discussion is organized from a consideration of the lowest-risk transactions through to a consideration of the highest-risk transactions. Thus, the due diligence investigation type increases in detail and complexity from the simple screen process to the transaction screen process, to the phase I environmental site assessment, to the environmental audit. The cost to the customer for compliance to the policy increases with the complexity of the due diligence investigation.

The policy directly guides the type and scope of the due diligence investigation to be conducted. In all cases, due diligence is strictly defined as the pretransaction investigation conducted to limit the environmental liability exposure of both the institution and its customers.

Checklist Method Guidance

The checklist method involves an initial due diligence evaluation by a trained employee of the institution. The actual checklist can be developed in-house, or the transaction screen process checklist may be used (see Table 5.2). When the ASTM checklist is used, the text of the standard practice should be purchased from the American Society for Testing & Materials at the address given in Chapter 5. This provides the necessary background materials and guidance. If the checklist is developed by the lending institution or consultants retained by the institution, then a manual should be prepared to accompany it. The manual should explain the institution's philosophy, in order to give the employee who is not involved in its development some additional background and explanation. If this process is to be successful, the employee must receive proper training from the environmental policy officer, perhaps supplemented with some outside course work.

Transactional Screen Process Guidance

The transaction screen process (TSP) is the next approach after the checklist to assess environmental liability on a site. It is a preliminary investigation that relies heavily upon information provided by governmental agencies and interviews of the owner, lessee, or occupants of the site. The TSP investigation is conducted by a qualified environmental professional who is on the institution list of qualified consultants or who can become qualified to meet the standards set by the institution. The primary work product obtained from a TSP is a completed checklist and a letter that provides the consultant's opinion regarding the site. The TSP process is described in detail in Chapter 5.

Internal evaluation of the TSP and the opinion letter is the next level of due diligence. When the TSP checklist and letter are received, they must be evaluated carefully to assess the risk in the transaction. If some evidence for site contamination is observed or is suggested by the records search, it may be necessary to require a full phase I environmental site assessment or to proceed directly with some on-site testing. The institution employee should review the following issues to assess the quality of the work product:

1. Is the company that performed the investigation on the institution approved list?
2. Is the professional who signed the letter licensed or can his or her qualifications be verified?
3. If the company that performed the investigation is not on the approved list, is there documentation provided to verify their qualifications?
4. Are the answers of the consultant, owner, and tenant to the questions on the list consistent?
5. Was any evidence for contamination reported, and was it verified?
6. Did the letter transmitted by the consultant agree with the answers to the questions on the checklist?
7. Was the language in the letter written by the consultant consistent with standard opinions given in the field of practice?

If it is found that the investigation was not performed in accordance with the appropriate ASTM standard, or if the company or professional that performed the investigation was not qualified, then the customer should be informed. This may require a new investigation or the production of additional verification materials.

Once the TSP has been accepted as a properly prepared document by the internal reviewer, the content of the TSP must be reviewed to assess liability exposure. If no evidence for a site environmental problem is found, then no further investigation is merited. If a problem is found, then the environmental officer should be informed, and a more rigorous review of the TSP must be undertaken. If there is a significant problem, then additional work should be mandated before the transaction is processed. When an actual contamination problem is found, a staged approach to the investigation and resolution of the problem is recommended. The strategies for resolution of contamination problems are discussed in Chapter 6.

Phase I Environmental Site Assessment Guidance

A phase I environmental site assessment is the primary due diligence investigative tool used to assess the potential for environmental liability. The standard scope of a phase I ESA is given in ASTM Practice E 1527, and a complete description of the procedure is given in Chapter 5. A phase I ESA is a technical investigation that is performed by a qualified environmental professional. It is recommended that ESA documents be accepted only from prequalified consultants for all internal institution transactions. Loan officers should inform customers at an early stage that an ESA is required and that the institution will accept only the consultants on the qualified list. This list should be provided to the customer without a recommendation as to which consultant to use. It is appropriate to list the consultants by geographic area, so the customer can choose a qualified consultant from a convenient location in order to save cost. The institution officer should never make a specific consultant recommendation or assist in the process by soliciting bids, because of the potential exposure to liability if the consultant makes a serious error.

All lending institution employees should know that a phase I ESA is not an insurance policy and that there will always be some risk associated with a property transaction. Therefore, the internal review of the ESA report and reliance letter is a critical part of the due diligence process. To simplify the consultant qualification process, many lending institutions require that the consultant retained by the customer be prequalified; otherwise, the phase I ESA report will not be acceptable. Some institutions maintain a more liberal policy and rely somewhat on the insurance coverage of the consultants to protect against errors that could expose customers to cleanup costs. The phase I ESA document should be read completely and carefully. The document should be reviewed in the context of the published ASTM standards, and the scope of the investigation should include all of the appropriate investigations. For example, if the property includes an old building, the ESA document should include an asbestos survey. The specific site conditions dictate the necessity for conducting specific additional environmental investigations (see Chapter 8). Once the scope of the ESA is determined to be complete and appropriate, the technical content of the document should be reviewed. The reviewer should assess the internal consistency within the report between the historical information and the observations and conclusions. One of the most common errors is finding that the investigation was done on the wrong property. This can be verified easily by searching the report for the description of known landmarks on the site and by reviewing the photographs in the report. Once the phase I ESA has been reviewed and found to be acceptable, the conclusions of the report must be considered in the credit extension evaluation.

Interpretation of the ESA report and conclusions is a critical step in risk analysis. If the investigation finds no evidence for any contamination, then the credit extension may be analyzed without further environmental considerations. However, if some evidence for contamination is found, then the institution must request additional information and follow a set procedure to analyze whether or not the perceived problem is real. If it is, the magnitude of the cleanup effort must be assessed. If any serious questions arise with regard to the content of the ESA report or the recommended procedures, the institution employee should request advice from the environmental policy officer. The environmental policy officer may request a second opinion on certain issues from other consultants and/or environmental attorneys retained by the institution. A description of various procedures for verification and cleanup of contamination is given in Chapter 6.

Environmental Audits Guidance

An environmental audit is a full investigation of an operating business to assess compliance with all applicable environmental rules and regulations. This type of investigation is commonly termed an *environmental compliance audit* or an *operational audit*. Environmental audits have been used for many years by major U.S. corporations to assess and maintain environmental compliance continuously. There is no specific scope of investigation that can be applied to an environmental audit, because the scope of each audit is tailored to the specific nature of the business. A manual describing how these investigations are conducted has been prepared by Cahill and Kane (1987).

An environmental audit is a very intensive investigation that can greatly assist a business owner or operator, but at the same time, it can cause exposure to regulatory agency actions. The lender may require a business to perform this type of investigation, but the lender must be aware that participation in the design of the scope and the methods used should be very limited. Any business conducting an environmental audit should seek to maintain confidentiality until management can assess the need for or ability to take corrective actions. If a regulatory agency were to obtain the information in the audit before the business initiated corrective actions, the agency could use the information to pursue one or more enforcement actions. Therefore, when a business plans to conduct this type of audit, an environmental attorney should be used who would act as the middleman to sign all contracts with consultants, pay the consultants, and receive the report. The audit team should make no direct contact with upper management until the final report is presented to the attorney and the attorney has reported to management. All interim reports should be labeled "draft report" and "privileged communication with legal counsel." Maintaining this degree of confidentiality is very important, because there must be time for management to react and correct any environmental deficiency without fear of immediate agency action. If a regulatory agency were to decide that a business did not pursue corrective actions in a timely manner, criminal actions could be brought against management. The lender should understand this process and not intervene in the confidentiality issue but should obtain sufficient information to assure due diligence. Perhaps the key piece of information that a lender needs is a verification that an operating business has an ongoing environmental auditing program. This serves as evidence that environmental issues are being managed adequately.

The scope of an environmental audit, which can be very complex, should describe all of the site operations. Particular emphasis should be placed upon the use, storage, handling, and transport of hazardous and toxic substances. The audit should assess compliance with all CERCLA and RCRA rules, along with a health and safety assessment for compliance with OSHA, when needed. There may be only a few environmental permits required for a site, or it may require scores of permits. The permit groups that require review are air, water, waste storage and disposal, storage tanks, and perhaps others, although no permits may be required in some of these areas. In the analysis of waste disposal practices, the names and locations of waste disposal haulers and disposal sites should be noted to assure that the business is a not potentially responsible party (PRP) in a Superfund site. A critical part of the audit involves accounting for the toxic and hazardous volumes that enter and leave the site (present and past). If there are any discrepancies, then a high potential for contamination or discharge to the environment exists. Most environmental audits contain the following items in the scope:

- Review of any previous site environmental work
- Assessment of scope consistency with the industry standards and methods
- An organization chart showing work assignments for various team members
- Compilation of all applicable environmental rules and laws
- An inspection of all facilities
- A review and evaluation of inventory and manifest records
- An evaluation of operational compliance
- An assessment of any possible violations of internal, industry, or legal standards
- A review of the findings with legal counsel and later with management
- Recommendations for procedures to correct any deficiencies and on future compliance monitoring

A lending institution may require an annual review of environmental compliance as a condition for credit extension. This requirement could include a new environmental audit each year, maintenance of an environmental compliance monitoring program internally, or provision of a letter guaranteeing compliance for each time increment (e.g., annual, quarterly, monthly), with an explanation concerning the methods used for evaluation of environmental compliance. If an institution requires an environmental audit each year and requires that the report be transmitted to the institution, great care must be taken to avoid direct management influence, as is very loosely defined in the Fleet Factors court decision (see Chapters 2 and 7). In many cases a business may decline to give the institution a copy of the complete audit report so that the document is not discoverable in litigation. A lending institution requirement for a copy of the complete audit report may make that institution noncompetitive in the high-risk market. A balance must be achieved between due diligence efforts and the cost to the institution in terms of business.

Review of an environmental audit report for a complex business operation requires a number of specialized skills that are not found commonly among the staff of a lending institution. These reviews will likely require outside consultants to assess the contents fully. These outside consultants must be required to sign confidentiality agreements to maintain the security of the report's contents, which could be very sensitive. There is no simple checklist that can assist in the review of these reports.

Documentation/Specific Industries

Environmental Agreements

Environmental agreements or clauses are necessary to define and clarify for the borrower the responsibility required by the lending institution as a condition of credit for environmental management of properties or operations. The environmental agreement applies to operating facilities and even to properties used as collateral. This agreement provides the lender with additional assurances that the borrower will comply with environmental laws and use due diligence in the management of acquisitions or other activities that could affect the security interest held by the institution.

The requirement that a borrower sign some type of environmental agreement or clause within credit documents is so common that an objection by a borrower may show an unsophisticated attitude toward environmental issues, signifying that the borrower is an unacceptable risk. An unsophisticated property owner or business operator is much more likely to incur substantial environmental losses, resulting in the inability to repay a loan.

Environmental clauses should contain a number of items, depending on the complexity of the credit extension and the special conditions. An example of a "free-standing" environmental agreement is given in Appendix B. All environmental agreements and clauses normally have at least the following elements:

- A description of the property or facility and its use and condition
- A limit to the borrower's increase of environmental risks without prior permission
- A statement that the borrower has complied with all applicable environmental laws and rules and will continue to do so
- A statement that there are no known hazardous substances on any of the properties or facilities listed
- A statement requiring the cleanup of any site environmental problems
- A requirement that the institution be informed of the discovery or occurrence of any environmental problems on the described properties or facilities
- A requirement that some monitoring or some acceptable form of assurance be provided to assure that all properties or facilities are in compliance with environmental laws or rules
- An agreement to allow institution personnel to inspect the property
- A requirement that borrowers indemnify the institution against environmental matters

The use of an environmental agreement, such as in the example provided, is the best way to state clearly the issues in lieu of special clauses, representations, or covenants. The indemnification clause within the environmental agreement requires the borrower, as a corporate officer and individually, to indemnify and make the lending institution whole in the event of a threatened or real loss resulting from the institution's relationship, when the institution was not at fault.

The Environmental Agreement provided does not allow for any exemptions; therefore, it must be modified to clarify existing site conditions. For example, there is a representation that no contamination exists on the site, and if some environmental problem does exist, the wording must be changed to read that the problem must be cleaned up. The requirement for monitoring to prevent future environmental problems will also require a modification of the agreement language. There are several addendums to the environmental agreement that should be included, as is shown in the checklist (see on the first page of Appendix B). If the activities conducted at the facility change or if the line of business changes to involve new or additional uses of hazardous or toxic substances, then either an addendum to the environmental agreement should be negotiated or a waiver letter utilized. The following are examples of situations that could be handled by either an agreement addendum or a waiver letter:

1. A borrower with extensive experience in the proper handling of hazardous or toxic chemicals requests institution approval to use a new set of chemicals for an existing or new operation,
2. A borrower experiences an accidental release of petroleum from an underground storage tank and immediately corrects the problem to the satisfaction of the appropriate regulatory agencies,
3. A borrower becomes subject to some new rule or law that requires the installation of some different pollution control equipment, which will reduce the risk for environmental liabilities.

In this part of the environmental manual, the circumstances should be outlined that require a new agreement, an agreement addendum, or a waiver letter. Also, the borrower should be informed regarding what types of environmental actions would result in the discontinuance of the credit arrangement.

Monitoring of Facilities Guidance

Monitoring credit extensions for environmental compliance is an important component of environmental risk management. The monitoring must be accomplished without the lender becoming directly involved in the management of the business. The environmental policy that defines monitoring requirements should use the same risk matrix as that developed to define the scope of due diligence for credit extensions. The risk matrix lists specific industry classifications with associated high-risk activities. The monitoring required should be based on how the borrower intends to manage environmental risk and whether the techniques used are in continuing compliance with current environmental rules and regulations.

There are three environmental investigative processes that can be used to monitor business activities, including the monitoring letter method, a phase I environmental site assessment, and an environmental audit. All of these investigation techniques have been described, with the exception of the monitoring letter.

The form and language of an acceptable monitoring letter from a borrower to a lending institution are provided in Appendix B. This letter would be transmitted to the institution at the time interval required in the credit conditions, along with the attached documents requested. The specific addenda to accompany the monitoring letter are defined in the environmental agreement. For example, if underground fuel storage tanks are present, the addendum to the monitoring letter should include such items as an updated insurance certificate (Petroleum Liability Insurance Program or equivalent), a certification of inventory records, a certification of monitoring records, and perhaps a pressure test certification. The monitoring letter should contain all of the necessary compliance information but should clearly indicate that the borrower, and not the lending institution, is operating and controlling the site environmental practices. Therefore, the language used in this letter must be carefully crafted to avoid a potential management influence problem, as was created by the Fleet Factors court ruling (see Chapters 2 and 7).

In most cases a monitoring letter is sufficient to maintain environmental awareness for both the borrower and the lender. However, when a change occurs on a site or an incident occurs that creates an environmental problem, the monitoring letter may be insufficient to truly assess environmental risk. In this case it is prudent to require a phase I ESA or an environmental audit. These documents would then be used both to assess environmental compliance and to revise the environmental agreement, as necessary.

The monitoring letter will include an assessment of the handling of specific materials, wastes, processes, and other activities conducted on each site. If the borrower has difficulty in providing the necessary information for the letter, then the due diligence environmental investigations conducted in the past or ongoing investigations may be insufficient for monitoring environmental compliance. This situation will require an upgrade of the intensity of on-site environmental investigation or perhaps the development of an environmental auditing program. The monitoring letter should describe the most effective environmental management methods being employed. Many industries have developed comprehensive "best management practices" for environmental issues. The monitoring letter should contain an assessment of current site practices and how they compare to the latest industry standards.

As part of the environmental policy manual, each lending institution should develop a series of industry data sheets to be used for analysis of monitoring letters. An example of a data sheet for agricultural facilities is given in Table 4.3. Each analysis data sheet should include a list of activities, the typical environmental risk components, a description of environmental concerns and potential violations, and the most recent best management practices used to control environmental risks.

Problem Assets

Managing Problem Assets

Foreclosing on a property or taking title in any form increases the exposure of a lending institution significantly. At this point, the institution becomes an owner and/or an owner and operator under CERCLA. The maintenance of a pure

Table 4.3 Example of an Industry Environmental Data Sheet

AGRICULTURAL FACILITIES

1. Activities: Farming — truck crops, citrus, orchards, trees, dairy farming, livestock, processing, etc.
2. Environmental issues:
   a. Fertilizer storage
   b. Pesticide handling and storage
   c. Mechanical repair facilities
   d. Petroleum storage tanks
   e. Vehicle/equipment cleaning activities
   f. Animal waste handling
3. Environmental Concerns: Soil, surface-water and/or groundwater contamination; pesticide-related injury to neighbors and other third parties; loss of permits for consumptive use of water, limitations on herd sizes, complete shut-down of operations, third-party actions caused by contamination from nutrients and pesticides.
4. Representative best management practices:
   a. Construction of surface-water management system with swales, holding ponds, and other features designed to prevent contamination with nutrients and pesticides.
   b. Maintaining detailed records of pesticide inventories, use, and application practices, show conformance of pesticide and fertilizer storage areas to modern designs.
   c. Regular inspection of fuel storage tanks used in the staging area, for pumping stations, and for wells in the fields. Provide some degree of containment for all fuel storage tanks.
   d. Develop and implement a livestock waste management plan.
   e. Maintain a list of required environmental permits and plan for renewals and to meet special conditions.

security interest causes minimal liability. In a workout situation, in consideration of the Fleet Factors decision, the lender may be determined to be an operator. The key solution here is not to take possession of the property or take an active rôle in the management of an environmental problem until determining the lender's environmental liability. Due diligence environmental investigations must be completed and evaluated by institution management prior to taking title to property in any form, including trust inclusion. A detailed discussion of the procedure that a lender should follow when a problem is discovered is presented in Chapter 6. The issue of acceptance of properties and businesses into a trust is covered in Chapter 7. There is no excuse for initiating foreclosure proceedings prior to completion of the appropriate environmental evaluations. If time is an issue, the foreclosure or acquisition should be delayed.

Whenever environmental problems arise, the institution's environmental policy officer should be informed and should assist in the development of the strategy to resolve the problem. The policy should address the factors that constitute the necessity to withdraw from a problem property and write down the asset. Commonly, the cost for preparing the appropriate environmental investigations to assess cleanup costs is well over $10,000, which may exceed the value of a property. There are, however, many instances in which special assets have been restored to full value, and the lending institutions have either fully or partially recovered their positions.

Internal communication with regard to a problem asset is critical to its successful resolution. The institution's environmental policy officer should be provided with at least the following information about the problem property:

- The name of the problem loan or property
- The estimated or appraised value of the property or collateral value if there is no environmental problem
- The book value of the asset
- An evaluation of the borrower's sophistication and attitude toward environmental matters
- A summary of the current and past uses of the property and general neighborhood
- Time constraints on resolution of the problem
- Any outlined work plan to deal with the problem

The environmental policy officer should receive all of this information via telephone, fax, or e-mail as quickly as possible, along with all environmental reports on the site. Upon review of the available facts, the environmental policy officer should determine whether the transaction can be processed without significant environmental liabilities or whether the problem must be given additional scrutiny. If the problem requires legal and/or technical expertise, an outside environmental attorney and/or consultant from the prequalified list should be retained to perform the appropriate reviews and studies. These professionals should also be interviewed to ascertain their expertise on the specific type of problem. The outside consultants retained will be involved with the site until the overall problem is resolved.

A detailed environmental policy manual may contain a description of the procedures used to resolve a contamination problem (see Chapter 6). However, since each environmental problem is unique, each will require a slightly different approach. There are some specific points, though, that the manual should contain. All environmental investigations should be conducted on an incremental basis, so that after each phase, an economic analysis can be made. As more information is obtained, it may indicate that it is not prudent to continue investing in solutions to a problem. The phased approach allows the institution to withdraw from the transaction at any time. The primary objective in the resolution of a contamination problem is to obtain a "no further action" letter from the appropriate regulatory agencies, thereby clearing the property for sale. Properties that are in some stage of cleanup or are in a "monitoring only" regulatory state still can be sold, but with greater difficulty. When a lending institution is contemplating a cleanup, it should negotiate agreements with the regulatory agencies before accepting the property. This will limit liability and allow more certainty in the economic analysis. If the agency takes an aggressive attitude toward a problem because it is a priority issue or if the agency is acting in an unreasonable manner, the institution may elect to withdraw from the deal rather than foreclose. Usually, the threat of leaving the site in a problem state without a viable party available to pay for the cleanup costs brings environmental agencies to the negotiating table.

The best method to deal with problem assets and the associated financial losses and liabilities is to conduct proper due diligence investigations prior to acquisition and the conveyance of a credit extension. It is the responsibility of the institution's officers and employees to enforce the policies related to the requirements for conducting TSPs and phase I ESAs, which are specifically designed to limit the institution's exposure to liability.

Selling/Leasing Problem Assets

It is sometimes possible to lease or sell a property while it is in the cleanup process. If the property is to be leased, the types of activities to be conducted on the site by the lessee must be scrutinized carefully. For example, if the site had been used as a plating facility and a cleanup of chromium and acid were currently underway, it might not be prudent to lease the facility to a business that would conduct the same activity, because they might add additional contamination to the site. This new contamination might be indistinguishable from the existing contamination. If similar activities were to be conducted on the site, the institution should require special disclosures in the environmental agreement and a high degree of environmental monitoring. A sophisticated lessee would also require the institution to sign an indemnification, exempting it from any liabilities emanating from the existing onsite environmental problem. Leases of a contaminated site should be carefully reviewed by an environmental attorney.

The sale of a contaminated property can be complicated by the phase of the cleanup and the issue of disclosure. A buyer of the site must be aware of the ongoing cleanup process, which could limit or delay proposed site activities. For example, if a buyer wished to build a new structure, an active remediation system could be located at a position that would preclude building or delay it indefinitely. Also, construction activities, such as excavation or dewatering, could cause the contamination plume to migrate, which would increase the cost of cleanup. Specific issues of the cleanup should be clearly stated in the terms of a sales contract. The specific parties responsible for the cost of cleanup should be identified (the institution, in this case). A sophisticated purchaser might require that an escrow account be established to contain a reserve to assure that the cleanup would be completed. The contract might also contain a provision on the completion date of the remediation. The sale of a contaminated property that is in some phase of active remediation would cause the institution to negotiate many rather complex issues that are not involved in a normal transaction. It might be necessary to retain an environmental attorney to assist in these negotiations.

The issue of disclosure in the sale of contaminated property is technically complex. In a case cited in Chapter 2, a lending institution that foreclosed on a property discovered contamination and sold the property to a third party without revealing the problem. After serious litigation, the court ruled that the institution was not liable under CERCLA. The revealing of a material defect on a property may or may not be required under strict interpretation of the law. The "let the buyer beware" principle is applicable in many states, and under CERCLA the institution may prevail in litigation. However, a quality lending institution must consider its ethical business standards and reputation. The purposeful sale of a property with a material defect is not a practice that either increases business opportunities or public trust. The institution's environmental policies should clearly state the disclosure policy and an ethics policy.

Glossary

There are a number of technical words and phrases that are commonly used when discussing environmental matters. All institution environmental manuals should contain a glossary, with current definitions of terms and a list of defined acronyms.

REFERENCES FOR FURTHER READING

Cahill, L. B. and Kane, R. W., Eds., Environmental Audits, 5th ed., Governmental Institutes, Inc., Rockville, MD, 1987, 656 pp.

Kammert, J. L., Lender liability/environmental contractual provisions in real estate transactions, in Annual Environmental Land Use Law Update, The Florida Bar, Tallahassee, FL, 1994, 11.1.

Motiuk, I. L. and Pritchard, J. A., Lender and Fiduciary Environmental Liability, Practicing Law Institute, Corporate Law and Practice Course Handbook Series, PLI Order No. B-4-7100, 1995.

Rothstein, R., Rethinking the joint and several liability of lenders under CERCLA, *Valparaiso U. Law Rev.,* Summer 1995.

5 MANAGEMENT OF CONTAMINATION LIABILITY

A lending institution can protect itself from environmental liabilities by adopting and implementing an environmental risk policy (see Chapter 4). This policy carefully defines the types of due diligence investigations that must be conducted to cover various types and sizes of business transactions. However, lending institutions are not the only businesses that need to understand environmental risk management methods. All business owners and operators should follow similar guidelines to manage risk and minimize liabilities. Additionally, professionals who rely on lending institutions should be familiar with environmental issues that create concerns for the lenders. Realtors must understand the types and details of information that lenders will expect to review in a transaction, and consultants providing services to parties in the transaction must understand the acceptable elements and methodologies involved in the due diligence process and how they correspond to the institution's environmental policy.

A due diligence investigation is defined as some type of standardized, site-specific environmental investigation, currently termed an *environmental site assessment*. The concept of due diligence investigation, or the environmental site assessment, evolved from the corporate environmental audit; the investigation was originally termed a *transactional environmental audit*. Liabilities created within the Comprehensive Environmental Response, Compensation, and Liability Act of 1980 (CERCLA) and the poorly defined "innocent landowner defense" created within the Superfund Amendment and Reauthorization Act of 1986 (SARA) motivated the business community to focus more effort on environmental issues. The environmental audit became a major business factor in the late 1970s and early 1980s (Cahill and Kane, 1987). The term *environmental audit* evolved from the Securities and Exchange Commission (SEC) audits of several corporations, including United States Steel Corporation (1977), Allied Chemical (1979), and Occidental Petroleum (1980), triggered by hazardous waste disposal issues and applied to operating facilities. The operational environmental audit currently plays an important role in lender-related transactions and will be covered in a separate discussion.

The environmental audit developed into two different types of investigations, the *transactional environmental audit* and the *operational environmental audit*. The operational environmental audit still maintains the same name. The transactional environmental audit became the *environmental site assessment* which has been further broken down into various types of investigations based on the scope of the investigation and the complexity of the property or business being investigated. The most common term for the initial site investigation has become *phase I environmental site assessment* (*ESA*). If additional information is required, additional phases are added, which may include the collection of soil and/or groundwater samples for chemical analysis or the completion of a preliminary assessment of contamination. However, the largest problem with the environmental site assessment concept has always been the lack of a standardized scope of the investigation.

In the late 1980s and early 1990s, various technical groups assembled experts on environmental issues from the major disciplines, including engineering, geology, hydrology, chemistry, biology, soil science, and a host of others. The first standard procedure for conducting a phase I environmental site assessment was published by the Society of Groundwater Scientists and Engineers (1991), the technical branch of the National Water Well Association. This standard, although quite comprehensive, was in some ways impractical and was not widely used. In 1993, the American Society for Testing and Materials (ASTM) published two separate standards for types of phase I environmental site assessments. The first standard was Designation E 1527, entitled "Standard Practice for Environmental Site Assessments: Phase I Environmental Site Assessment Process" (ASTM, 1993; revised in 1994). The second standard published was Designation E 1528, entitled "Standard Practice for Environmental Site Assessments: Transaction Screen Process" (ASTM, 1993). These compiled standards were widely accepted throughout the lending industry and today form the basis for most lending institution provisions on phase I environmental site assessments. ASTM Standards E 1527-94 and E 1528-93 are being modified and updated on a regular basis; therefore, it is important to obtain the latest printed standard from the ASTM, which is located at 100 Barr Harbor Drive, West Conshohocken, PA 19428-2959.

What Types of Transactions Should Require an Environmental Site Assessment?

An argument could be made that virtually any transaction involving real property should somehow trigger a phase I environmental site assessment. However, there are practical issues regarding real versus perceived risks involved in a transaction and the cost of the environmental site assessment as it relates to the overall transaction cost. These issues are normally debated by the management of a business; the resultant policies are written in that institution's environmental risk manual. However, for those businesses and professionals that do not have a written policy as a guide, there are certain facts that must be considered in terms of risk. A list of real property and/or business transactions that require some type of environmental site assessment is given in Table 5.1. This is not an all-inclusive list and there is no recommendation concerning whether the scope of the environmental investigation should be a transaction screening process or a full-scope phase I environmental site assessment.

Table 5.1 Types of Transactions That Should Require an Environmental Site Assessment

1.	Industrial property sales
2.	Industrial property purchases
3.	Commercial property purchases
4.	Operating commercial property sales (?)
5.	Large non-residential property purchases
6.	Special residential property transactions
7.	Lessor of industrial or commercial properties
8.	Lessee of industrial or commercial properties
9.	Acceptance of trust properties or businesses
10.	Acceptance of inheritance properties or businesses
11.	Acceptance of gift properties or businesses
12.	Refinancing of industrial and commercial properties
13.	Financing of high-risk businesses
14.	Prior to foreclosures
15.	Acquisition of public lands

Based on the information presented in this text, it should be quite clear that a phase I environmental site assessment (ESA) should be required for the purchase of all industrial or commercial properties. Some exceptions could occur if the properties were previously unused or if the transaction involves a very small facility not including any high-risk business activities. There are some specific cases where the acquisition of established residential properties should require at least a transaction screening process or even a phase I ESA. The trigger for an investigation of a residential property could include

- The age of the property (Old structures may contain asbestos and/ or lead paint that could require the new owner to expend capital, affecting his or her ability to pay the mortgage.)
- The type of heating system in the residence (Some large residences have underground storage tanks to supply fuel for furnaces.)
- The physical location of the residential property (A Love Canal home is an example of a high-risk location, as are areas where there are no zoning laws and the residential property borders industrial properties.)
- Activities conducted on the property by the owner, such as repairing cars or discharging chemicals into a septic tank system

Commonly, the due diligence in a residential property transaction can be accomplished by simply asking a few key questions about the residence and about past activities.

There are some cases in which the seller of a property or business should obtain at least a phase I environmental site assessment before closing the deal. The most important transaction type requiring this action is probably the sale of an industrial operation (or a complex commercial operation, like an old shopping center) to another party that will operate it using similar practices. Commonly, there are provisions placed in the sales contract to protect the seller from future environmental problems on the site. However, if an environmental action were brought against the purchaser at some point in the future, the seller could be brought back into the liability framework if the purchaser declared bankruptcy or is unable to pay for the entire cost of the cleanup. Also, sophisticated purchasers require that environmental warranties be placed in the contract, in case a problem is found after the sale is closed. A phase I environmental site assessment by the seller prior to the closing of the transaction is a valid due diligence action if it is conducted at a sufficient level of detail to assure that the site was left in an environmentally acceptable state, free from significant contamination. If the environmental site assessment is only a cursory investigation, then it is not useful and does not provide protection against future liability claims. If a site has been operated for many years, the environmental site assessment might require considerable collection of on-site data to determine the condition of the soils and groundwater. There is some risk in performing an "exit" environmental site assessment, because if some contamination is found, this fact must be disclosed to the purchaser in the transaction process. However, as a basic rule in business, the advantage always goes to the entity with the most knowledge, providing the ability to negotiate from this position.

The purchaser of a large parcel of property, even if it is raw land, should require a phase I ESA. In many documented cases, the purchasers of large parcels who did not have a phase I ESA performed ended up with very large problems. Some potential problems can only be found through detailed knowledge of the local history. An example of a potential problem with currently unused land was the location of a railroad tie–making operation, where the wood was treated by soaking it in unlined pits containing creosote. These facilities were located miles from any populated site and even large distances from the railways. When site vegetation grew back after several decades, the problem lay in the ground, to be discovered only by a future land user. Another type of problem occurs when a large parcel of land has been used at any time for agricultural operations. This history should trigger a full phase I ESA, because of the many regulated chemicals used by growers and ranchers. The size of a parcel that will trigger the need for a phase I ESA is again determined by the institutional environmental policy.

Other transactions that should trigger phase I ESAs are leases. When leasing an industrial or commercial property, the lessee should always require at least a phase I ESA, particularly when a similar operation will be conducted on the property. If the lessee of an industrial property allows a discharge of a regulated substance on the property and a regulatory agency investigation finds that a large part of the site is contaminated with the same substance as the discharge, the agency will assume that the lessee is the entity that caused the contamination, because the lessee cannot document the predischarge site condition. A lessee of an industrial site must know the condition of the site prior to signing the lease and beginning on-site operations. It is recommended that the lessee still obtain at least a phase I ESA, even if the lessor gives an environmental warranty in the lease. The lessor of the property also should conduct a phase I ESA on the site prior to signing the lease, in order to be excluded from liability of activities conducted on-site by the lessee. If the lessor is also the property owner, then some right of access to conduct additional on-site monitoring of activities and/or the monitoring of groundwater quality should be a part of the lease conditions. The lessor must be quite careful, however, not to become designated as an operator under the definitions given in CERCLA or subsequent case law, as evidenced by the activities conducted on the site. If the site is quite complex, it is unlikely that only a phase I ESA will be sufficient to protect the parties to a lease, and actual monitoring of water quality may be necessary. In certain cases, a potential lessee of a property should consider carefully if it wishes to lease a property to conduct similar activities if there is any reasonable possibility that the site may contain contamination for which liability may be disputed.

Of major concern to both lending institutions and any other entities that accept responsibility for trust management is the liability associated with environmental issues. Once an institution accepts real property into a trust, including an operating or closed business, the trustee may become owner and/or operator of the business or may be held liable for on-site contamination if no one will accept title to the property. Trust management and environmental liability concerns are discussed in greater detail in Chapter 7. Based on recent experiences by lending institutions, all industrial or commercial properties to be placed in a trust should trigger a phase I ESA prior to acceptance by the trustee.

Acceptance of real property as part of an inheritance or as a gift has become problematical. The liabilities under CERCLA are so punitive that even an individual accepting the inheritance of the family business or property can be placed in great financial jeopardy. If the properties are industrial or commercial, or if they are large, a phase I ESA should be conducted on them prior to acceptance. A case in point involves the donation of the large parcel of property in the western United States to an environmental organization to add to a protected wilderness area. The gift property was accepted, but piles of highly contaminated mine tailings were later discovered on the property. The environmental organization was forced to spend a great deal of money to contain the problem and suffered considerable embarrassment. There are similar examples of universities accepting gifts of property, only to find major contamination liabilities instead of the expected windfalls. Whenever there is a doubt, conducting a phase I ESA or even a TSP is an inexpensive way to gain will some control over environmental risk and liability.

The acquisition of public properties is a commonly neglected area within the framework of environmental liability management. Environmental issues are very common in the acquisition of rights-of-way for expansion of existing highways, because gasoline stations and other commercial activities are located adjacent to the roads. Many states have adopted policies to assess entire rights-of-way prior to acquisition under eminent domain proceedings. Also, the acquisition of utility rights-of-way to construct water mains, sanitary sewers, or telephone cable systems can bring considerable liability to local or state governments and to public companies. Construction tends to facilitate movement of contamination, thereby exposing people to toxic or hazardous substances and possibly causing contaminants to move across property boundaries, creating exposures to third party actions. An example of a utility easement problem occurred in New Mexico, where gasoline leaked into some PVC conduits containing fiber optic cables. The gasoline traveled over one-half mile from the source through the conduits, and the fumes entered the basement of a house, which subsequently exploded when a light was turned on. The telephone company that owned the conduit was held liable, in addition to the gasoline station. Prior to land acquisition for easements, every local government should perform either a TSP or a phase I ESA for the entire right-of-way tract.

There is a whole series of lending transactions that tend to trigger the necessity for TSPs and phase I ESAs, including refinancing, financing of credit lines for high-risk businesses (with or without properties as collateral), and foreclosures. The risks involved in these transactions should be evaluated within the context of the risk policy. Any property or business owner knowledgeable about environmental risk will ask the lending institution at an early stage what specific ESA requirements will be requested and what consultants are acceptably qualified in risk policy to perform the work. The requirements for environmental investigations of various property types prior to refinancing tend to be similar to those prior to financing. The issue of foreclosure can be quite complex, but in nearly all cases, a phase I ESA should be required and necessary evaluations should be made to assure that the property or business has greater value than the cleanup and other associated costs (see also Chapters 4 and 7).

Determining which transactions will require an environmental investigation can be accomplished through the simple application of common sense. If toxic or hazardous substances are used or were used or stored on a property, a prudent lender or purchaser will conduct an environmental site assessment or at least a transaction screening process prior to purchase or financing. A complex business transaction should include competent, experienced, professional environmental consultation to avoid potentially costly mistakes.

TECHNICAL ASPECTS OF THE TRANSACTION SCREEN PROCESS

The simplest form of environmental site assessment is the transaction screen process (TSP). General standards for conducting a TSP are given in Designation E 1528-93 "Standard Practice for Environmental Site Assessments: Transaction Screen Process" (American Society for Testing and Materials, 1993).* The TSP process is specifically recommended for use in relatively simple property and/or business transactions when the property is unlikely to contain significant sources of contamination. Whether to use a TSP or a phase I ESA depends on the degree of risk involved in the transaction and the specific contents of the risk policy of the institution or business involved in the transaction. Much of the documentation on the TSP process refers to the liabilities created by CERCLA, with additional liabilities caused by petroleum product storage or use on the site to be investigated.

* Quotes from Designation E 1528-93 are reprinted with permission, on the copyright held by the American Society for Testing and Materials (ASTM), 100 Barr Harbor Drive, West Conshohocken, PA 19428-2959. Copies of this standard may be obtained from ASTM (phone, 610-832-9585; fax, 610-832-9555).

It is important to note that this type of environmental investigation may satisfy the narrow definition of due diligence under SARA as applied to the CERCLA liabilities, but many states do not recognize *any* type of innocent landowner exemption under CERCLA enforcement activities. Therefore, the TSP may be used more appropriately in some states than in others for similar-sized transactions. Legal research specific to the state and local program statutes and rules must be conducted before adopting this process as part of an environmental risk policy.

Technical Scope and Process

The TSP leads to a completed checklist that includes twenty questions regarding the site and surrounding properties, three regarding contaminated sites within public regulatory files in the vicinity of the site and some past site-use data. Answers to the questions determine whether the site is cleared, with minimal risk of contamination, or whether additional inquiry is needed. The scope of a TSP is very limited in terms of the technical issues to be investigated, the sources of information on which the opinion is based, and the ability to independently verify the information obtained. The checklist adopted by ASTM for the TSP investigation is given in Table 5.2, with the permission of the ASTM.

In this approach to an environmental investigation, the key variable is the experience of the individual conducting the inquiry. This person is defined within ASTM Standard E 1528 (Section 3.3.11) as

> a person possessing sufficient training and experience necessary to conduct a site reconnaissance, interviews, and other activities in accordance with Practice E 1527, and from other activities, having the ability to develop conclusions regarding recognized environmental conditions in connection with the property in question. An individual's status as an environmental professional may be limited to the type of assessment to be performed or to specific segments of the assessment for which the professional is responsible. The person may be an independent contractor or an employee of the user.

A TSP conducted by an inexperienced individual or one with a vested interest can lead to a total lack of liability protection and, even worse, a false sense of security. When an independent contractor is utilized, it is important that the lending institution be informed of the qualifications and experience of the contractor and its employees. As previously discussed, the insurance coverage carried by the contractor is also important, but the very nature of the inquiry and limits on verification of information place very little liability on the contractor.

If the TSP is conducted by the staff of the lender, the information should be strictly limited to internal use when deciding whether or not to proceed with the transaction. If the information is given to a prospective buyer, for example, the lending institution could inherit some unwanted liability if undiscovered contamination is found on the property or business at a later time. This same principle also applies to realtors and other parties involved in the sale or acquisition of properties. It is very important to have a competent professional perform the TSP,

Table 5.2 Transaction Screen Process (TSP) Questionnaire for ASTM Standard E 1528 (ASTM, 1993)

Description of Site: (Address)

Question	Owner			Occupant(s)			Observed during site visit		
1. Is the property or any adjoining property used for an industrial use?	Yes	No	Unk	Yes	No	Unk	Yes	No	Unk
2. To the best of your knowledge, has the property or any adjoining property been used for an industrial use in the past?	Yes	No	Unk	Yes	No	Unk	Yes	No	Unk
3. Is the property or any adjoining property used as a gasoline station, motor repair facility, commercial printing facility, dry cleaners, photo developing laboratory, junkyard or landfill, or as a waste treatment, storage, disposal, processing, or recycling facility?	Yes	No	Unk	Yes	No	Unk	Yes	No	Unk
4. To the best of your knowledge has the property or any adjoining property been used as a gasoline station, motor repair facility, commercial printing facility, dry cleaners, photo developing laboratory, junkyard or landfill, or as a waste treatment, storage, disposal, processing, or recycling facility?	Yes	No	Unk	Yes	No	Unk	Yes	No	Unk
5. Are there currently, or to the best of your knowledge have there been previously, any damaged or discarded automotive or industrial batteries, or pesticides, paints, or other chemicals in individual containers of greater than 5 gal in volume or 50 gal in the aggregate, stored on or used at the property or facility?	Yes	No	Unk	Yes	No	Unk	Yes	No	Unk

Reprinted with permission of ASTM.

6. Are there currently, or to the best of your knowledge have there been previously, any industrial drums (typically 55 gal) or sacks of chemicals located on the property or at the facility?	Yes	No	Unk	Yes	No	Unk	Yes	No	Unk
7. Has fill dirt been brought onto the property that originated from a contaminated site or that is of an unknown origin?	Yes	No	Unk	Yes	No	Unk	Yes	No	Unk
8. Are there currently, or to the best of your knowledge have there been previously, any pits, ponds, or lagoons located on the property in connection with waste treatment or waste disposal?	Yes	No	Unk	Yes	No	Unk	Yes	No	Unk
9. Is there currently, or to the best of your knowledge has there been previously, any stained soil on the property?	Yes	No	Unk	Yes	No	Unk	Yes	No	Unk
10. Are there currently, or to the best of your knowledge have there been previously, any registered or unregistered storage tanks (aboveground or underground) located on the property?	Yes	No	Unk	Yes	No	Unk	Yes	No	Unk
11. Are there currently, or to the best of your knowledge have there been previously, any vent pipes, fill pipes, or access ways indicating a fill pipe protruding from the ground on the property or adjacent to any structure located on the property?	Yes	No	Unk	Yes	No	Unk	Yes	No	Unk
12. Are there currently, or to the best of your knowledge have there been previously, any flooring, drains, or walls located within the facility that are stained by substances other than water or are emitting foul odors?	Yes	No	Unk	Yes	No	Unk	Yes	No	Unk
13. If the property is served by a private well or nonpublic water system, have contaminants been identified in the well or system that exceed guidelines applicable to the water system or has the well been designated as contaminated by any government environmental/health agency?	Yes	No	Unk	Yes	No	Unk	Yes	No	Unk
14. Does the owner or occupant of the property have any knowledge of environmental liens or governmental notification relating to past or recurrent violations of environmental laws with respect to the property or any facility located on the property?	Yes	No	Unk	Yes	No	Unk	Yes	No	Unk

Table 5.2 Transaction Screen Process (TSP) Questionnaire for ASTM Standard E 1528 (ASTM, 1993) (Continued)

Question	Owner			Occupant(s)			Observed during site visit		
15. Has the owner or occupant of the property been informed of the past or current existence of hazardous substances or petroleum products or environmental violations with respect to the property or any facility located on the property?	Yes	No	Unk	Yes	No	Unk	Yes	No	Unk
16. Does the owner or occupant of the property have any knowledge of any environmental site assessment of the property or facility that indicated the presence of hazardous substances or petroleum products on, or contamination of, the property or recommended further assessment of the property?	Yes	No	Unk	Yes	No	Unk	Yes	No	Unk
17. Does the owner or occupant of the property know of any past, threatened, or pending lawsuits or administrative proceedings concerning a release or threatened release of any hazardous substance or petroleum products involving the property by any owner or occupant of the property?	Yes	No	Unk	Yes	No	Unk	Yes	No	Unk
18. Does the property discharge waste water on or adjacent to the property other than storm water into a sanitary sewer system?	Yes	No	Unk	Yes	No	Unk	Yes	No	Unk
19. To the best of your knowledge, have any hazardous substances or petroleum products, unidentified waste materials, tires, automotive or industrial batteries or any other waste materials been dumped above grade, buried and/or burned on the property?	Yes	No	Unk	Yes	No	Unk	Yes	No	Unk
20. Is there a transformer, capacitor, or any hydraulic equipment for which there are any records indicating the presence of PCBs?	Yes	No	Unk	Yes	No	Unk	Yes	No	Unk

Government records/historical sources inquiry			
21. Do any of the following **federal** government record systems list the property or any property within the circumference of the area noted below:			
National Priorities list - within 1.0 mile?	Yes	No	
CERCLIS list - within 0.5 mile?	Yes	No	
RCRA TSD facilities - within 1.0 mile?	Yes	No	
22. Do any of the following **state** record systems list the property or any property within the circumference of the area noted below:			
List maintained by state environmental agency of hazardous waste sites identified for investigation or remediation that is the state agency equivalent to NPL - within approximately 1.0 mile?	Yes	No	
List maintained by state environmental agency of sites identified for investigation or remediation that is the state equivalent to CERCLIS - within 0.5 mile?	Yes	No	
Leaking Underground Storage Tank (LUST) list - within 0.5 mile?	Yes	No	
Solid waste/landfill facilities - within 0.5 mile?	Yes	No	
23. Based upon a review of **fire insurance maps** or consultation with the local fire department serving the property, all as specified in the guide, are any buildings or other improvements on the property or on an adjoining property identified as having been used for an industrial use or uses likely to lead to contamination of the property?	Yes	No	N/A

This questionnaire was prepared and completed by:

Name:____________________

Title:____________________

Firm:____________________

Address:____________________

Phone Number:____________________

Date:____________________

Table 5.2 Transaction Screen Process (TSP) Questionnaire for ASTM Standard E 1528 (ASTM, 1993) (Continued)

If the preparer is different than the user, complete the following:
Name of User:
User's Address:
User's Phone Number:
Preparer's Relationship to Site:
Preparer's Relationship to User (Principal, Employee, Agent, Consultant):
Copies of the completed questionnaire have been filed at:

____

____

Copies of the completed questionnaire have been mailed or delivered to:

____

____

Preparer represents that to the best of the preparer's knowledge the above statements and facts are true and correct and to the best of the preparer's actual knowledge no material facts have been suppressed or misstated.

Signature Date

Signature Date

Signature Date

Note: Copies of this standard may be obtained from ASTM (phone: 610-832-9585, fax: 610-832-9555). From American Society for Testing and Materials, Standard Practice for Environmental Site Assessments, Designation E 1528-93: Transaction Screen Process, ASTM, 100 Barr Harbor Drive, West Conshohocken, PS 19428-2959, 1993. With permission.

even if it costs a few hundred dollars more; otherwise, the institution appears not to be really serious about liability management.

Based on the ASTM standard, the first twenty TSP questions are posed by the "environmental professional" to the property owner and occupants, if applicable. The site is then visited, and the questions are answered independently by the professional conducting the investigation. In many cases it is not possible to verify answers to the questions given by the owner or occupants during the site inspection, because certain activities conducted in the past may no longer be conducted or the entire land use may have changed. The last three questions are answered by making an appropriate inquiry of the regulatory agency files to determine if any contaminated sites lie on the property or within a certain critical radius. The professional conducting the investigation may perform the agency inquiries by accessing the computer data files directly, by agency visits and direct file reviews, or by subcontracting the agency file search to an independent company supplying that service. The last question involves a search for stored toxic or hazardous substances on the site and adjacent area using fire insurance maps (Sanborns or others) or by contacting the fire marshall for assistance. These maps are commonly available for larger, older municipalities at public libraries, at fire departments, or at a centralized risk management facility. There are many communities, however, that do not have this information available.

The Interview Process

Even an experienced environmental professional can be fooled by an owner or occupant of a property under investigation. In many cases it is not possible to verify the information given in response to the first twenty questions of the TSP. The wording of the questions can lead to misunderstandings, and how the questions are posed to the owners or occupants can cause judgment errors to occur. If the TSP questionnaire is to be used properly, interviews should be conducted in person to allow the interviewer to gauge the reaction of the person answering the question, although ASTM Standard E 1528 does not specifically suggest this method and, in fact, allows telephone interviews. If the person is extraordinarily nervous or the answers appear to be inconsistent, the environmental professional should note this information, and if some of the facts can be independently verified, this should be accomplished. If someone is purposely trying to hide significant information, it is quite difficult to ascertain whether or not the truth is being told. One technique to assess consistency in knowledge of the property is to ask a few simple questions with regard to the property, such as a question concerning the color of a building, or concerning how long the person has occupied the land or building, or some other obvious question with regard to the property or neighborhood. The environmental professional asking the questions should be quite familiar with the property before the interview, and if possible, the site inspection should be conducted before the interview. The questions may be asked in the order given on the TSP questionnaire (Table 5.2) or in any order deemed reasonable by the environmental professional. In order to assess the consistency of the answers of the person being interviewed, a good technique is to ask several of the questions two or even three times at random during the interview process. Any inconsistencies in the answers should be noted. If the answers appear to be in conflict or if the interviewer suspects that the person being interviewed is not telling the truth, it may be appropriate to request the owner or occupant to sign the form. Normally only the user and preparer of the TSP questionnaire are required to sign the document. This additional signature provides some additional legal protection. If there is a real contamination problem, a case could be made for misrepresentation or fraud.

Since a major part of the TSP evaluation is the interview, the environmental professional should determine that the TSP was adequate to ensure that the site does not contain a significant environmental problem, although this is not specifically required by the ASTM standard. If the owner or occupants of the property are not knowledgeable, are not cooperative, or give conflicting answers to the questions, then the environmental professional would normally recommend that a full phase I ESA be conducted on the property or business. If a concerted effort is made to locate and interview the owner and occupants of the property, but they cannot be located or choose not to provide information or answers to the questions, then the TSP cannot be completed, and the recommendation would be for a full phase I ESA.

Regulatory File Search Issues

The regulatory file search answers questions 21 and 22 of the TSP. Some states maintain the information required to answer these questions in a geographic data base, filed by latitude and longitude and/or by the township–range system. However, many states and local governments maintain their regulatory action files based solely on the names of the individuals and/or companies against which the environmental action was filed. Since the TSP does not require a title search or an abstract, it can be quite difficult to determine the names of former owners or operators to check for environmental problems. Sometimes a cooperative regulatory agency person can obtain this information. However, it is important to maintain a degree of confidentiality in the TSP process, so asking a regulatory agency employee directly about a specific property is not an appropriate action, unless it is a last resort to obtain the information. Before mentioning to an agency the specific site location and business name being investigated, it is wise to discuss this action with the client and/or their attorney. In states or other localities where the agency actions are not computerized and where the information is filed solely on the basis of formal name, the TSP may not be a practical tool for an adequate due diligence investigation.

There are a number of data base companies that provide environmental regulatory agency searches, including but not limited to the CERCLIS list, RCRA TSD facilities, state environmental citations, UST registrations, and landfill–solid waste facility locations. This part of a TSP can be subcontracted to data base companies, as long as an adequate legal description of the property is available. To make the computer search, some of the data base companies do require an accurate longitude-latitude position, which can be obtained from U.S. Geological Survey topographic maps or by making a position determination using a hand-held Global Positioning System instrument. It is important to note that there are very significant variations in the quality of information obtained from various private companies that provide this type of information. Users of these data base companies should know how often the data base is updated, what agencies are monitored, how the information is obtained (by direct computer link and/or on-site agency checking), and how the internal data search is compiled. Any company using a data base search firm to obtain agency action information must understand that they become the primary party responsible for the conclusions based on *all* information provided.

Some larger, sophisticated companies maintain their own computer links to agency data files and obtain updates of the various federal, state, and local agency regulatory files. These companies also conduct information searches of the files by location and/or geographic position at agency locations. If the regulatory information is to be obtained by direct search at one or more agencies, certain routine protocols should be followed. An appointment should be made and questions asked with regard to file access, whether certain files are missing because of confidentiality, the timing of file updates and whether the files are complete. Both TSPs and phase I ESAs are confidential investigations, so care must be taken to protect the interest of the client or borrower.

There are also data bases available, such as the fire districts and fire maps previously mentioned, to locate stored hazardous or toxic substances. Past business occupancies can commonly be obtained by using the local business directory service (Polk Directory) or a computerized occupational license or certificate of use file. Power company files can be accessed to determine if any previous transformers on the site contained PCBs, the answer to question 23.

The Site Inspection

In the TSP investigation, the site inspection is used primarily to verify the answers given in the questionnaire. The key to obtaining a high-quality site inspection is for the environmental professional to be an experienced observer with some imagination. The site inspector may have some knowledge of the natural direction of groundwater flow beneath the site, general industrial practices of the past and present uses that could cause contamination, and what types of on-site waste disposal activities could cause contamination.

Many sites inspected using a TSP investigation are vacant and relatively small in size. Because the scope is limited and a detailed site inspection can be readily accomplished, it is important to view the ground carefully for obvious indicators of contamination, such as dead vegetation or stained or altered soil (Figures 5.1 and 5.2). Also, since the review of historical aerial photographs is not required, evidence should be sought to determine whether the site was ever occupied in the past by a building, was used as some type of construction staging area, or was ever farmed. These determinations are prime indicators that some

Figure 5.1 Vegetation is dead in the dark middle ground of the photograph. There is some association between the pipe exiting the building and the dead vegetation.

type of chemicals were used or stored on the site. The site must be inspected for any past excavations (see Figure 6.1), including ponds, lagoons, or infilling of these excavations. Since the TSP investigation is quite limited and the answers to these questions may be impossible to obtain, the observations made on the site are critical to determine the need for additional investigations.

When a site is paved or a building is present, the site inspector should look for some of the same evidence as described above on the site, such as stained soil and/or dead vegetation. If a building is present, the site should also be searched for vent pipes, indicative of underground fuel storage tanks. A determination should be made with regard to the waste disposal system currently and formerly used by the building. It is important to know if the building ever used a septic tank wastewater disposal system and, if it did, for what period of time and for what corresponding site uses. The site should also be inspected for floor drains that do not drain to the wastewater system (French drains). There are a number of other possible indicators of contamination, such as the occurrence of drums or other solid waste such as discarded oil cans, pesticide containers, or other labeled debris. It is common for many multistory buildings to have emergency generators that may have either underground or aboveground fuel storage tanks. If a building contains an elevator, the inspector should determine whether the system contains a hydraulic ram that could leak fluid into the ground.

A more detailed discussion of the site inspection is given in the description of the phase I ESA. A general guide to the site inspection is also given in the text of Designation E 1528 (ASTM, 1993).

Figure 5.2 The soil is stained severely from the edge of the vegetation line outward. This appears to indicate the discharge of a chemical or petroleum product.

Advantages of the TSP Investigation

The primary advantages of a TSP are that it can be accomplished rapidly and inexpensively and that it is truly a scanning process to determine general site characteristics. It is most useful as an internal tool of a lending institution, as long as the inspector is sufficiently trained to obtain satisfactory results. A TSP investigation can be conducted within a few days, assuming that the regulatory information can be obtained rapidly and that the owner and occupants of the site are available and cooperative.

Disadvantages of the TSP Investigation

There are some obvious deficiencies in using TSP as a due diligence environmental investigation. The analysis of the site history as described in the TSP scope could lead to substantial liabilities. For example, if the property is unimproved, with little evidence of past environmental problems and no known past land uses of a high-risk nature, the TSP investigation will probably find that it will not require additional investigation. Despite the preliminary investigation, the site may have contained a past easement for a local landfill. (Thousands of landfills are not listed in the public records.) This information would only be available in the title information or from inspection of old aerial photographs. If any type of building is present on the site other than a residence, the TSP may not be an appropriate environmental investigation. For example, the occupation history of a small, older strip shopping center cannot be evaluated adequately using a TSP. Any type of structure on a property suggests a number of environmental issues that must be evaluated, such as radon gas, asbestos, and in older buildings, indoor air pathogens. The TSP is a useful tool for the simplest property transactions and for determining which properties within a portfolio will require additional investigation.

There is another important disadvantage that all lending institutions must consider when using the TSP. If a consultant inspects the wrong property or commits some other act of gross negligence, virtually no liability can be assigned to the consultant if contamination is found on the site at a later time. The consultant must rely upon an interview process that requires little verification of facts, and if facts are withheld by the owner or occupants or if they do not have a complete knowledge of the past history of the site, the consultant cannot be held responsible for not finding contamination. Therefore, it is imperative that the lending institution environmental policy carefully define the uses of the TSP that are appropriate.

Discussion

The transaction screen process (TSP) is a limited scope environmental site assessment created by the American Society of Testing and Materials Standard (E 1528-93) to meet the due diligence provision of CERCLA and to standardize a general screening process. It is important to recognize its deficiencies, so that the TSP is used only for appropriate sites, which are very simple and have a very low potential for being contaminated. It is important to repeat the ASTM's recommended use for the TSP given in E 1528-93 (section 4.1), which reads:

> 4.1 Uses — This practice is intended for use on a voluntary basis by parties who wish to assess the environmental condition of commercial real estate. While use of this practice is intended to constitute appropriate inquiry for purposes of CERCLA's innocent landowner defense, it is not intended that its use be limited to that purpose. This practice is intended primarily as an approach to conducting an inquiry designed to identify recognized environmental conditions in connection with a property, and environmental site assessments that are more or less comprehensive than this practice (including, in some instances, no environmental site assessment) may be appropriate in some circumstances. Further, no implication is intended that a person must use this practice in order to be deemed to have conducted inquiry in a commercially prudent or reasonable manner in any particular transaction. Nevertheless, this practice is intended to reflect a commercially prudent and reasonable inquiry.

The American Society for Testing and Materials states that the TSP has some useful purpose, but that the appropriate use of the process must be decided by the parties to a transaction. The decision-making process leading to use of no environmental investigation, a TSP, a phase I ESA, or a more complex environmental investigation is based to a great extent on common sense and should be incorporated into the environmental risk policy. The ASTM Standard's repeated assertions that TSPs constitute "appropriate inquiry" for purposes of the CERCLA "innocent landowner" provision is legally debatable. First, depending on which jurisdiction the property lies in, there may or may not be any real "innocent landowner" defense for CERCLA actions, and in many states, such as Florida, this defense has not been adopted in the state law. Local government programs, in many cases, do not recognize the "innocent landowner" defense. The primary reason to perform this or any other type of environmental investigation on a property should not be to create an illusion of legal defense but to find out if there is any great risk of site contamination, with the associated liability. The TSP as a tool for defense against CERCLA action is not appropriate.

TECHNICAL ASPECTS OF THE PHASE I ENVIRONMENTAL SITE ASSESSMENT

The most common type of environmental investigation to assess the potential occurrence of toxic or hazardous substances on a property is termed the *phase I environmental site assessment* (ESA). As previously discussed, the scope of the phase I ESA was debated for many years prior to the general adoption of the American Society for Testing and Materials Designation E 1527-94, "Standard Practice for Environmental Site Assessments: Phase I Environmental Site Assessment Process" (ASTM, 1994). Although the phase I ESA scope acceptable to most lending institutions generally follows the standards set by the ASTM, there are notable exceptions that appear in the risk policies or manuals of many institutions.

The phase I ESA is primarily an investigation that assesses the potential that contamination is present on a site or that actually verifies the presence of contamination on some sites via the discovery of actual documentation. The scope can and should be modified, depending on the types of sites and/or land uses being investigated. A standard phase I ESA of a chain of gasoline stations may indicate that additional testing will be required at each site investigated. In this case, the scope of the environmental investigation practically should include an evaluation of inventory records at each site, a review of recent and past underground storage tank pressure tests, a review of the records of agency inspections of the facility, and some initial testing of soil and groundwater quality in the vicinity of the tanks and the lines connecting the tanks to the pumps. The scope of an environmental site assessment should start with the ASTM Standard, but again, common sense must be used in considering the circumstances when deciding on modifications to the scope. Additional tests that may be required depend on the location and size and/or age of existing structures, including tests for radon gas or asbestos, pathogenic-biological air quality assessments, limited chemical testing of building materials for lead paint or urea fiberboard, and limited testing of soil and/or groundwater for known contaminants.

Each of the subject areas included in a phase I ESA are discussed in this text in the approximate order of their appearance in a typical report. A general outline for a standard phase I ESA report is given in ASTM Standard E 1527-94 as Table X2 on page 24 (Table 5.3). Many lending institutions prefer their phase I ESA reports in different formats that conform to specific requirements, but all of the information discussed in this text should be contained in each phase I ESA report.

Table 5.3 Recommended Table of Contents and Report Format for a Phase I Environmental Site Assessment (ASTM, 1994)

X2.1	**Summary**	
X2.2	**Introduction**	
	X2.2.1	Purpose
	X2.2.2	Special Terms and Conditions
	X2.2.3	Limitations and Exceptions of Assessment
	X2.2.4	Limiting Conditions and Methodology Used
X2.3	**Site Description**	
	X2.3.1	Location and Legal Description
	X2.3.2	Site and Vicinity Characteristics
	X2.3.3	Descriptions of Structures, Roads, Other Improvements on the Site (including heating/cooling system, sewage disposal, source of potable water)
	X2.3.4	Information (if any) Reported by User Regarding Environmental Liens or Specialized Knowledge or Experience (pursuant to Section 5.)
	X2.3.5	Current Uses of the Property
	X2.3.6	Past Uses of the Property (to the extent identified)
	X2.3.7	Current and Past Uses of Adjoining Properties (to the extent identified)
	X2.3.8	Site Rendering, Map, or Site Plan
X2.4	**Records Review**	
	X2.4.1	Standard Environmental Record Sources, Federal and State
	X2.4.2	Physical Setting Source(s)
	X2.4.3	Historical Use Information
	X2.4.4	Additional Record Sources (if any)
X2.5	**Information from Site Reconnaissance and Interviews**	
	X2.5.1	Hazardous Substances in Connection with Identified Uses (including storage, handling, disposal)
	X2.5.2	Hazardous Substance Containers and Unidentified Substance Containers (including storage, handling, disposal)
	X2.5.3	Storage Tanks (including contents and assessment of leakage or potential for leakage)
	X2.5.4	Indications of PCBs (including how contained and assessment of leakage or potential for leakage)
	X2.5.5	Indications of Solid Waste Disposal
	X2.5.6	Physical Setting Analysis, if Migrating Hazardous Substances are an Issue
	X2.5.7	Any Other Conditions of Concern
	X2.5.8	Site Plan (if available)
X2.6	**Findings and Conclusions**	
X2.7	**Signatures of Environmental Professionals**	
X2.8	**Qualifications of Environmental Professionals Participating in Phase I Environmental Site Assessment**	
X2.9	**Optional Appendices (for example):**	
	X2.9.1	Other Maps, Figures, and Photographs
	X2.9.2	Ownership/Historical Documentation
	X2.9.3	Regulatory Documentation
	X2.9.4	Interview Documentation
	X2.9.5	Contract Between User and Environmental Professional

Reprinted with permission of ASTM.

Qualifications of Professionals Conducting Phase I ESAs

A vast number of firms and individuals are currently performing phase I ESA investigations, but unfortunately, only a few of these actually understand the philosophical concepts of the process and are capable of producing a high-quality report that really provides a competent level of due diligence. A discussion of the consultant selection process is included in Chapter 4, within the context of the environmental risk manual, and in the technical discussion of the TSP (this chapter). The credentials of both the company and the individual conducting a phase I ESA should be carefully inspected before the investigation is authorized.

There is no guarantee within the framework of ASTM Standard E 1527-94 that the investigation will be conducted in a professional manner, even if the general standards are completely met, because the quality of an investigation is only as good as the professional effort and expertise of those who conducted it.

One of the weakest provisions of ASTM Standard E 1527-94 is Section 6.5, entitled "Who May Conduct a Phase I." It is important to review the text of this section of the standard, because it affects the quality of the product and the liability loopholes that can be used by those performing a phase I ESA. Section 6.5 reads as follows:

> 6.5.1 Environmental Professional's Duties — The interviews and site reconnaissance, as well as the review and interpretation of information upon which the report is based and overseeing the writing of the report, are all portions of a Phase I Environmental Site Assessment that shall be performed by an environmental professional or environmental professionals. If more than one environmental professional is involved in these tasks, they shall coordinate their efforts.
>
> 6.5.2. Environmental Professional Supervision — Information for the records review needed for completion of a Phase I Environmental Site Assessment may be provided by a number of parties including governmental agencies, third-party vendors, the user, and present and past owners and occupants of the property, provided that the information is obtained by or under the supervision of an environmental professional or is obtained by a third-party vendor specializing in retrieval of the information specified in section 7. Prior assessments may also contain information that will be appropriate for usage in a current environmental site assessment provided the prior usage procedures set forth in sections 7, 8, and 9 are followed. The environmental professional(s) participating in the site reconnaissance and responsible for the report shall review all of the information provided.
>
> 6.6.2.1 Reliance — *An environmental professional is not required to verify independently the information provided but may rely on information provided unless he or she has actual knowledge that certain information is incorrect or unless it is obvious that certain information is incorrect based on other information obtained in the Phase I Environmental Site Assessment or otherwise actually known to the environmental professional.*

A key term used throughout this part of the ASTM Standard is *environmental professional*, which is defined in section 3.3.11. The text term definition quoted directly from the standard is as follows:

> 3.3.11 Environmental Professional — A person possessing sufficient training and experience necessary to conduct a site reconnaissance, interviews, and other activities in accordance with this practice, and from the information generated by such activities, having the ability to develop conclusions regarding recognized environmental conditions in connection with the property in question. An individuals's status as an environmental professional may be limited to the type of assessment to be performed or to specific segments of the assessment for which the professional is responsible. The person may be an independent contractor or an employee of the user.

Based on the information provided in ASTM Standard E 1527-94, the environmental professional may be educated or uneducated, can come from any discipline, may not even know what groundwater contamination is, may not understand the flow of groundwater, may not recognize the basic signs of potential contamination, and may be qualified to conduct "only part of the investigation." This definition of an environmental professional contains no real statement of qualifications at all. Although the format of the ASTM report does require incorporation of the résumés of the person or persons performing the investigation, there is no way to determine the level of input to the investigation or even if the person providing the résumé even worked on the ESA. Based on the language in section 6.5.1 of the standard, an environmental professional must perform or supervise the performance of the investigation. One question comes to mind is how does an environmental professional "supervise" the performance of a site inspection? Here again, the standard does not provide quality assurance. In fact, the issue of "reliance" is mentioned in a context that implies that the environmental professional can rely on any information, with no necessary verification of facts, and then be absolved of all liability. Based on the key provisions of Standard E 1527-94, it is clear that every user of a phase I ESA must develop a minimum standard of quality and a consultant qualification procedure that will satisfy the level of due diligence required by its own environmental risk policy. Conformance to the ASTM standard may not necessarily provide quality control for an ESA report. Additionally, if a consultant arrives at conclusions based solely on unverified, hearsay information, the wording in the standard implies a release from liability, yet this so-called protection will evaporate in a legal proceeding.

Terms and Limiting Conditions, Contractual Responsibilities

In the introduction of a phase I ESA, it is very important to clearly identify the person or entity authorizing the work product and the specific scope of services, including work items omitted from the scope by design or by the specific request of the authorizing entity. Also, a reference to the contract between the performing party and the client or authorizing party, any special terms and conditions, any limitations and special exceptions of assessment, any limiting conditions, and the methodology used should be included. The primary cause of misunderstandings and/or litigation between the party providing a phase I ESA and the party authorizing the work is a lack of insight into the nature of the scope of the investigation and the liability protection given by the ESA. Therefore, the scope of the contract should be repeated verbatim in the ESA report, in order to avoid misunderstandings and to state clearly what was requested and what was completed.

A phase I ESA report is not an insurance policy and cannot be treated like one. The report is the result of a scientific investigation with a specific scope designed to minimize liabilities from environmental hazards. There is no financially viable type of environmental investigation that will completely abate the liability that can arise in the property transfer business. Some of the more cautious have additionally requested some limited testing of soil and groundwater for contamination as part of a phase I ESA, but even this approach does not guarantee that unwanted contamination is not present. The only way that a site may be designated as "clean" is to run a variety of geophysical surveys, to drill hundreds of closely spaced test borings to obtain soil analyses, to install numerous test wells to obtain groundwater quality samples, and then to analyze the samples for several thousand potential contaminants at a laboratory. Even after sustaining an expense many times the value of the property, there may still be some risk that something was missed. The general approach to the phase I ESA as provided by the ASTM Standard is far more practical than the "pin cushion" testing approach and provides a reasonable degree of liability limitation and assurance.

The description of the phase I ESA scope should reference the ASTM Standard, if appropriate. Any exceptions should be described for any normal scope item that has been deleted from the investigation. The reasoning behind the deletion should be explained. For example, a title search is a normal part of a phase I ESA. If it is deleted from the scope of the investigation, there should be a valid reason, such as the timing of a closing date required by a lending institution that precluded the ability to obtain the information in a timely manner. One very important, rather common omission is the asbestos investigation of properties containing structures. If the asbestos investigation has not been conducted, there must be a very good reason. The language in the report should state the reason, which may be as simple as, "The building was constructed in the past year and according to current regulations, does not contain asbestos," or "The client indicated that the asbestos investigation was not necessary," because that level of assurance was not necessary. The consultant and/or the lending institution performing the investigation must be aware that any omissions from the normal standard of practice could bring substantial liability to the consultant; therefore, the justification must always be based on scientific reasoning or on a direct request from the entity that authorized the investigation. It is the responsibility of the consultant to educate the client with regard to the work scope needed to minimize future problems; the omission language may not be sufficient to protect the consultant from claims of negligence, especially if an omission was made on a very necessary part of an ESA. A lending institution must very carefully review any exceptions to a standard scope of a phase I ESA in the context of common sense and the environmental policy manual.

The basic provisions of the contract between the entity performing the ESA and the user should be repeated in the text of the ESA. It is common to place this language in the appendix of the report and to highlight any exceptions to the normal phase I ESA scope in the first part of the report. The purpose of this language is again to avoid misunderstandings between parties involved in the preparation and use of the report.

Some consultants place some limitation of liability statement within the early text of a phase I ESA. This language does not really provide any special liability protection to the preparer of the investigation, but it can alert the user that the document cannot be used as some type of insurance policy. The liability protection for the consultant is to follow closely the scope of the contract, complete all items listed in the scope, and provide all documentation obtained in the report.

It is common to acknowledge the persons providing information in the phase I ESA investigation near the beginning of the report. This list of persons may include agency personnel, interviewees, the property owner, or property tenants or users. The acknowledgement list should include all persons who have assisted, unless they specifically request to remain anonymous. The list is a portion of the investigation documentation.

Site Description — Introduction

The site description includes a substantial amount of information. Based on the ASTM report outline given in Table 5.3, this section of a phase I ESA contains

- The location and legal description of the property
- The site and surrounding vicinity characteristics
- Descriptions of structures, roads, site improvements (including heating/cooling system, wastewater disposal, source of potable water, site drainage direction and characteristics)
- Information on environmental liens or actions filed against the property or special experience
- Current uses of the property
- Past uses of the property (duplicated to some degree in the records review)
- Current and past uses of adjacent properties
- A site map or plan

Each of these subject areas is significant and is accorded an individual discussion. Information to assess the property is obtained from a records review, a site inspection (reconnaissance), and interviews with various knowledgeable parties.

Site Description — Location and Legal Description

The first priority is to locate the property accurately on topographic maps and aerial photographs and then to obtain a street address and detailed legal description. One of the most common errors that occurs in the performance of phase I ESA investigations is doing a site inspection of the wrong property. When a site is located in an urban setting, it is relatively easy to locate the correct property by the street address or building description, but when the property is located in a new development, is vacant land, or is a large parcel described by a metes and bounds survey, the exact location may be quite difficult to ascertain. The ESA investigator must know the exact boundaries of the property, even if this requires that the owner stake or flag the boundaries. Questionable boundary delineation could cause the report to contain erroneous information, including a possibly significant exception in the conclusions.

The legal description of the property should be reproduced exactly in the report text. If the legal description is very lengthy, it may be placed in the appendix and simply referenced in the body. Location of the site on a U.S. Geological Survey topographic map and on aerial photographs is necessary to determine local drainage patterns and the site history.

Site Description — Site and Vicinity Characteristics

The general conditions on and surrounding a site give a good indication of the potential for finding contamination. The connection between general conditions and environmental problems is obvious in many circumstances. If the property is unused and is completely surrounded by unused land, then the phase I ESA investigation should concentrate more on historic records than on the site inspection, because there may be little evidence on site of any past activities. If the property is located in an industrial area, next to a gasoline station, near a junkyard, or even adjacent to a cemetery, the location can have a significant impact. On-site structures and easily observable activities bear greatly on the emphasis and direction of the ESA investigation. The same environmental professional who performs the initial investigative work on the site should conduct the site inspection, because the direction of the site investigation and interviewing process is based on details of the aerial photographs and topographic maps.

A determination must be made concerning the most probable direction of groundwater flow, so that potential impacts of off-site land uses may be assessed. Some knowledge of groundwater hydrology is useful at this stage, because although in many cases the groundwater flow direction in the surficial aquifer (from land surface to some depth below it, determined by the occurrence of the first confining bed; see Chapter 3) follows the slope of land surface across the site or the regional topography or slope of land surface, the presence of drainage features, such as rivers, canals, ditches, or even underdrains, can greatly influence groundwater flow direction, so that it may be opposite the slope of the land or at some angle to it. Some companies currently offering information on records have also attempted to provide groundwater flow directions from topographic maps as part of their service. Again, without local knowledge, an accurate assessment of flow direction cannot be made. It is best to view the topographic map while in the field making observations and to check with other sources, such as the U.S. Geological Survey or state agencies that regulate water, before any conclusion is drawn. Once the groundwater flow direction is determined, off-site activities in the upgradient direction must be inspected carefully to assess the contamination potential.

Site Description — Description of Features and Structures

There are some particular observations of the site and features that should be reported. It is quite a simple matter if the site is vacant and surrounded by unused land. However, when the land uses on the site and on surrounding properties are both intensive, this part of the ESA becomes important. Certain site features, particularly drainage, are important because they control the movement of contaminants to some degree. The presence of drainage ditches, canals, dikes, impoundments, and retention or detention areas all should be noted. If a well is used as the water supply for the site, the size (diameter), depth, and aquifer used should be determined. Information must be obtained about the history of wastewater disposal on the site. If the site has always had a connection to a municipal or industrial wastewater treatment facility, then there is usually no problem (with the exception of collection system leaks). If the site is currently or was in the past connected to a septic tank or cesspool wastewater disposal system, the location of the entire system should be noted as well as the length of time it was in use. Sometimes historic use of these systems can be observed directly in the field if the adsorption field is elevated or the top of the tank is exposed. Larger facilities may contain an on-site wastewater treatment plant and effluent disposal system, which should be noted with a location and description. Any information on the operational history of the system, including sludge clean-out schedules, should be obtained. In older buildings, it is necessary to view or request information on the cooling system. Depending on the type of system used or its age, this could be a source of contamination. Old cooling systems that utilize a cooling tower can be a source of indoor air contaminants, such as pathogenic bacteria (Legionella).

Site Information — Environmental Liens, Spills, or Mishaps

The records review and interviews process should enable the documentation of any known environmental actions that have been taken against the owner and/or tenants. Despite the statement in the ASTM Standard that information can be relied upon without verification in order to draw conclusions, it is good practice to verify information obtained from a landowner and/or tenant with regard to environmental liens, spills of hazardous or toxic substances, or agency actions against the owners or operators of the site or facility. If any type of reportable spill has occurred, there should be associated documentation in the company and regulatory agency files that can be obtained. In the case of fires, the local fire marshall's office should have the records. Spills that occurred prior to 1980 may not have been recorded, so little if any information may be present in agency files. In this case, interviews may be the only available tool to reveal the occurrence.

A search of environmental agency files will normally reveal any actions that have been brought against the site (see Records Review subsections, this chapter). In some states or local government jurisdictions, agency actions are not compiled on a physical location basis (by latitude-longitude or by township-range-section), but on the basis of individual or corporate names. In this case, it is necessary to use the information obtained from the property title search to obtain all of the existing and previous owner names in order to search the agency files. U.S. Environmental Protection Agency lists, such as CERCLIS, are geography-based and are easy to search. If a geographic search is used, the legal description of the property must be accurate.

Site Information — Current Uses of the Property

A simple description of the character and use of the property should be contained in the phase I ESA report. If the property is unused, the description should include the condition of the site. For example, the site is "cleared and adjacent to an interstate highway in a partially developed industrial park." Another example is, "the site is unused and is covered by a native pine forest with a few acres of wetland marsh occurring in the northwest corner." The description should be concise, accurate, and specific about what is there. If the property is developed, the type of land use should be stated clearly. For example, "the site contains a 700,000 square foot shopping mall constructed in 1988 with four outparcels each containing a gasoline station." In the case of multiple land uses, each use should be individually described, with the approximate area and location. The locations of all land uses within complex properties should be clearly delineated on the site map contained in the report.

Site Description — Past Uses of the Property (Site History)

One of the most important parts of the phase I ESA is the site history of land uses. It is also perhaps the most difficult information to obtain for certain rural sites and complex urban sites. Contamination is discovered on many sites through historical research rather than from the site inspection, because many times there is no physical evidence of contamination. A partial list of sources for historical land use information is given in Table 5.4. The wording in ASTM Standard E 1527-94 with regard to historic land uses and practices on a site implies that the acceptable level of investigation be limited to "reasonably ascertainable" information. The exact wording of E 1527-94 with regard to land use is as follows:

> 7.3.2 Uses of the property — All obvious uses of the property shall be identified from the present, back to the property's obvious first developed use, or back to 1940, whichever is earlier. This task requires reviewing only as many of the standard historical sources in 7.3.4.1 through 7.3.4.8 as are necessary and both reasonably ascertainable and likely to be useful (as defined under Data Failure in 7.3.2.3). For example, if the property was developed in the 1700's, it might

Table 5.4 Sources of Historical Land Uses Information

1. Abstracts
2. Title searches
3. Aerial photographs
4. Fire department records
5. Fire insurance maps
6. Property tax files
7. Business directories
8. Local street address directories
9. Building department records
10. Zoning department records
11. Certificate of use files
12. Disaster preparedness agency files
13. Local historical society files
14. Library — historical books
15. Newspaper files
16. Specialized clubs or groups (Railroad Society)
17. Trade groups (Cattlemans Association, Dairy Farmers Association, etc.)
18. Interviews

> be feasible to identify uses back to the early 1900's, using sources such as fire insurance maps or USGS 7.5 minute topographic maps. Although other sources such as recorded land title records might go back to the 1700's, it would not be required to review them unless they were both reasonably ascertainable and likely to be useful. As another example, if the property was reportedly not developed until 1960, it would still be necessary to confirm that it was undeveloped back to 1940. Such confirmation may come from one or more of the standard sources specified in 7.3.4.1 through 7.3.4.8, or it may come from other historical sources (such as someone with personal knowledge of the property; see 7.3.4.9) However, checking other historical sources (see 7.3.4.9) would not be required. For purposes of 7.3.2, the term "developed use" includes agricultural uses and placement of fill. The report shall describe all identified uses, justify the earliest date identified (for example, records showed no development of the property prior to the specific date), and explain the reason for any gaps in the history of use (for example, data failure).

Although the standard with regard to historical land use is reasonably clear, in practice a generally poor job has been done on the historical research section in ESA reports reviewed by the author. The definition of "developed use" is somewhat problematic, since some of the worst contamination sites in the southern United States have been associated with temporary facilities located in rural settings, such as railroad tie dipping vats or cattle dipping vats. The process of harvesting timber may not be a land use of concern, but if railroad ties were manufactured or turpentine stills were temporarily located on a site, the historic records may not note these activities, even though the liabilities exist.

One of the most useful tools in researching properties with a long land use history is the abstract of title (abstract) or, to a lesser degree, a title search. An abstract is a complete documentation of the ownership history of a property, including recorded leases, deeds, mortgages, and easements. The abstract goes back in time to the first recorded deed and contains many clues to historic land uses. The most obvious land use information that can be obtained from an abstract is the company name with an implied use, such as ABC Oil Company, Big Dirty

Chemical Company, or XYZ Fertilizer Company. Some of the early land use descriptions include clues to past land uses. For example, "The north property boundary ran from the section corner to the barn and turned south to the turpentine still." The abstracts also contain gas and oil leases and timber leases in rural areas. Special easements are also recorded for uses like petroleum pipelines. If an agreement has been made between a landowner and a local government to conduct some special activity on the property, such as temporary placement of a landfill, the information is recorded in the abstract. In large land deals, an abstract is commonly available and can be borrowed from the attorney handling the closing of the deal. If an abstract is not available, the next best document is a title search. As indicated in the wording of the ASTM Standard E 1527, the ownership of the property should be traced to when the site was unused or to 1940, whichever is more complete. When ordering a title search, it is imperative that all information on recorded leases and easements be included. The title search may not contain all of the documents recorded on a given property, but it should be adequate for ownership research.

Aerial photographs are very useful tools in researching historic land use after 1940. Aerial photographs are available for most of the United States beginning in the 1940s, when the U.S. Soil Conservation Service, the Department of Agriculture, and a few other agencies photographed most of the country to establish land uses. These older photographs are available from the U.S. Department of Agriculture in Colorado Springs, CO. U.S. Geological Survey topographic maps are also made using aerial photographs to form the base map, and land uses can often be assessed using these maps. The U.S.G.S topographic maps can be purchased from the Publications Distribution Center in Denver, CO, or can be reviewed in many public libraries. Most cities and counties in the United States use aerial photographs to assess property taxes and to map changes in land use. These photographs are taken every 1 to 5 years, depending on the growth rate and the sophistication of the local government. These photographs are available for a nominal cost at the local courthouse or government building in the zoning or land development department. Other sources of historic aerial photographs include the U.S. Department of Transportation, the state and local government departments of transportation, the U.S. Coast and Geodetic Survey (Department of Commerce, National Oceanic and Atmospheric Administration), the U.S. Air Force and other military units, and the National Aeronautics and Space Administration. There are also commercial services that can provide aerial photographs for a fee (REDI Maps and others). Review of a succession of aerial photographs shows the history of the property. It is most effective to use the aerial photographs in the interview process to form a basis for inquiry of knowledgeable persons.

Historic research on large parcels that appear to have minimal use in the near past sometimes must be conducted using history books found in the local public library. This research is sometimes necessary when trying to assess past land use practices (older) that could have impacted larger, rural parcels. If the historic research indicates a limited access to a large rural parcel, chances are good that no significant contamination has occurred. There are exceptions, of course, such as certain agricultural or railroad operations (tie-making operations). However, if there was no road or railroad access, then further research may be unnecessary. Once a property becomes accessible, there is always the possibility that the site could be affected by some less intense land use or by illegal dumping. The very process of constructing roads has created a significant number of contamination sites. Staging areas where heavy equipment was stored, fueled, and/or maintained commonly contain hydrocarbon and/or solvent contamination. The construction dates of all roads, railroads, and other accesses can be found in the library, at the local department of transportation, from aerial photographs, or from interviews. Information on the railroad system can be obtained from special clubs, such as the Railroad Preservation Society. Historic information on past agricultural practices can be obtained from the Cattleman's Association, the Dairy Farmers Association, the Fruit and Vegetable Growers Association, and other organizations.

Properties within intensely developed areas with a long history of land uses must be researched through a variety of sources. Aerial photographs alone will not yield the information necessary to determine the operations housed within the structures or what other activities may have been conducted on a property. In order to obtain the history of uses within structures, it is necessary to research some or all of the following sources: fire department records, fire insurance maps, property tax files, business directories (Polk's and others), local street address directories, building department records, zoning department records, certificate of use files, and disaster preparedness agency files. Information collected from these sources should then be confirmed through interviews with knowledgeable people. The fire department and fire insurance records are more directed to the storage and use of toxic and hazardous substances and are considered to be the optimum sources of information. However, there are many areas of the United States where these types of records are either unavailable or incomplete. The completion of historic research in these areas will require the use of the other sources of information mentioned. Any site with a long and varied use history will be difficult to assess and will require an appropriate budget for research. The party to a transaction who commissions an ESA report for such a property based upon a "low ball" price may not be getting the desired level of protection from contamination-related liabilities.

One very difficult land use type to assess for past history is an older (over 20 years) strip shopping center, which may have included "high risk" businesses, such as dry cleaning facilities or others, that could have discharged toxic or hazardous substances into an on-site wastewater disposal system. It is often relatively easy to research the wastewater disposal practices on the site and the time of hookup to a municipal system. However, it may be difficult to find the use history of every individual unit rented within the shopping center. If the ownership of the facility has changed one or more times, internal records on use may not be available. Even if the records are complete, there may be no connection between the activities or store types and the formal names. For example, if the record states that unit 1 was occupied by “Mae's,” the question remains as to whether this is a restaurant, a flower shop, or a dry cleaner. Use of internal records, directories, and other sources may yield only a partial history; only personal interviews can confirm the overall use of each unit. Sometimes old telephone directories will yield this information. The other issue involves coordinating the records of use with the history of wastewater disposal to assess the potential for contamination. This correlation of records can be very difficult and, commonly, the least expensive method for assessing the potential for contamination is to test the soil and groundwater for a variety of chemical compounds. Testing in that case would be limited to the on-site wastewater disposal area. There are occasions when a complete history simply cannot be determined, so the report should contain an explanation with a special condition.

The investigator must be very careful about how the historic land use information is presented in the report, because the use, storage, or sale of toxic or hazardous substances does not necessarily mean that contamination is present in the soil or groundwater. The land use information must be placed in the context of the site inspection to determine if further research is required. If the facility is no longer in existence and several high-risk land uses were present, then further investigation may be necessary. However, if the site contained no physical outlets for potential contaminants to enter the soil or groundwater, then no further research is required.

At present, the leading cause of litigation against consultants performing phase I ESAs is the omission of historic information that indicates a high-risk land use. The most commonly omitted businesses that carry a high likelihood of contamination are dry cleaning and photographic print shops.

Site Description — Current and Past Uses of Adjoining Properties

Research on properties adjoining the primary ESA site is an instrumental part of every phase I ESA. A common question often raised is how far off the site is far enough. In the records search section of the ASTM Standard E 1527 (Section 7.2.1), the radius of research for known hazardous waste and waste disposal facilities ranges from 0.5 to 1 mi. The language in Standard E 1527 covering this section of the phase I ESA is as follows:

> 8.4.1.3 Current Uses of Adjoining Properties — To the extent that current uses of adjoining properties are visually or physically observed on the site visit, or are identified in the interviews or records review, they shall be identified in the report, and current uses so identified shall be described in the report if they are likely to indicate recognized environmental conditions in connection with the adjoining properties or the property.
>
> 8.4.1.4 Past Uses of Adjoining Properties — To the extent that indications of past uses of adjoining properties are visually or physically observed on the site visit, or are identified in the interviews or record review, they shall be noted by the environmental professional, and past uses so identified shall be described in the report if they are likely to indicate recognized environmental conditions in connection with the adjoining properties or the property.
>
> 8.4.1.5 Current or Past Uses in the Surrounding Property — To the extent that the general type of current or past uses (e.g., residential, commercial, industrial)

of properties surrounding the property are visually or physically observed on the site visit or going to or from the property for the site visit, or are identified in the interviews or record review, they shall be noted by the environmental professional, and the uses so identified shall be described in the report if they are likely to indicate recognized environmental conditions in connection with the property.

8.4.1.6 Geologic, Hydrogeologic, Hydrologic, and Topographic Conditions — The topographic conditions of the property shall be noted to the extent visually or physically observed or determined from interviews, as well as the general topography of the area surrounding the property that is visually or physically observed from the periphery of the property. If any information obtained shows there are likely to be hazardous substances or petroleum products on the property or on nearby properties and those hazardous substances or petroleum products are of a type that may migrate, topographic observations shall be analyzed in connection with geologic, hydrogeologic, hydrologic, and topographic information obtained pursuant to records review (see 7.2.3) and interviews to evaluate whether hazardous substances or petroleum products are likely to migrate to the property, or within or from the property, into groundwater or soil.

The records research indicates that a radius of 0.5 to 1 mi should be used to locate the very bad contamination sites, and the ASTM Standard states that what can be seen visually off-site is important within the context of the topography and hydrogeology. Therefore, no clear guidance is provided in the ASTM Standard to answer the basic question of how far off-site to assess current and past land uses. It is important to use logic and common sense to answer this question. First, if the topography is flat and the surficial aquifer does not have high permeability, then the potential for the migration of contaminants from off-site sources onto the property is not high, and the investigation of adjoining properties can be minimized. Another issue is the age of the operations being conducted in adjoining and adjacent areas. Even if the groundwater movement in an area is slow, perhaps only a few feet per year, when a land use with a potential contamination problem has been operating for decades, it should be investigated if it is upgradient and within 0.5 to 1 mi from the property. The most critical direction to search for off-site contamination potential is in the upgradient groundwater flow direction. For example, if the topography or hydrogeologic record indicates that the groundwater flow direction is from north to south across the property, then the land uses north of the property are the ones that should receive the most scrutiny. The higher the slope of land surface and the higher the permeability of the surficial aquifer, the longer the distance that requires research in the upgradient direction. A knowledgeable hydrogeologist can estimate the groundwater flow velocity to determine a reasonable maximum distance to search. If the average groundwater flow velocity is 10 ft/year and the oldest upgradient land use has been present for 10 years, then the maximum reasonable search distance may be only 100 ft. The environmental professional should be quite careful in this type of analysis, because of the potential errors that can be made in the groundwater flow velocity estimate and because outside influences from man-made features, such as a municipal wellfield or a series of individual wells, can greatly alter both the direction and speed of groundwater flow. It is often impractical and time-consuming to use a fixed radius of search around a site. This guideline should only be used when the groundwater flow direction is unknown. Current and past land uses should be discussed using compass directions in the context of the most likely groundwater flow direction.

Current and past land uses can be determined using methods similar to those described for the on-site current and past land use assessment (see previous discussion). Current use information can be obtained from directories, fire department records, and certificate of use records. The sources of past land use history are given in Table 5.4. It is often necessary to confirm or obtain past off-site land use information from interviews. When using the interview process, the environmental professional must recognize that misinformation may be obtained, particularly when there are disputes between neighboring businesses or owners (see discussion on interviews).

Site Description — Site Rendering, Map, or Site Plan

Every phase I ESA should contain a map and/or a copy of a current aerial photograph showing the property and the surrounding lands. The map should contain a north arrow and a bar scale. (Written scales are not useful, because copying alters the scale dimensions to some degree.) Each off-site land use on the area map should be labeled and adequately identified, if there is any discussion of the use in the report. It is often necessary to have a large-scale detail map of the site, particularly if the site is complex, with many locations discussed within the report text. The detail map should also contain a north arrow, the proper locations of all structure and features, and a bar scale.

Records Review

The due diligence environmental investigation of a property includes a review of public records of the site and the surrounding properties. ASTM Standard E 1527 references the records search within the context of using "reasonably ascertainable/standard sources" of information. Records should be searched for land to a radius similar to the radius of the off-site historic land use investigation previously described in this text. There are designated minimum search distances for specific types of contaminated sites mentioned in the standards, but the records search area should be based on a logical approach to the specific site conditions. The most important considerations are the topography and hydrogeology of the site and local area and the types and ages of on- and off-site land uses that have a high potential to cause contamination.

The value of the records search depends on the accuracy and usefulness of the information compiled. Much of the information obtained in an ESA investigation comes from public records, but the source agencies offer no guarantee that the information is either accurate or up-to-date. ASTM Standard E 1527 implies that the environmental professional is not responsible for any mistakes made by the source agencies, but should make a "reasonable effort" to compensate for these errors by consulting some other sources of information. An environmental professional is responsible for correcting obvious errors in public data files, such as correcting the location of a gasoline station actually across the street from the property that the agency shows to be a mile away. The environmental professional is also responsible for determining the proper location of the property in order to initiate the records search. If a computer data base search is run using an incorrect site location, obviously the information will be inaccurate. To check the accuracy of a search, the investigator can locate both the site and a known contamination site in the vicinity. If the known site does not appear in the search, then the investigator knows that the data base must be checked; either the site location is wrong or the computer data base is inaccurate or not up-to-date. The environmental professional must check the timing of the most recent update of the information base to assure that it is no older than 90 days. The environmental professional is responsible for establishing a quality control procedure to ensure that information will be crosschecked. Sometimes the interview process can be used to authenticate information from another source.

Several methods commonly used to search for environmental data on or around a property include direct access of regulatory agency data systems and public records or retaining of a specialty company that offers this type of search (see regulatory file searches in the TSP discussion). Whether the records search is conducted in-house or is outsourced, the environmental professional and the company producing the report are fully responsible for the accuracy of the information.

Records Review — Standard Environmental Record Sources, Federal and State

Standard environmental records in each state and local government jurisdiction may be accessed. Some specific environmental records require searches of a radius of 0.5 to 1 mi, as recommended in ASTM Standard E 1527. However, the search radius should be tied to the hydrogeologic setting of the specific property. In most cases, a computer search using a radius of 1 mi from the property boundaries is sufficient when researching the following lists: federal National Priorities, federal CERCLIS, federal RCRA TSD facilities, RCRA generators, federal ERNS, state hazardous waste sites, state landfill and/or solid waste disposal facilities, state leaking underground tanks, state registered underground tanks, and state hazardous waste generators (large and small). Local governments also maintain lists that tend to be more current of these types of facilities. Research of both the active facilities lists and closure records should not be neglected.

Some environmental records are filed according to a specific type of problem or land use. Records of toxic or hazardous substance discharges can sometimes be found filed according to the facility or individual name and/or the geographic location. The investigator must determine the methodology used in the regulatory filing system prior to initiating a search of these records or risk missing significant information. Ongoing toxic or hazardous waste assessments and remedial actions are usually recorded in both the federal and state data bases, depending on the size of the site and whether there is overlapping jurisdiction. Information on contaminated wells and other local information can usually be found at the local or state government environmental protection agency or the health department. The records of wastewater disposal facilities permits issued through local and state governments can be located at the appropriate agencies.

Storage and handling of toxic and/or hazardous substances require permits or notifications in most state and local government jurisdictions, information that can be found in several of the data sources listed in Table 5.4. The best sources of these data include records of fire departments, planning and zoning departments, local environmental and health departments, regional planning agencies (in Florida and several other states), and some regional water supply agencies. Local or regional power companies maintain data on the location of transformers containing PCBs. Transformers that do not contain PCBs are currently labeled by many power companies.

Records Review — Physical Setting Sources

The primary source of physical setting information is the U.S. Geological Survey topographic map for the area being investigated, which is readily available for purchase and can be reviewed at most university or public libraries. U.S.G.S. topographic maps are specifically identified in ASTM Standard E 1527 as a mandatory source of information. Geologic maps, groundwater level and flow maps of the surficial aquifer, soil conservation service maps, and specialized aerial photographs containing topography and/or environmental information also offer physical setting information. It is often useful to include a color copy of a portion of the topographic map, with the site location highlighted in the final ESA report.

Records Review — Historic Use Information

A detailed discussion of the historic land use research of a property and adjoining properties appeared earlier in the text. A list of the sources for historic land use information is given in Table 5.4. It is often necessary to confirm the historic use of specific properties with the interview process. The most reliable sources of historic land use information are active or retired government engineers and employees, local historians, and other individuals who are not a party to the transaction in any way.

Site Investigation (Information from Site Reconnaissance and Interviews)

A physical inspection of the site is perhaps the most important part of a phase I ESA. While ASTM Standard E 1527 uses the term *site reconnaissance*, there is more to the site visit than a cursory view of the property and facilities by the environmental professional. The qualifications of the environmental professional conducting the phase I ESA become a real issue at this stage of the investigation. Many different types of scientists and engineers can become qualified to conduct an inspection of a simple site, one with a minimal number of uses and operating facilities. A single individual can adequately conduct the inspection of an unused property or commercial tract containing an office building. However, when the inspection is complex, involving a very large property with multiple uses, such as a farming operation or an industrial manufacturing facility, an individual environmental professional is usually not qualified to perform an unassisted inspection and evaluation of the property. An individual inspector may miss important features of a complex site. The environmental professional must have some familiarity with the type of industry or land use and must understand the activities and processes being conducted on the property. The site inspection and analysis of a complex site should be made by a team of experts from a variety of disciplines to obtain meaningful results. The experience and background of the site inspector should be carefully matched to the complexity of the property.

Some basic property inspection practices routinely used by environmental professionals, include the following:

1. Prior to the site inspection, the environmental professional should review the setting by inspecting the site location on a topographic map and determining the most likely direction of groundwater flow.
2. Some aerial photographs of the site and the area surrounding the site should be reviewed prior to the site visit, and the most current aerial photograph should accompany the investigator to the site.
3. The owner and/or operator of the property should be informed of the inspection time and their presence requested on the site during at least part of the inspection, and the tenants of a property should also be contacted.
4. The current property uses and the general land uses in the vicinity should be well known.

Prior to the inspection of a complex property, an approach to the inspection should be planned, and members of the technical team should be assigned responsibility for various aspects of the inspection. If the site covers several hundred or more acres, it is obvious that every square foot of the site cannot be inspected in detail, so the property may require an aerial inspection using a helicopter or a small airplane. A prepared environmental professional going into the field should bring at least the following tools: a recent aerial photograph of the site, a field notebook and several pencils, a tape measure (100 ft length is usually adequate), a camera (the best type is one that places the date on the photograph), color film, a compass, a safety kit, a small auger, and a shovel. Special circumstances may require additional equipment, such as a 4-wheel-drive vehicle, an organic vapor analyzer, a respirator, and any other specialized equipment as indicated by the information gathered prior to the inspection.

If the environmental professional is likely to come in contact with hazardous or toxic substances, he or she should have adequate safety training. This training should at least include the standard OSHA 40-hr safety course required for persons who work on RCRA hazardous waste cleanup sites, although this is not a specific requirement of the ASTM standards. The environmental professional must be trained to recognize a potentially hazardous or dangerous situation and take appropriate precautions. It is not advisable for a single environmental professional to inspect a site known to be hazardous. Safety considerations alone dictate that a team should complete these inspections. The environmental professional is responsible for having the appropriate safety gear available for use.

A systematic inspection of the property sometimes entails walking the complete perimeter before inspecting the interior of the site and any structures or activities being conducted there. This allows a view of off-site uses and gives a general impression of the site as a whole. The impressions of the site should be recorded in the field notebook or on a tape recorder. Color photographs provide the best documentation for observations made on the property with the compass directions and the locations of the photographs recorded. Every observation should be meticulously documented with regard to the site condition and any evidence of contamination. Field documentation and records are commonly used in litigation as evidence.

Only the most recently dated inspection of the site and the adjacent properties is valid. The environmental professional should give the exact date(s) and time(s) of the site inspection in the report. Also, all photographs taken to document site conditions should contain the date of the inspection. Documentation of the inspection date is very important, because the consultant and/or lending institution cannot be held responsible for any changes in site conditions after the inspection has been completed. There have been cases in which an owner or operator has attempted to hide or "dress up" site conditions between the inspection and time of the closing. Site inspectors must protect themselves from unscrupulous behavior and from potential liabilities that arise after the inspection. The most effective protection for all parties who provide or use a phase I ESA is proper documentation of facts that includes meticulous notes and photographs.

Site Inspection — Hazardous Substances in Connection with Identified Uses (Including Storage, Handling, Disposal)

All on-site uses of hazardous and toxic substances must be identified and verified from direct observation or interview. The investigator must determine where the substances are stored and whether there is any pathway for a spilled substance to enter the soil or groundwater on, beneath, or around the site. The substances found should be inventoried, along with notes of storage locations, so that this information may be included in the report. This level of inspection is usually not necessary on an unused site unless there has been a history of land use with a high potential for contamination. If the site is no longer in operation, then the types of substances used on-site must be determined by the interview process.

The appearance of the site is the first indication of the potential for contamination. A messy and dirty site indicates that an owner or operator did not care about details, and there may be a higher potential for contamination. Opened containers of hazardous or toxic substances may indicate potential pollution and careless workplace attitude.

Any site that has the status of either a generator or a small quantity generator of hazardous waste production must be carefully inspected. The investigator should review the records for delivery of hazardous or toxic substances and the quantities of those substances that are shipped off-site for disposal as waste. All storage facilities should be inspected to assess containment, compatibility of substances, cover, and any other factor that could have allowed a discharge to occur. This includes both the storage of the unused substances and the waste products from operations.

The history of on-site wastewater disposal and internal drainage of the structure must be determined, when it is discovered that hazardous or toxic substances are stored and used on the site. A well-managed site may contain stored hazardous or toxic substances used for maintenance or in some industrial process, but that fact does not necessarily equate to high potential for contamination. There must be some pathway for contamination to leave the building and enter the ground. If toxic or hazardous substances are being stored outside of a structure or containment area and on unpaved ground, the substances are probably in the soil and/or groundwater. Even if these substances are being used in an area contained with a cement pad or asphalt, if the area is uncovered, runoff from rainfall will cause the migration of the substance into the surface drainage system. Evidence for direct input of contaminants into the soil includes dead vegetation (Figure 5.1), stained soil (Figure 5.2), pipes leading from a building directly to the soils or a drainage area (Figure 5.3), and uncovered storage drums, such as waste oil drums (Figure 5.4). There are many other types of evidence of direct discharge of hazardous or toxic substances (see discussion on petroleum storage). Potential points of discharge within the interior of structures include all sinks, sumps, and floor drains (Figure 5.5). If any type of on-site wastewater disposal system has been used at any time, there is a direct pathway for contamination to enter the soil. All floor drains or the outlets for any sumps must be checked to assess their ultimate discharge location. The existence of underground storage tanks that have contained any type of hazardous or toxic substance raises questions, particularly if the facility is more than 10 years old. If no reasonable pathway exists for an interior stored or used substance to enter the soil or groundwater, then contamination is unlikely.

Sometimes there is an overreaction by the site inspector to the discovery of minor evidence of contamination. A small oil stain or a grease spot is not necessarily an indication that a major contamination problem exists. If the stains exist, they should be documented and photographed. If there is no corroborative evidence of fuel or solvent use on the site, the environmental professional should dig with a shovel or auger into the stained soil to check the depth of penetration. If the stain is persistent, further testing may be deemed appropriate. The site inspector must use common sense when recommending additional work to test for contamination.

Figure 5.3 Pipe leading from the interior of a structure into the ground. Pipes like this commonly provide conduits for potential contaminants to enter the soil and groundwater system.

Figure 5.4 A 55-gal drum and 5-gal buckets containing waste oil at the exterior of a building with no overhead cover. A rainfall event would cause the oil to overflow onto the ground, thereby causing a contaminant problem.

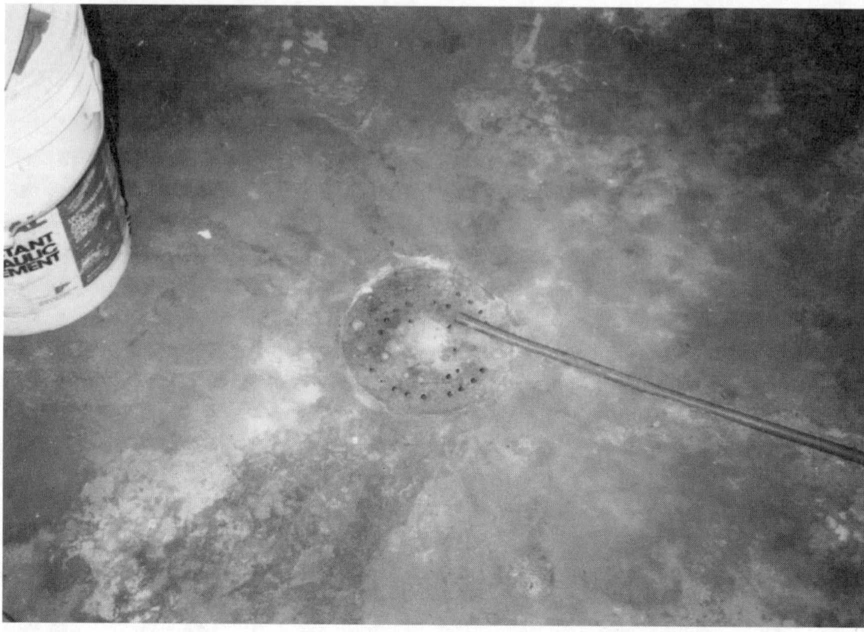

Figure 5.5 An interior floor drain that leads to a French drain. Note that an overflow pipe directs unknown substances into the drain. French drains occur in the soil with a direct connection to the groundwater.

Site Inspection — Hazardous Substance Containers and Unidentified Substance Containers (Including Storage, Handling, Disposal)

The temporary and ultimate disposal locations for hazardous and toxic substance containers on a site should be determined. Whenever any debris and solid waste are observed on a site, the material should be described and a search made for container labels. If 55-gal (or other size) drums are located on a site, it should be noted if the containers are empty or partially full and if there is any information available on what substance is contained within them. Great caution should be used when assessing the contents of drums, and any sealed full or partially full drum should not be opened by a field inspector. The presence of empty hazardous or toxic waste containers in piles of solid waste is a strong indicator that site contamination may have occurred.

Whenever large quantities of hazardous or toxic substances are known to have been used on a site, the disposal of the containers must be researched. Some large sites, such as agricultural facilities, commonly have a private landfill, where pesticide and other chemical containers are or were placed. There are some other ways that waste materials and containers can cause soil and/or groundwater contamination, even if the waste is being carried off-site for disposal. The temporary storage of the waste must be contained to prevent the entry of rainfall, which could form a leachate that may leak directly into the ground. The site inspector should view the location of dumpsters or other storage facilities to assess the potential for leakage (Figure 5.6). If the dumpster is not located in a contained area or the top is open to rainfall or if liquid can be observed flowing from the base of the container, then contamination may be present. Another cause of contamination is the unprotected or uncontained temporary storage of special waste containing leachable chemicals. For example, the lint waste from a dry cleaning operation may be bailed and placed outside for disposal. Rainfall enters the bail and causes a discharge of perchloroethylene. The lint discharge problem can also occur via air ducts, with the residual cleaning chemical being leached from the lint into the groundwater system.

Figure 5.6 An uncovered dumpster containing empty industrial waste containers is leaking fluids onto a paved area. Each rainfall event washes the potential contamination into the soil.

Site Inspection — Storage Tanks (Including Contents and Assessment of Leakage or Potential for Leakage)

One of the largest contributors to soil and groundwater contamination in the United States is leakage of hazardous and toxic substances from underground and aboveground storage tanks. The most common type of leaking tank is an old (particularly more than 10 years old), steel tank filled with fuel. Even brand new tanks constructed of fiberglass have shown leaks. Any fueling areas near storage tanks also must be assessed to search for contamination.

There are a number of ways that petroleum can enter the ground to cause contamination:

- Direct entry via a leak in a storage tank
- Direct entry via a leak in the plumbing connecting the tank to areas of use or fuel pumps
- Direct inflow at fuel input portals (no overfill protection and/or spill containment)
- Direct entry from major spills occurring at fueling locations
- Indirect inflow via minor spills and rainfall runoff into the drainage system
- Direct inflow from surface storage tanks that do not have proper containment

A common mistake made by environmental professionals in assessing contamination from tank facilities is to search only in the near vicinity of the tank, instead of tracing the piping system and researching the area in which the fuel was dispensed. The storage tank facility begins at the filling portals. In the field, the environmental professional should open each filling portal and check the area between the pipe leading to the tank and the vault containing the cover (Figure 5.7). The area between the interior pipe and the larger diameter vault should be sealed with a nonpermeable material or should contain a reducer bushing. If the area contains soil with the odor of hydrocarbons or solvents and no seal is found, there is a high potential that contamination is present. There should be some records on the construction of the tank, fuel inventory records, and perhaps some pressure test data. If no high-quality data exist and there are no monitoring wells surrounding the tank area, then it must be assumed that some contamination could be present, and additional testing is required. The largest percentage of hydrocarbon leaks are caused by faulty plumbing in the piping connecting the tanks to the fuel pumps. If the entire piping system is constructed of fiberglass with double-wall protection, then there is probably no leak. However, if the piping is made of steel and is old, it is likely that contamination is present. Even relatively new plumbing can leak if some of the fittings were installed with incompatible metals, such as threading standard steel pipe directly into stainless steel or brass. In this case, rapid electrolytic corrosion occurs, which can cause a leak to develop in less than one year. Another common defect in a new system that results in fuel discharge into the ground is a faulty check-valve (a pin-hole in the ball valve). Contamination caused by human error has occurred at gasoline stations, such as when the driver of the fuel truck connected to a monitoring well instead of the fueling portal accidentally pumped a full 8000 gal of gasoline into the ground instead of the storage tank. All underground storage facilities can have leak problems, regardless of age or construction design. If there is no record of inventory control, no adequate monitoring well system, and no past evidence of proper monitoring, then the site may be contaminated. Although this discussion centers around hydrocarbon storage facilities, the same principles apply to underground storage tanks containing dry cleaning solvents or any other hazardous or toxic substance.

If there are no records of underground storage tanks on a given site, the site inspector still must be alert to observable evidence that can indicate their existence. If a site is paved and near any major intersection of roads, it is reasonable to expect that a service station was once present. Even the front area of an old,

Figure 5.7 A fuel portal containing an overfill protector. The rubber boots surrounding the fuel pipe are sealed to the pipe to prevent fuel discharge into the soil between the wall of the vault and the interior pipe. This is a common conduit for fuel contamination of the soil and/or groundwater.

historic country store may have contained a gasoline pump with an associated tank. A very diagnostic piece of evidence is the presence of one or more stand pipes (Figure 5.8). All underground tanks have vent pipes, which can be free-standing or may be attached to the side of a building (Figure 5.9). On older urban sites, the only way that underground tanks can be found is through detailed historic research or by a geophysical survey (magnetometer survey).

Sites with aboveground storage tanks must be inspected for possible pathways of contamination from the tank to the ground, particularly in the containment area beneath and surrounding the tank. During the interview process, the owner or operator should be questioned about when the tank was installed and when the containment was built or improved. Again, many of the leaks in this type of system occur in the piping between the tank and the dispensing area. If there are no monitoring wells surrounding the facility, it is necessary to test the site for contamination. Common defects in the containment system include insufficient volume to contain a major leak, no overfill protection on the pipe leading into the tank, location of the filling portal outside the containment area, and positioning of an open drain at the base of the containment area.

Spillage near fueling areas is perhaps the most common hydrocarbon contamination problem related to storage tanks. The fueling area in most modern service stations is well contained, and the ground is covered by asphalt or cement. Most of the spillage occurs onto the paved area, where it evaporates before it can

Figure 5.8 Air vent pipes connected to underground fuel storage tanks. All underground fuel storage tanks must have some type of ventilation. Whenever standing pipes like these are observed, it is likely that an underground fuel storage tank is or was present.

enter the surface-water management or groundwater system. However, when a fueling area is temporary, there may be no containment. This is common at farms, mining sites, and large construction sites for roads, bridges, dams, or other facilities. Some of the worst, often undiscovered areas of contamination occur in the staging areas near construction sites. A maintenance and equipment storage area with a temporary fuel storage facility is commonly placed at some central location immediately adjacent to a construction site. This facility is sometimes located near barrow pits or on a leased property. Sometimes, staging areas are formally leased and recorded in a property abstract or chain-of-title. When assessing vacant but disturbed lands located near roads or other large facilities, the environmental professional should interview knowledgeable persons to determine if the site was ever used as a construction staging area.

Figure 5.9 Vent pipe connected to the side of a house. This subtle pipe leads to a 500-gal underground fuel storage tank.

Site Inspection — Indications of PCBs (Including How Contained and Assessment of Leakage or Potential for Leakage)

Polychlorinated biphenyls (PCBs) are organic chemicals used principally as nonconductors in transformers and other electrical equipment. Modern electrical equipment does not contain oils having high concentrations of PCBs. If there are any transformers on a site, the local power company should be contacted to obtain information on the type of non-conducting fluid used in the transformers. Large industrial complexes may have numerous electrical facilities, which will require considerable research and may actually require testing of the transformer fluids. This type of testing is a dangerous, highly technical operation and should not be attempted by anyone other than a specialist. Many power companies are currently labeling their new transformers with "no PCBs" in clear blue lettering to assist in assessing their potential for contamination.

PCB contamination also occurs on old power company storage sites and staging sites. These sites were used to store or perform maintenance on transformers. Any properties located next to a power substation containing very large transformers may require special investigation and an interview with power company representatives to assess past activities and to determine whether any spills occurred.

A few industries used PCBs in manufacturing certain equipment. The valances of florescent light fixtures once contained significant quantities of PCBs. Past use of PCBs is determined by obtaining detailed histories of the products manufactured and by interviewing former or retired employees.

Site Inspection — Indications of Solid Waste Disposal

Any site containing scattered debris or solid waste is likely to contain some contamination. The investigator must identify the solid waste found on a site and the overall solid waste disposal practices used by existing or past users of a site. A general discussion of obvious poor waste disposal practices is given in a preceding section covering hazardous substance containers.

Solid waste disposal practices are an important issue on large rural properties and old, large manufacturing facilities. It is important to know the locations of the existing municipal landfills and their distance from a site being investigated. If a rural site is large and is located 50 mi from the nearest known landfill, it is likely that solid waste disposal may have occurred on site. Most old agricultural facilities contain at least one landfill on site. The old landfill commonly can be located on aerial photographs, by finding concentrations of debris, or through the interview process. When inspecting an old manufacturing facility, if the existence of the facility predated the installation of the first local landfill, then it is likely that some type of on-site solid waste disposal facility was used. Some of the older facilities used an incinerator and then used the resultant ash as fill beneath internal roads or for use during winter months on roads to allow movement across ice. Sometimes the ash was placed in large piles, exposed to possible leaching. Commonly, the ash from these old incinerators still contains high concentrations of hazardous and toxic substances that tend to leach into the soil or groundwater. It is necessary to determine the past solid waste disposal practices on a site prior to the inspection in order to know what type of features occurring on the site may be significant.

Site Inspection — Physical Setting Analysis, if Migrating Hazardous Substances Are an Issue

As previously stated, it is very important to understand the general flow direction of groundwater prior to beginning a site inspection, in order to know which off-site areas are of most concern. If the on-site or off-site inspection or the overall ESA process indicates that some contamination is present, then the direction and rate of movement of groundwater must be estimated. This initial assessment should be qualified in the report in terms of what known factors it is based upon and what additional information is needed to confirm it. If the contamination is located on-site, the groundwater flow rate must be used to estimate the possible size of the plume or to assess whether contamination has moved beyond the property boundaries, causing the addition of potential third-party liability actions. If the contamination is located off-site, the initial assessment should be used to estimate the potential for migration onto the site or whether contamination has already occurred on the site from off-site sources.

The information used to make the initial assessment includes the topographic conditions on and adjacent to the site, the geology of the surficial aquifer underlying the site, the depth to the water table, any drainage features on or adjacent to the site that could influence the rate and direction of groundwater flow, and the rate or volume of contaminant inflow. All information used to make the estimate should be carefully documented in the report, again with the qualifications given concerning the deficiencies of the estimate.

Site Inspection — Any Other Conditions of Concern

There are some sites that are affected by specific or unusual conditions, such as a site that lies between a municipal wellfield that withdraws water from the surficial aquifer system and an unlined municipal landfill. Although there is currently no evidence that the leachate plume from the landfill has reached the property, based on the current wellfield pumping rate and unknown expansion plans, there is a high likelihood that contamination will reach the property at some time in the future. Another special circumstance is the location of a property in an area of general contamination. There are many areas where the groundwater system is contaminated with solvents or agricultural chemicals beneath several square miles of occupied land. It is important to note the nature of the known contamination and whether there is any history of the on-site use of this type of substance.

The special circumstances described may or may not create potential liabilities for the current or future owners, operators, or tenants of the property being investigated. The phase I ESA report should contain all of the available information and documentation and, when necessary, a recommendation for some limited testing. However, no opinion should be rendered by the environmental professional on the potential liability of the client, because this type of opinion must be rendered by a qualified environmental attorney. These situations, which are legally complex, may require considerable analysis before professional advice can be rendered.

Site Inspection — Site Plan

All information found during a site inspection should be referenced to a site plan containing the locations of all structures and potential problem areas. While ASTM Standard E 1527 implies that a site plan is necessary "if available," a site plan or map is always necessary to provide a complete and reviewable document. The site plan should contain a consistent scale (bar scale), a north arrow, and sufficient detail to allow the reader of the report to locate all features discussed in the report. However, a properly scaled drawing is not always available, and to prepare such a drawing could significantly increase the cost of the ESA report.

Discussion of Special On-Site Investigations: Asbestos, Clean Air/Pathogens, Construction Materials

A phase I ESA conducted on any site that contains a building may require some type of investigation of the interior building materials, depending on the age and use of the structure. Issues of concern include the presence of asbestos, urea fiberboard, or lead paint, and the existence of radon gas or pathogenic bacteria. If these issues are significant in the ESA process, the contractor should so state in the proposal to perform the phase I ESA investigation. If the user of the phase I ESA does not wish to investigate these issues, then a statement to that effect should be contained in both the contract and the final report. If the structure is old and subject to problems with these substances, then some special exceptions and qualifications should be contained in the report if they are not investigated.

The asbestos issue is quite complex; the specific future use of the structure bears greatly on the degree of detailed information required (see Chapter 8). Commonly, an asbestos survey of the structure is not required by the purchaser when an ESA investigation is conducted on a site containing an old structure slated for demolition. This omission can be very costly, because when the structure is removed, special provisions must be made to limit emissions of asbestos into the local atmosphere during demolition. Additionally, the asbestos material is considered to be a "special waste" that may require that special landfill disposal measures be taken. In the case of the demolition of an old hotel in Miami, the process was stopped when asbestos was discovered on the site by a regulatory agency, and the company owning the structure was fined and nearly faced criminal charges. Ultimately, the asbestos in the structure had to be removed before demolition could proceed, resulting in a cost of over $1 million. The necessity for an asbestos survey must be determined in the context of the building use. If the building will be used as a work place in which it is possible that the workers could come into contact with airborne asbestos, then an asbestos survey should be accomplished as part of the phase I ESA. There are specific licenses and certifications required to perform both consulting work and remediation on asbestos.

Construction materials other than asbestos can become liability issues. In the interior of an old structure, perhaps 20 years old or older, certain materials such as urea fiberboard or lead paint may have been used. Within the context of a phase I ESA scope, a survey to locate these materials may be necessary if the structure will be demolished, modified, or continue in commercial use.

The occurrence of radon gas is another health issue related primarily to existing structures. It is not reasonable to require or perform radon gas surveys on raw land, because the accumulation of radon gas within a structure is a function of the structure design and the degree of ventilation provided. Many states have conducted surveys to designate areas with high potential for radon gas problems. A phase I ESA conducted on a site containing a structure in a radon gas high risk area should contain this information in the report document. When existing buildings are involved, the most common remedial action to eliminate a radon gas problem is to provide additional ventilation of the structure in order to decrease the buildup of unacceptable concentrations.

Accumulations of pathogenic bacteria in old buildings is a relatively rare occurrence, but it may be necessary to address this issue during a phase I ESA. Pathogenic bacteria tend to concentrate in the air handling systems of old buildings containing cooling towers as part of the air conditioning system. Old hotels or buildings with no direct outside ventilation are most prone to this problem. An interior survey for pathogenic bacteria requires a highly sophisticated expert in the field and should not be attempted by a phase I ESA inspector. Interior clean air surveys are not commonly included in a phase I ESA, but in a large-scale acquisition, results from a survey may be necessary in order to review the long-term financial viability of the deal, especially if costly modifications of the air handling system are necessary.

Discussion of Off-Site Investigations and Land Uses

The level of inspection necessary for off-site land uses is always a question in the phase I ESA investigation process. In ASTM Standard E 1527, the language pertaining to the off-site investigation implies that the degree of detail necessary is limited to what is "visually or physically observed" adjoining the property or in the surrounding area. In a complex setting there may be numerous potentially problematic land uses surrounding the site being investigated. The activities conducted on these sites may be unclear. There is a tendency for some site inspectors to attempt a physical inspection of the adjacent property. The inspector must understand that the uninvited entry onto private property is called trespassing and is a crime. Care must be taken to gather as much information as necessary with regard to land uses and activities conducted on properties adjacent to the site, within the framework of reality. Off-site information should be obtained mostly by records research and from interviews, without direct entry onto the property. Again, the extent of the off-site investigation is determined by the hydrogeologic characteristics of the area and by common sense.

Discussion on the Interviewing Process

A key part of the phase I ESA involves obtaining and verifying information during the interview process. Therefore, the environmental professional conducting interviews must be familiar with the questions that should be asked and the information that requires verification. There are several persons who should be interviewed in order to obtain all of the available information. The owners and occupants of the property should be interviewed to assess current and past operations and practices on the property. If the property is used for an operating business, then various employees of the business must be interviewed. If a business was operated in the past, some research must be completed to find an employee or a person knowledgeable about that business operation. If the environmental agency records are incomplete and some action has been filed against the owner or operator of the property or business, it may be necessary to interview regulatory agency personnel to determine the status of the on-site environmental problem. When it is difficult to discover some facts about the property, it may be necessary to interview some neighbors, an elderly, long-term resident of the community, or the local neighborhood "busybody." The list of persons who should be interviewed depends on what information is necessary to answer the basic questions about the property. In all cases, the information obtained in the interview process should be attributed to the source, and the sources should be acknowledged in the report, unless a person specifically requests anonymity.

The interview of the property or business owner can be quite challenging, depending upon the nature of the transaction that triggered the necessity for the phase I ESA. If the owner is sophisticated and must sign some type of environmental waiver agreement and an affidavit stating that the property is free from any environmental problem, the owner generally tends to be cooperative and answers questions candidly. If the owner of the property is involved in an "as is" condition sale to an unsophisticated purchaser or if the phase I ESA was initiated by a lending institution in a refinance deal, the owner may not be very cooperative, and the answers to questions may vary from lack of knowledge to outright lies. It is necessary for the environmental professional to understand the transaction and be fully aware of the demeanor of the owner. Some of the questions that must be asked are contained in the TSP screening questionnaire (see Table 5.2). Many other questions should be asked about the site operations, including

- The past and present wastewater disposal methods
- The existence of past environmental records and documents and the availability of copies
- The existence of agency actions
- The on-site use of hazardous or toxic substances
- The past and present location of chemical storage facilities
- The condition of the site upon purchase
- The past or current existence of any underground storage tanks associated with fuel storage for a heating system or emergency generator
- Any specific question with regard to anything observed on the site during the inspection

Although ASTM Standard E 1527 allows interviews to be conducted by telephone or by writing, if the site contains an operating business, the interview is best conducted in person and, if possible, at the site. It should be documented in the report if the owner is uncooperative, refuses to be interviewed, or gives dubious information that is later verified to be in error. Incorrect or false information given by the owner could lead to a recommendation for on-site testing or to an inconclusive opinion about the site based on incomplete information.

Interviews with tenants or other site personnel are often very useful. When the tenant of the property is involved in a complex business, he or she should be treated in a similar manner to the owner, because vested self-interests may cause the tenant to slant answers to his or her advantage. A similar set of questions should be asked of the tenant and/or site operator as is asked of the owner. In a complex site operation, it is necessary to interview the site manager, operations manager, environmental manager, plant manager, or whoever has responsibility for the facility. It may not be as helpful to interview the president of the corporation, if he or she does not have a high level of knowledge about the specific property involved. It is important to understand that the site manager may not always be absolutely cooperative, because his or her job may be in jeopardy over site issues. The manager of an operating facility may not always be the best information source. Lower level employees tend to give direct, honest answers to questions, as long as they are satisfied that their job status is not in jeopardy and as long as they are not intimidated by the interview process. In this case, the interview should be conducted in the field during the site inspection, and the environmental professional should avoid appearing like management by not wearing a coat and tie. It is important to obtain permission from the appropriate party prior to initiating on-site interviews. Several interviews with workers should be obtained using the same set of questions in order to contrast and compare the information for consistency in the site practices. The interviews should be formatted to include questions from on-site observations. For example, if there is a vehicle repair facility on the site and the waste oil disposal tank is located a few hundred feet from the repair shop, a question should be included regarding the use of the waste oil facility. When asked about how the waste oil disposal occurs, the site manager may reply that the oil goes into the waste oil disposal drum. The on-site foreman will verify the manager's response, but the mechanic could very well answer that the waste oil facility is too far away, so he drops the oil in the sink or throws it over the fence located only 20 ft away. Common sense must be used in the interview process, particularly when dealing with an operating site.

Sometimes it can be quite difficult to get information on a particular site. For example, if excavation was done on a property in past years and the present owner of the site has no knowledge about what was done or the reason for the excavation, information might be limited. A records review might also not produce an answer. It is then time to find a neighbor who lives or lived near the property, or perhaps an elderly person who clearly recalls the history of the area. A friendly call or visit with this person can often provide the needed answers. The excavation could turn out to be the old farm landfill or the cattle pond. The investigator must be cognizant when interviewing neighbors, because if some purposeful misinformation is given (as in neighborhood dispute issues), incorrect information could be placed into the phase I ESA report. The most common sources of environmental complaints against operating facilities come from neighbors, recently fired employees, or workers involved in labor disputes. It is always a good idea in the interview process to ask about the past relationship of the interviewee to the property, the facility, or the owner.

A most useful information source in a community is a local retired business person or city or county engineer who lived in the area for many years. Many consultants who perform ESAs maintain a list of these people with whom to check on dates of road construction, when drainage improvements were installed, and other useful historic information. These unbiased third parties are often the best sources of local information.

Employees of regulatory agencies are often interviewed about environmental violations and actions filed against property owners or operators. It is very important in this process not to reveal confidential information about the subject property. The environmental professional conducting the investigation is not working for the agency but for a private client. If information is purposely or inadvertently given to the agency by the environmental professional and some type of agency action results, the individual environmental professional or the consulting company may be liable for damages based on contractual agreements (i.e., interference in a property transaction and devaluing a property during a transaction). There are some legal issues regarding disclosure of contamination that are covered later in this text.

Obtaining the most accurate information possible during an interview requires that the environmental professional be open-minded, knowledgeable about the property, and have a friendly demeanor. Too often, inexperienced environmental professionals are overly assertive, acting more like police investigators than business people. The interview should be a crosscheck of other information sources and should take place after a review of certain records and after or concurrent with the site inspection. Since many interview subjects are quite busy, it is important to conduct the interview in a timely manner and to take adequate notes or to record the interview (with the permission of the person being interviewed). Followup interviews should be conducted only when a new question arises or when there is a conflict in the facts. It is usually not wise to confront an owner or operator with conflicting facts from the answers previously given. A tactful question or two about the subject could elicit a more complete or truthful response. In complex sites, the owner or any given tenant or operator may not be aware personally of all of the activities being conducted, so it is wise to ask for the names of any other people who could be helpful. There is no substitute for experience in the interview process. An experienced interviewer can effectively glean the facts about a site without causing stress to the interviewee.

Findings and Conclusions (Recommendations)

All phase I ESA reports must have a section containing a concise statement of the findings, with conclusions and an opinion statement related to site environmental conditions. If the Standard ASTM E 1527 format is used (Table 5.3), this section is given at the end of the text, but a better position for this material is at the beginning of the report to make it as user friendly as possible.

The content of the findings and conclusions, which is the meat of the report, must truly reflect the opinion of those environmental professionals involved. In Standard E 1527, the ASTM recommends that one of the following two statements be used as the opinion:

> 11.6.1 — "We have performed a Phase I Environmental Site Assessment in conformance with the scope and limitations of ASTM Practice E 1527 of (insert address or legal description), the property. Any exception to, or deletions from, this practice are described in Section ( ) of this report. This assessment has revealed no evidence of recognized environmental conditions in connection with the property", or 11.6.2 "We have performed a Phase I Environmental Site Assessment in conformance with the scope and limitations of ASTM Practice E 1527 of (insert address or legal description), the property. Any exceptions to, or deletions from, this practice are described in Section ( ) of this report. This

assessment has revealed no evidence of recognized environmental conditions in connection with the property except for the following: (list)."

These two fairly nebulous statements do not give the user of the report a true indication of the relevant site conditions. The phrase "recognized environmental conditions" has little meaning in the context of the phase I ESA investigation and must be limited to the real scope of the investigation. A phase I ESA report should never contain absolute statements, such as the statement that the site "is clean," or "no toxic or hazardous substance contamination exists," because there is always some risk associated with unknown conditions. The opinion statement should not contain legal conclusions or any implication of legal conclusions. However, the opinion statement should be balanced in the context of the site size and the activities conducted.

Phase I ESA report authors tend to concentrate on the negative aspects of a property, with little consideration of the magnitude of these aspects in the context of site size. One example would be a phase I ESA conducted on a 10,000-acre farm, which found a few potential contamination problems affecting a total of about 1 acre of the entire property. The rather ambiguous wording of the ASTM language states that no problem was found, with the exception of problem a, b, and c, with a minimal explanation. The problem could range in seriousness from a grease spot to the Love Canal, with no way for the reader to assess it without reading every word of the report. A more precise and reasonable opinion statement would be, "A Phase I Environmental Site Assessment was conducted on a 10,000 acre farm in (*location*) in conformance to ASTM Practice E 1527. No evidence for contamination with toxic or hazardous substances was found on most of the property, with the exception of a 1 acre area containing three possible contamination problems. (Describe potential problems)." A brief explanation of the available facts supporting the conclusions should be given at this point.

After reading the findings and conclusions of a complex phase I ESA, the reader is often confused about what to do next. It is appropriate in the findings and conclusions or in a separate letter to make some recommendations to the report user of how to resolve any qualifications or how to confirm or deny the presence of contamination. It is usually prudent for the ESA investigator to inform the ESA user of any adverse findings prior to the delivery of the final report in order to resolve as many issues as possible. If some potential environmental issues remain and are described in the report, a series of recommendations should be made about a possible resolution of the problems, which may involve some preliminary sampling and analysis of soil and/or groundwater. It is not possible to assess the potential cost of remedial measures within the framework of a phase I ESA investigation if a contamination problem is discovered. Estimated costs of contamination cleanup without supporting hydrogeologic and water quality assessment should be viewed within the context of the qualifications. If a contamination problem is discovered, there is a general procedure that should be followed (see Chapter 6).

The findings and conclusions section of the phase I ESA report should be no more than a few pages in length, depending on the size and complexity of the site. Findings or conclusions should be completely explained in the text of the report. If the findings and conclusions section is lengthy, as in the case of a complex site, it may be more appropriate to place this section at the end of the report and begin with a one- or two-page executive summary.

Signatures of Environmental Professionals

The environmental professionals conducting a phase I ESA should be clearly identified, and the person in charge should sign the document. In many states, if a licensed professional geologist or engineer performs the ESA investigation or is in charge, the individual must sign and seal the document in the manner required by the appropriate state law. One of the current deficiencies of the phase I ESA process is that only senior personnel of the company performing the investigation usually sign the document. This is not the intent of the ASTM Standard, nor is it sound technical practice. The senior person signing the document should be the secondary signature and should be indicative of review. The signature(s) should be located on the first page of the report beneath the cover. The title of the person should be given under the name, along with any information on the professional license held by that person.

Qualifications of Environmental Professionals Participating in Phase I Environmental Site Assessment

A brief résumé of the individual(s) conducting the phase I ESA investigation should be included in the report text or as part of the appendix. This résumé should include, at a minimum, the following information: name, degrees, name of the school, dates of graduation, major field of study, summary of experience, number of years of experience in each job area, and experience in the phase I ESA and general environmental field. The résumés placed in the report must include those of the environmental professionals who performed the investigation, rather than just some principals in the firm that was contracted to perform the investigation.

Optional Appendices

A number of items should be found in the appendix of the report, including site photographs with captions, a copy of the contract containing any exceptions to ASTM Practice E 1527, detailed information on the chain of property ownership, interview documentation, and any other information deemed to be appropriate. The appendix should contain all pertinent documentation in support of the conclusions reached in the report. The site photographs should illustrate all significant environmental features of the property. Any information not contained in the report text or appendix should be retained in the project file for a period of at least 5 years for the purpose of liability protection or litigation support.

Advantages of the Phase I ESA

Based on the extraordinarily punitive nature of existing environmental laws governing hazardous and toxic substance contamination, the phase I environmental site assessment is the only reasonable method of providing some protection for property purchasers or lending institutions. If a phase I ESA is completed by a competent environmental professional following the ASTM or other well-prepared guidelines, it is likely that any major contamination affecting a property will be discovered.

The biggest single problem with the phase I ESA in the past was the lack of a common scope of investigation and a consistent reporting method. The general adoption of ASTM Designation E 1527 by the lending industry has provided a common scope of investigation. While some weaknesses in the ASTM Standard have been pointed out or criticized in this text, it is still the best overall guideline for preparation of a phase I ESA, and it will be revised in the future. The scope of an ESA investigation should be modified based on the specific conditions of the property, which may cause a deviation from the scope of the original ASTM Standard scope. Use of the phase I ESA within the framework of the lending institution environmental policy provides the institution with considerably less exposure to environmental damages.

Disadvantages of the Phase I ESA

A phase I environmental site assessment is not an insurance policy against any and all environmental liability in a property transfer or a financial deal. There is always some degree of environmental liability risk when dealing with real property, because it is simply not possible to check and test every square foot of a property for every potential contaminant.

Although ASTM Designation E 1527 provides a common reference frame for the scope of a phase I ESA, it cannot assure the quality of the investigation and report. Designation E 1527 is filled with language suggesting that if the standards are met, there is little liability for the entity performing the investigation. The issues of quality assurance and liability regarding performance are perhaps the most significant problems with the current concept of the phase I ESA. When the ASTM Standard became generally accepted, a number of marginally qualified "environmental professionals" entered the field to perform these investigations. Although these larger numbers have driven the cost of the phase I ESA down, quality assurance is not possible with the less expensive provider of the service, and the higher-paid, senior environmental professionals have been eliminated from the process. These quality control problems and the competition pressures have caused well-managed lending institutions to require prequalification of consultants, with checks of personnel and insurance (see Chapter 4). The problem of poorly prepared phase I ESAs is acute at this time, particularly inadequate research in the site history for past sources of contamination. Also, the issue of fraud has entered the practice, with certain unscrupulous individuals being paid to document a "clean" property. An inadequately prepared ESA does not provide the user with any real protection against future claims for environmental remediation costs.

Discussion

Since the creation of environmental liabilities through a series of federal and state laws, lending institutions have sought ways to minimize exposure to environmental liabilities. In the day-to-day process of lending on real property or to businesses owning and operating on real property, the phase I environmental site assessment has proven to be useful in providing an acceptable degree of liability management. It is clear that the phase I ESA must be utilized within the framework of an institutional environmental risk policy that is accepted and used by all institution loan officers and operating personnel. The lending institution should police the quality of phase I ESA documents used by clients and strictly enforce all provisions of the internal environmental policy. The environmental policy should be perceived by lending institution personnel as a guideline that serves and assists the lender and its customers. The loan officers and marketing personnel should educate less sophisticated clients about the environmental risks they may face and how the lending institution may assist in helping to reduce risk.

The phase I ESA process is still evolving, and it is anticipated that substantial changes will occur in ASTM Designation E 1527 and the standard methods used as a framework to complete these investigations. These revisions will improve the quality of the final phase I ESA product and provide better protection to lending institutions and other users. The current problems with poor quality work products ultimately will be corrected by the legal process. Many thousands of lawsuits are being filed each year against companies that provided deficient phase I ESA reports. Also, state agencies and professional regulators have taken an interest in the possible regulation or licensing of the individuals and companies in this business. The best protection for the user of phase I ESAs is to understand the process, use common sense, and ask questions if something is not understood. The issue of environmental liability is not something to fear but something to be managed.

REFERENCES FOR FURTHER READING

American Society for Testing and Materials, Standard Practice for Environmental Site Assessments, Designation E 1528-93: Transaction Screen Process, The Author, Philadelphia, PA, 1993, 31 pp.

American Society for Testing and Materials, Standard Practice for Environmental Site Assessments, Designation E 1527: Phase I Environmental Site Assessments Process, The Author, Philadelphia, PA, 1994, 24 pp.

Ashton, D. A., Chauncey, W. H., Goss, F. D., McCubbin, J. A., Porter, P. E., Purcer, S. B., and Redinger, C. F., *Environmental Evaluations for Real Property Transactions,* Government Institutes, Inc., Rockville, MD, 1989, 250 pp.

Association of Ground Water Scientists and Engineers, Guidance to Environmental Site Assessments, Ground Water Scientists and Engineers, Dublin, OH, 1992, 72 pp.

Bureau of National Affairs, BNA's Environmental Due Diligence Guide, The Author, Washington, D.C., (updated monthly) 1995.

Cahill, L. B. and Kranc, R. W., Eds., *Environmental Audits,* 5th ed., Government Institutes, Inc., Rockville, MD, 1987, 656 pp.

Missimer, T. M., Transactional and operational audits/assessments of farms and agricultural facilities, Natl. Symp. Pest. Fert. Containment, Design Manage. Conf. Proc., Mid-West Plan Services, Iowa State University, Ames, IA, 1992, 36.

Moskowitz, J. S., *Environmental Liability and Real Property Transactions,* John Wiley & Sons, New York, 1988.

6 MANAGEMENT OF CONTAMINATED SITES

There are a number of ways a lender can address the decisions that must be made to manage the risk in a particular deal to avoid involvement in the actual cleanup of a contamination problem. The lending institution risk manual should provide some guidance about how to manage various aspects of the contamination cleanup issue, but it is important for the loan officer or upper management of the institution to understand the options available and what information is needed to make an informed decision. Too often the general policy of a lending institution is to avoid a problem out of fear or ignorance by exiting a complex deal as fast as possible instead of assessing the risk, inserting the proper protective language, and completing the deal. A contamination cleanup problem should be viewed as a challenge to management, not as a hopeless situation. The lender must clearly understand when to stay in a deal and when to cut losses and exit.

Strategies on how to manage contamination cleanup issues depend greatly on when the problem is discovered, the information available, and the nature of the relationship between the lending institution and the property. Three specific situations involving contamination cleanup issues will be discussed in this chapter. First, contamination is discovered during a phase I environmental site assessment on property being considered for a loan. Second, contamination is discovered on property owned by the lending institution. Third, the lending institution is faced with making a decision on the foreclosure of contaminated property. Each of these scenarios requires a different strategy with some common management themes. Because every contamination problem encountered is unique to a large degree from both a technical and business perspective, the same approach does not apply to each problem. What is important is the strategy and how to proceed after each piece of information is added.

CONTAMINATION FOUND DURING A PHASE I ENVIRONMENTAL SITE ASSESSMENT: THE ART OF SALVAGING A DEAL

Some evidence for contamination is found in 20 to 30% of phase I ESA investigations, depending on the geographic region of the country and the duration and intensity of land use. Only a small portion of the potential problems lead to substantial contamination cleanup costs. As stated in the previous chapter, there is a tendency for preparers of phase I ESAs to focus the report conclusions on the problems found and not on the uncontaminated portion of a property, thereby implying a pervasiveness of the problem that may not be accurate. This approach commonly causes lenders to overreact to specific situations in a negative way. A well-informed lender will tend to use the facts relating to a specific problem and a little common sense to save the deal and satisfy all parties involved.

Verification of Contamination

During a phase I ESA, many types of evidence of contamination on a property may be discovered, ranging from a minor oil stain in the soil to a pile of open, half-filled drums of hazardous and toxic chemicals. The first observation of a potential problem can be very misleading. Before the contamination panic button is pushed, there must be some verification that contamination actually exists on the site. A sophisticated consultant who performs a phase I ESA will not wait until the report is complete to inform the client about potential contamination on a property, but will contact the client and make a recommendation to do some verification testing. If a potential contamination problem is described in the ESA report and remains unverified, the time required to perform the testing and analysis could cause failure of the deal or an excessive delay in the closing time.

The first step in the verification process is to confirm the presence of contamination by the collection of soil and/or groundwater samples for chemical analyses. This type of work is commonly called a phase II ESA investigation. When soil and water samples are collected for chemical analysis, it is absolutely necessary that the samples are collected using scientifically acceptable techniques, according to a written quality assurance plan. This plan describes the techniques to be used for sampling and analysis, the chain of custody procedures, and other methods used to assure that the samples are not altered. Therefore, the company retained to do the verification work must be able to prove that it has the proper experience to do this type of work and that it has a written quality assurance plan (or gives evidence that it has accepted and adheres to the appropriate EPA and/or state procedures) and a health and safety plan, which requires evidence of proper safety training. Any lender involved in this phase of environmental work should request these documents before any work is authorized. The laboratory performing the chemical analyses must have the appropriate certifications, which should be verified before any work is authorized. The labeling and delivery of samples from the field to the laboratory should be carefully controlled, and standard chain of custody methods should be used.

The verification process is a relatively straightforward procedure. If the soil is stained and there is an odor of hydrocarbons, then a few soil samples should be collected and tested in the field using a calibrated organic vapor analyzer or other appropriate equipment before samples are collected for chemical analysis. Where soils are stained with hydrocarbons, an auger hole can be drilled at the stain location to assess the depth of penetration before collecting samples for analysis. If the problem is persistent, then sampling should occur using the proper field techniques. If the type of the potential contaminant is known, the chemical analyses can be targeted to the substances suspected. Sometimes a number of chemicals have been used on a property, and the potential contamination site may be a landfill or a septic tank that would have received a large number of different substances. In this case, it is necessary to perform organic compound scans and a suite of other analyses, such as those for selected heavy metals, on the soil and water samples collected. After the results of the chemical analyses are received, the concentrations of the substances must be compared to the appropriate regulatory standards to determine if a contamination problem exists. In certain cases, this may require the assistance of legal counsel to determine the applicable standards.

Upon analysis of the data, many potential contamination sites are eliminated from concern. However, if some samples show marginal results or if there is a conflict in the results, it may be appropriate to resample and analyze the samples before any further action is taken. Some sample analyses will yield results that clearly indicate contamination at a given location. When site contamination is verified, a meeting should be held between the buyer and seller and perhaps with a lending institution if they are involved at this point in the deal.

Initial Negotiation Between Buyer and Seller

When the presence of contamination is verified on a property, there must be some information exchanged between the buyer and seller (or between any parties involved in a transaction, including lessors and lessees). In the case of a refinance deal between an owner/operator or a lessor and a lending institution, a meeting should also be held at this time. A number of issues must be resolved, including the following:

1. Is there sufficient time to deal with the contamination problem within the context of the sales contract?
2. Since additional testing and analysis of the contamination problem will be necessary, who will pay for this work?
3. Does the seller (or other party) wish to use the same consultant to minimize cost, or do they wish to hire an independent consultant?
4. Does the discovery of contamination require any disclosure of the problem to a regulatory agency?

These same questions must be discussed between the lending institution and the owner/operator or lessee if they are the parties in the deal.

The issue of time in a transaction can lead to some very complex legal problems. In most sophisticated land deals, there is a clause in the sales contract allowing an inspection period of up to 90 days or some other time. Also, there is a clause that covers environmental problems found during the inspection period and the terms and conditions placed on the buyer to allow withdrawal from a deal without penalty. In a complex land deal or purchase of an operating company, the inspection period should be long enough to allow the performance of a phase I ESA and any additional work required to allow an economic assessment of any contamination problem to be made. Other environmental issues, such as the presence of wetlands or endangered species, must be investigated within this time frame. The inspection period and environmental clauses should allow a prospective purchaser to withdraw from the deal without penalty at any time during the period preceding the contractual closing date.

The timing and phase I ESA issues are not usually problems when parties are dealing in good faith. However, an example of what can happen can be seen in a case in which a prospective purchaser signed a contract to buy a large parcel of vacant land and placed a substantial sum of money in escrow. An inspection period of 120 days was placed in the contract, but no real environmental conditions clause was included. The buyer proceeded with minor environmental inspections of the property but did not authorize a phase I ESA until required by a lending institution with only 45 days remaining on the contract. The ESA investigation revealed some potential contamination from solid waste partially buried on the site, which included some discarded pesticide containers and hydrocarbon containers. Some phase II ESA testing on the property was completed by the purchaser without the knowledge and consent of the owner. With the closing less than 5 days away and armed with some chemical data that indicated some minor contamination and an observation of a "sheen" on an excavation that "could be" petroleum, the purchaser met with a state regulatory agency and revealed the information, again without the knowledge of the owner. The agency informed the owner that the property contained a violation of solid waste disposal laws and some possible contamination. At this point, the purchasers requested an extension of the closing date and a reduction in the purchase price of the property. The owner of the property declined to extend the closing date, claimed the purchaser deposit of over $1.5 million, and began negotiations with the regulatory agency with regard to cleanup of the property. The problem involved only the disposal of solid waste at the local landfill, and after several rounds of testing, no significant contamination of the soil and groundwater was found on the site. The purchaser then filed suit against the owner to reclaim the deposit monies. After a jury trial, the court ruled that the purchaser violated the sales contract by not pursuing the phase I ESA in a timely manner, that the ESA methodology (phase II) was not in accordance with acceptable standards, and that the purchaser interfered in the transaction by revealing information to a third party (the state environmental agency) without permission of the owner (tortuous interference). The owner was allowed to retain all of the deposit monies, and the purchaser also had to pay for court costs. A number of important lessons can be learned from this example. First, the wording of a sales contract must be carefully constructed and must contain an environmental liability clause. Second, a phase I ESA should be performed on a site in a timely manner, perhaps as soon as the contract is signed, to allow time for additional work if required. Third, it is not appropriate for a purchaser to reveal any information to a third party without permission of the property owner unless there are very special circumstances (see disclosure discussion).

When phase II ESA work must be done, it is necessary for the purchaser and owner of the property to meet to discuss the testing procedures and to determine who will pay for the testing costs. It is necessary for the purchaser to obtain permission to perform testing on the site and to give the owner a plan, including a complete description of the proposed testing program. If the program is agreeable to both parties, then the issue of cost allocation should be discussed. Commonly, the purchaser of the property will pay for most of the costs, and a sophisticated owner will request duplicate samples and pay for these analyses. Sometimes the purchaser and owner will divide the costs equally. The equal division of cost may involve the use of a common consulting company. If so, the parties (including any lender) should clearly specify the tasks to be performed by the consultant on behalf of all parties. Provisions should also be made as to whom, if anyone, the consultant can represent in the event of disputes.

Disclosure Issues

Another issue involving both the owner and purchaser is that of disclosure of discovered contamination. In the event that a spill of a hazardous or toxic substance in reportable quantities is documented or observed, the owner has a direct legal obligation to report the problem within guidelines given in both federal and state laws. There are guidelines for the spillage of numerous chemical compounds, which include the minimum volume of the substance that triggers reporting and the time frame in which the spill must be reported. For example, if 50 lb of tetrachloroethylene is spilled, which is above the reporting volume of 1 lb in RCRA 3001, then this spill must be reported within 24 h. If a spill is not reported in a timely manner, a property owner can face both civil fines and possible criminal charges.

During a phase I ESA, the potential contamination found is usually the result of past site activities and cannot be directly related to a spill. Therefore, the necessity to report verified contamination is not clear. First, any real or perceived obligation to report contamination is the responsibility of the owner and/or operator of the site and not the purchaser or the purchaser's consultant. When contamination is discovered with adequate verification, before any reporting is done to a regulatory agency, it is necessary to consult an environmental attorney for legal advice on reporting requirements. A decision to report should be made in a timely manner to avoid violation of specific provisions contained in federal and state laws. One specific guideline that should be followed is that if the contamination problem poses an imminent health or safety hazard, then the problem should be reported immediately, and action should be taken to warn the public. Most sophisticated property owners or business operators are aware of the potential liabilities of contamination, especially when a potential third party action for damages is involved. Therefore, most sophisticated property owners report a discovered problem to the appropriate regulatory agency using legal counsel and/or consultants. However, there are cases when contamination is discovered and the owner is informed but refuses to allow disclosure to an agency. Because of confidentiality clauses in many contracts, the purchaser and the consultants may not be permitted to disclose the problem and could face litigation if the disclosure is made without permission of the owner. The key issue here is whether there is an "imminent" health and safety issue caused by the presence of the contamination. Under the licensing laws of many states, attorneys, engineers, and geologists may be required to report serious health or safety issues to the local environmental protection or health agency. An ethical decision must be made about what is an "imminent" risk. A clear example would be the difference in risk between a hydrocarbon contamination problem located a mile from the property boundary on flat ground as opposed to a pesticide disposal pit located next to a school, which uses a shallow well for water supply. Unfortunately, it is often not possible to define clearly the health and safety risks caused by a verified but poorly defined contamination problem. If the owner refuses to disclose a potentially serious problem to the appropriate environmental agency, a purchaser or its consultant should confront the owner with the issue directly and inform the owner (possibly in writing) that he or she may be legally or morally obligated to report the problem. Any party involved in a disclosure issue should consult with a qualified environmental attorney.

Saving a Deal When Site Contamination Is Involved

Phase II ESA testing reveals that one or more contamination problems exist on a property. The purchaser of the property and the property owner are both informed of the problem and now need to find a solution that can allow the deal to proceed. The purchaser and/or lender must decide if they wish to continue to pursue the property and under what circumstances. The owner is now faced with the dilemma of cooperating in a cleanup that could lead to substantial cost, and with knowledge of the problem, the owner cannot sell the property to another purchaser without disclosure (depending on the state and situation). The user of the ESA report should request that the consultant make some possible recommendations for resolution of the problem or suggest various options to resolve the problem. At some point in time, the issue of agency involvement must be discussed, because the problem cannot be resolved without the appropriate regulatory agency approvals.

There are ways to save the deal and proceed with the transaction on contaminated properties. The extent and nature of the contamination and the local hydrogeology determine the possibility of an acceptable solution. Some possible solutions to save the transaction are as follows:

1. The owner agrees to indemnify purchaser and to clean up site (also, occasionally a purchase becomes a lease/purchase with the owner obligated to clean up site before purchase occurs).
2. The contaminated part of the property and a buffer area are excluded from the deal.
3. The owner establishes an escrow account to cover the estimated costs of contamination cleanup.
4. The purchaser takes responsibility for the cleanup cost, with a corresponding reduction in the purchase price.
5. The purchaser and owner agree to split the cleanup costs.

6. The purchaser and seller agree to split the cleanup costs and pursue a cost recovery action against the party that caused the problem.

In a number of large property transactions, a relatively small area of the site contains a contamination problem. If the contamination will take several months or even years to clean up but both the seller and the purchaser wish to proceed with the transaction, the relatively small contaminated site can be excluded from the transaction and remain owned by the seller until the problem is resolved. The outparcel may then be conveyed at a later time. In order to complete this type of resolution successfully, both parties in the transaction need to know the approximate areal extent of the contamination and the approximate direction and rate of migration. Once this information is available, the size of the parcel to be excluded can be determined. A buffer area should be left between the contaminated site and the land to be sold, in order to cover any potential errors in contamination mapping or in time estimates for movement of the plume. The agreement should also contain a provision that the seller must pursue timely cleanup and attenuate the movement of any contamination plume as soon as practical. The seller must obtain a right of access to the contamination site from the purchaser in order to perform the necessary testing and remediation work. The right of access may also include provisions for placement of additional monitoring wells on the purchaser's property if required by a regulatory agency. If the rate of contamination movement is difficult to ascertain, the purchaser may require the installation of several monitoring wells along the boundary between the purchased property and the excluded parcel to give additional protection to the purchaser. The water quality in these wells would be monitored as part of the agreement.

An example of this type of agreement is illustrated in Figure 6.1. A 40-acre parcel of commercial property is involved (area inside of dark line). A developer has an option to purchase the property and has absorbed the costs of planning, site design, and rezoning. Upon obtaining the necessary permits to proceed with the project, the developer arranges the financing for the property, and the lending institution requires a phase I ESA. A small landfill is discovered in the southwest corner of the property. The landfill was formally used by the local government to dispose of solid waste, including agriculture waste products. Some phase II testing reveals the presence of some elevated concentrations of heavy metals. The field testing and an analysis of the site hydrology show that the groundwater flow direction is to the south or southwest (photographs are compass oriented). The purchaser wishes to close on the deal as soon as possible to proceed with development. An agreement is reached to exclude the former landfill site, including a buffer strip about 200 ft wide. The seller and the purchaser agree that the contaminated site will be purchased from the seller as soon as the site is released for no further action by the state environmental regulatory agency.

This type of solution would be problematic if the contamination site is located at a key point on the property or if the contamination will rapidly migrate onto other parts of the property. The purchaser must determine if design changes can

Figure 6.1 A 40-acre site is shown within the outlined area on aerial photographs taken in 1966 and 1986. Note that an old excavation was filled in between 1966 and 1986. This was verified to be an old landfill with associated contamination. The groundwater flow direction was measured to be south (down), and the area of the landfill with a buffer was excluded from the transaction.

be made to avoid use of the contaminated part of the property and if construction on the site will in any way affect movement of the contamination, which could create liability for the purchaser. The migration issue can be mitigated if the seller agrees to attenuate movement of the contamination using a barrier or some treatment method.

Another common method of managing a contamination problem during a property transaction is the establishment of an escrow account, funded by the proceeds of the transaction. The purchaser and seller agree to a specific amount of money to be placed in an escrow account to be used to finance the cleanup costs as they are incurred.

A number of issues must be negotiated before this method can be used to resolve the contamination problem. First, the approximate cost of the cleanup must be estimated based on the information available. The accuracy of the estimate will always be subject to debate, so additional contractual issues must be included. The seller can require that interest be paid on the balance of the escrow funds until the contamination problem is resolved or until there are no funds left in the account. Any funds remaining after the cleanup is completed would be returned to the seller. However, if the escrow account funds are insufficient to cover the cost of cleanup, the seller may be obligated to cover the additional costs, the purchaser may share in the obligation, or the purchaser may cover all additional costs. There must be clear agreement about which party will take primary responsibility for management of cleanup activities and for how the escrow account draws will be made. In all cases, the seller needs to have review capacity over every aspect of the cleanup procedure, because the seller may be responsible for all or part of additional costs or may be able to receive any remaining funds. If the purchaser takes primary responsibility for the cleanup actions, there should be some negotiated time frame during which the cleanup will be completed (within reason) and some indemnification agreement in the event that actions of the party managing the cleanup incur any third-party liabilities arising out of the cleanup activities. (Purchasers should be indemnified for past spills and cleanup activities.) Also, the seller must be protected from additional costs for the cleanup that are caused by the site activities of the purchaser. For example, if the purchaser is constructing structures that require dewatering to place an elevator shaft or a basement and the dewatering activity causes the movement of the contamination plume, which in turn causes the cost of remediation to increase, then the seller should not be responsible. It is clear that the use of an escrow account to cover contamination cleanup costs is most complicated from both technical and legal viewpoints. Therefore, legal assistance should be sought before entering into this type of agreement. If any other more favorable options are available, they should be pursued before the escrow account method is used. The concerns of the lender in this overall agreement must also be satisfied, further complicating the solution.

A less complicated remedy to the contamination problem is for the purchaser to make an investigation of the problem to a degree sufficient to estimate the cleanup costs, including management and inconvenience costs. The purchaser would then deduct this cost from the property contract price. In this case, the seller must agree to the estimated costs and must pursue an indemnification agreement, leaving no liability to the seller under any reasonable circumstance. This solution is less complex but often fails because the parties cannot agree to the cleanup and other costs. The indemnification issue is very important, because if the purchaser has some future financial problem, the cleanup liability could go back to the seller under certain provisions of CERCLA.

A divided cost for cleanup of a contamination problem is another complex solution. Many of the same issues discussed in using the escrow account method must be resolved when pursuing a jointly funded cleanup. One party must take the lead in management of the cleanup activities. Some economy can be achieved by using the same consultant and cleanup contractor for the site, but both parties should be represented by independent legal counsel and consultants. Critical to a jointly funded cleanup is a method of resolving internal disputes so that the project can proceed smoothly and in a timely manner. Delays to cleanup of contamination caused by internal friction can provoke regulatory agencies to file sanctions or fines against all parties involved. If the buyer and the seller agree to jointly fund the cleanup and jointly pursue a cost recovery action against the party that originally caused the contamination, the cleanup procedure must follow the provisions given in the National Contingency Plan (NCP), or the courts may deny the cost recovery action. If it is a CERCLA action, other common-law and state statutory claims exist. This type of solution can be very complex legally, and well-qualified environmental law specialists should be used in the process.

Discussion

A well-informed lender can complete a complex deal involving contaminated property if there is an understanding of the problems on the property, if a clearly defined approach is used to solve the problem, and if a sufficient amount of information is available on which to base a decision. The lender must judge the sophistication of the borrower in these situations to assess whether the borrower understands the issues and liabilities before assistance is given to save the deal. It may be a poor investment of time and effort to continue negotiations between a lender and one or more unsophisticated parties who seem intent on avoiding rather than facing a contamination problem in a logical manner. In the rare cases when a deal is destroyed by contamination or other environmental issues, it is usually because an unsophisticated party is involved in the deal. Withdrawing financial support from a deal takes no training or imagination. Profits are lost and business relationships destroyed by a timid approach to management of contamination issues during a property transfer.

CONTAMINATION FOUND ON INSTITUTION-OWNED PROPERTY

In many ways a lending institution can be exposed directly to a contamination problem. Lending institutions that own a number of physical facilities may have old buildings with numerous potential sources of site contamination. During extensive mergers and acquisitions within the lending community over the past decade, many properties that were acquired were not checked for potential contamination prior to the acquisition. Some large, diversified institutions that include lending in their list of services (such as insurance companies) may also own investment properties, such as agricultural facilities, commercial buildings, and shopping centers. When contamination is discovered on property owned by a lending institution, it is imperative that action be taken as soon as possible to avoid exposure to regulatory fines and/or third-party actions. Lending institutions are particularly susceptible to these types of actions, because they are generally viewed as "deep pockets." A well-constructed environmental risk manual will contain some guidelines for the internal investigation of institution-owned properties for any potential contamination.

Discovery of Contamination Problems/Environmental Auditing

It is important for every lending institution to have full and complete knowledge of the environmental compliance of institution-owned facilities. Sophisticated institutions now have an environmental policy so that prior to the acquisition of new properties a phase I environmental site assessment is performed. Therefore, the institution also systematically investigates all properties acquired or obtained through foreclosure before the environmental policy was adopted. In the case of a publicly owned institution, an assessment of environmental exposure may no longer be voluntary but may be a near-term requirement of the Securities and Exchange Commission as part of the annual filing of Form 10K at the end of each fiscal year (the rule mandating that the disclosure of environmental liabilities will be enforced).

The systematic investigation or environmental auditing of institution-owned properties should be prioritized, beginning with the highest risk properties and ending with the lowest risk properties. It is recommended that the properties be separated into four categories — industrial, commercial, unused, and residential. Most of the residential properties can be eliminated unless they are over 40 years old or are very large, with possible underground fuel storage facilities for heating. The most intensely used industrial properties would be first on the priority list for investigation, and all other industrial properties would be included in the first tier of inspections. The next group is the commercial properties, which should be prioritized by age and land use intensity. Unused properties should be given some scrutiny based on their location or the history of the surrounding land uses. Agricultural facilities should be included with the high priority industrial properties. It is necessary to budget for this type of work and only undertake investigations where immediate or prompt action can be taken to remedy a discovered problem. If an institution discovers contamination and does not take action in a prudent manner, the management and the institution may be subject to both civil and/or criminal actions.

Environmental auditing of existing facilities should be conducted in a manner similar to the procedure followed in a phase I ESA, with the addition of an operations analysis where appropriate. An environmental audit of a site is, however, a much more detailed and complex investigation than a phase I ESA.

The investigation should be planned with considerable detail before it begins. Outside legal counsel should be engaged to manage any newly instituted environmental auditing program. Any consultants retained to perform the environmental auditing procedure should be contracted and paid by legal counsel, with all work products provided only to legal counsel. This procedure is necessary to temporarily protect the institution from legal discovery of certain information until timely action can be taken to correct the problem. The exact scope of the investigation should be determined based on objectives set by the institution management. A written list of tasks should be developed to cover each objective fully. In most cases, the primary objective of the investigation is to determine the exposure of the institution to liabilities associated with the occurrence of existing contamination or on-site practices that are causing or could cause a discharge of contaminants. A detailed site history should be developed to determine if hazardous or toxic substances were used on the site in the past and if there were any discharges into the environment (see Chapter 5). In conducting an operational or compliance audit of an existing facility, it is necessary to perform a detailed site analysis, including inspection, direct observation of site activities, interviews with site management and general personnel, and analysis of records, including the Manufacturers Safety Data Sheets (MSDS) on chemicals used on site, deliveries and disposal of toxic or hazardous substances, and disposal practices for solid and hazardous substances. The site inspection should also include a detailed analysis of site storage facilities for toxic and hazardous substances. Guidelines for performing and managing these investigations are published in a variety of sources (Blakeslee and Grabowski, 1985).

Managing a Contamination Problem

If some contamination or other environmental problems have been found in the process of investigating institution-owned properties, unless the institution has a staff that includes properly trained and experienced environmental professionals, it will be necessary to retain a team of experts to evaluate the problem and resolve it in the most cost-effective manner. This team may include an environmental attorney and a qualified consulting firm, which has the expertise necessary to solve the problem. The lender should take care that these experts have the proper credentials and experience, because not every attorney practices environmental law and not every engineering or geological consultant has experience in the evaluation and remediation of soil and groundwater contamination problems. The policy for the hiring of outside consultants contained in the institution environmental policy manual should be followed (see Chapter 4).

A series of questions must be posed at the beginning of the investigation to determine the magnitude of the problem and the potential exposure. These questions are

1. Does the contamination require disclosure to an environmental agency?

2. Which agency or agencies need to be informed and when must they be informed?
3. What is the nature of the contaminant, and does it have the potential to cause an immediate health or safety problem?
4. What is the rate and direction of contamination movement, and will it rapidly move off site (beyond the legal property boundary)?
5. What is the size and extent of the problem?
6. Who is or was responsible for the problem?
7. What are the options for cleanup of the problem, and how much will it cost to complete the cleanup?
8. How long will it take to clean up the problem, and will the cleanup process disrupt business activities?
9. Can the party who caused it be identified?
10. Is there any possibility for a cost recovery action against the party that caused the problem?

The possible legal requirement to report a discharge or contamination problem immediately to a regulatory agency or health department is a serious issue. As a legal question that must be governed by federal and state statutes, as discussed earlier in this chapter; as a technical question it examines the chemical or biological nature of the contaminants, how rapidly the contamination problem is moving, and in what direction it is moving. Because the institution is the property owner, it is responsible for reporting a contamination problem based on advice of legal counsel and the consulting team. The specific agencies to be informed depend on the legal jurisdiction and must be properly researched. If counselors advise the institution that reporting is not necessary but the environmental policy officer is not comfortable with that advice, he or she should obtain another opinion from another environmental attorney, perhaps with experience in the specific type of contamination problem being evaluated. It can be done without discussing specifics of the problem. Prior to the implementation of any site remediation, disclosure of the problem to various agencies will be required in order to dispose of waste products legally.

When contamination is discovered, it is necessary to determine rapidly if the groundwater is contaminated and, if so, the size of the problem and the direction of contamination plume movement. It is time to test the soil and groundwater at the most probable origin of the problem, to map the contamination plume, and to determine the direction and rate of movement. This is termed *assessment of the problem*. If the problem requires disclosure to a regulatory agency, then the contamination assessment plan may require preapproval by the agency before work can begin. If the contamination problem is the result of a spill or the origin of the problem is clearly defined, an agency may be informed and some type of initial remedial action may be undertaken. In the case of a hydrocarbon fuel spill, the initial remedial action may simply involve the immediate excavation of contaminated soil, transport of the soil to a disposal facility, and decontamination. If the problem is acute and has the potential to move rapidly off site, then some type of immediate containment measure may be necessary. If the problem is extensive but poses no threat to the health and safety of on-site personnel and is not going to rapidly move off site, then a more cost-effective plan may be developed to assess the problem. The assessment phase involves the measurement of the contamination in the soil and groundwater, the mapping of the contamination plume, and the determination of the direction and rate of movement. If a consultant comes to the lender with a plan to install hundreds of monitoring wells and collect hundreds of samples to assess the problem, the lending institution environmental policy officer should evaluate the plan carefully and possibly obtain a second opinion. The assessment phase often involves the collection of several soil samples, measurement of soil gases (in the case of organic volatiles) in the field, construction of several monitoring wells to obtain water samples for chemical analysis, and collection of any other necessary information. The assessment may be phased so that only data necessary to generally understand the problem is collected in the first phase. Then, more extensive sampling may be conducted, if necessary, to further map the vertical and horizontal extension of the contamination plume for development of cleanup strategies.

Prior to the development of cleanup strategies, it is important to determine who is responsible for the contamination problem. If, during normal operation of a banking facility, contamination occurred because of a leaking fuel storage tank used to supply the emergency generator or the hydraulic fluid leaked out of the elevator ram, the fault lies with the institution. However, if a third party, such as a vendor, accidentally caused the problem by careless overfilling of a fuel tank or some other similar problem, the institution may have to take prudent and immediate action, but certain legal procedures must be followed to assure reimbursement for the spill. Also, the institution may not be at fault for contamination found beneath properties purchased for building sites or in foreclosure proceedings. If the polluter can be determined and if the polluter is still financially solvent, some type of cost recovery action may be possible. If a CERCLA cost recovery action is planned involving a federal court suit, then any cleanup procedure must follow the guidelines given in the National Contingency Plan (NCP). There are other cost recovery actions that do not require adherence to the NCP, such as a RCRA 7002 citizen's action or a suit in a state or local court under common law or state statutory causes of action, such as nuisance. However, if any type of cost recovery action is contemplated, then experienced legal counsel should be retained and involved from the beginning of any assessment or remedial site activity. If the contamination problem discovered on the site originated from an off-site location, some action to attenuate the further movement of the plume may still be a prudent action, but the problem should be reported to a regulatory agency before any remedial activities are initiated. In this case, the institution has the right to file a legal action against the polluter for cleanup costs and additional punitive damages under common law, such as trespass. If the off-site polluter is insolvent, then the institution could become responsible for cleanup of the contamination beneath its site.

Once financial responsibility has been ascertained and a detailed assessment has been made, it is time to determine the most cost-effective method of cleaning up the contamination problem. The various possible cleanup strategies must be evaluated to assess *all* of the costs involved, including not only the direct costs of remediating the site but also the opportunity costs for business losses caused by site activities. Often, a slow, methodical cleanup of a site using bioremediation or other techniques can be accomplished at some reduced cost, compared to the more conventional excavate-and-burn or pump-and-treat strategies. However, the time required to complete a cleanup may be a real issue, especially if access to a structure is curtailed during site activities or if a major parking facility cannot be used or business is interrupted by any other means. It may be far less expensive in the long run to remove the contamination problem at a more rapid rate, when the business disruption expense is considered and added to the overall cost. Also, costs are incurred when the institution faces a contamination issue and in-house personnel are occupied for hours, days, or weeks by the matter until it is resolved. It is recommended that great care be taken in the evaluation of each cleanup strategy posed and that institution operating personnel be consulted during the decision-making process. It is necessary, however, to make a decision within a prudent time frame in order to avoid problems with environmental regulators and to avoid increased costs associated with a migrating plume; the bigger it gets, the more expensive it is to remediate.

Avoiding Future Contamination Problems from Operational Activities

Every lending institution should have a policy in place that explains the safeguard measures to be taken to avoid future contamination liability from existing operations. There are several different operational issues that must be treated individually, including operation of existing physical facilities, acquisition of new properties, including mergers with other institutions, and foreclosures. The issue of acquisitions is covered in both Chapters 4 and 5. The primary protection of the institution from environmental liability during acquisitions is the same as in any other business; the due diligence investigation is used to minimize exposure by conducting the appropriate scope phase I environmental site assessment. The issues involved in foreclosure have been covered in Chapter 4, and additional information is given later in this chapter. The primary subject of this discussion is how to minimize environmental liability exposure from existing physical operations.

An uninformed lending institution employee may question the need for operational due diligence, because the institution is not an industrial manufacturing operation or a retail business operating a high-risk service, such as selling fuel or changing oil. The lending institution of today is a complex, diversified company that may resemble a small city. Every large building housing a lending institution contains numerous hazardous and toxic substances used in daily operations. A typical building has a fuel storage tank to supply an emergency generator and a maintenance department that stores various lubricants and solvents used inside of the structure, and also pesticides, paints, and other chemicals used on the exterior of the building. In very large complexes, there may even be a machine shop in the maintenance facility. It is important that all of these facilities be in full compliance with all environmental laws and that waste products are disposed in a proper manner. Common items such as fluorescent light bulbs can no longer be sent to the local solid waste disposal facility.

Perhaps the best way to demonstrate the need for environmental awareness in an operating facility is to give some examples of what can happen if no attention is given to operating environmental issues. In case 1, a small branch bank lies in a rural area outside a major city. The bank's wastewater disposal occurs via a septic tank-adsorption field. The bank has a small maintenance facility, which is used to service about a dozen other small branch facilities. The employees bring a variety of small equipment to the central maintenance facility for repair. They use about a dozen different solvents and degreasers in daily work. The excess waste products are washed into a sink. After 30 years of operation, the branch is sold, but a question about the septic tank wastewater disposal system is raised in a phase I ESA. Contamination is discovered, with a resulting cost of $250,000 for cleanup. In case 2, a high rise complex in a northeastern city is the headquarters for a multinational corporation that has operated at the facility for 30 years. About 20 years ago, the facility required the replacement of several large transformers on the exterior of the building for an upgrade of the electrical system. The transformers were owned and included as part of the structure. A contractor was hired to remove the old transformers and replace them with new ones. The old transformers, containing polychlorinated biphenyls, were transferred to a disposal company for placement in a hazardous waste facility. About 15 years after the transformer disposal, the corporation was served with legal notice that it was a Potentially Responsible Party in a CERCLA contamination case at the site of the former disposer of the transformers. The result was a settlement with two environmental agencies, costing about $1 million, with about $500,000 in legal fees and about 5 man-years of nonproductive staff time. In case 3, a small lending institution located in the Midwest called for the delivery of heating oil for a branch facility. The regular driver was not available, and when the substitute arrived at the facility, he found three different possible fueling portals. In a hurry, he opened one of the pipes and discharged 500 gal of fuel into a vent pipe, carrying the fuel into a basement area. The fumes from the fuel made a dozen employees very ill. The cost of the cleanup was borne mostly by the vendor, but a series of third-party actions were brought against the institution and the vendor. Since the fuel portal was not properly labeled, the institution paid legal costs and a $50,000 settlement. There are dozens of other examples that can be cited that point to the need for operational due diligence at lending institution facilities.

The most prudent way to minimize operational environmental liabilities is to use the environmental audit. This process was described previously for use in discovering any lingering environmental liabilities in existing physical facilities and properties. The scope of an original operational environmental audit should be accomplished by outside personnel, attorneys, and consultants and then taken over for implementation by an internal environmental manager. The scope of such environmental audits can include analyses of physical facilities, solid and hazardous waste storage and disposal practices, and wastewater disposal practices, as well as indoor clean air analyses, assessment of special issues, such as asbestos and radon gas, and consideration of a variety of health and safety issues. It is very important that if any contamination or health and safety problems are found during the audit, prompt action be taken to make the necessary corrections. Therefore, the budget for this type of effort must be carefully considered, because if a substantial and expensive problem is discovered, the lack of action by management could lead to civil or criminal liabilities for both the company and the individual managers. Possible third-party actions might be taken by employees in the case of safety issues. Once a facility is in full compliance with existing environmental rules and regulations, the institution can delegate the responsibility for monitoring environmental conditions to trained employees. It is recommended that most institutions obtain an outside environmental audit every 3–5 years to assure continued compliance. This external check will assure compliance to any new environmental rules and laws, will assess the performance of the internal environmental manager, and will provide a check of any changes to the physical facility that may affect compliance.

Discussion

Most lending institution managers and loan officers are well aware of environmental liabilities in the transaction process and in the issue of foreclosure. However, there is a tendency for institution operating personnel to ignore environmental issues at institution-owned facilities. Each lending institution should be sure that it does not have an existing environmental liability problem on any of its properties. If a contamination problem originating on institution property crosses a property boundary or if an employee of the institution becomes ill because of exposure to a contaminant, the financial liabilities could be quite extreme.

FORECLOSURE OF CONTAMINATED PROPERTY

Some very costly contamination problems have been acquired unknowingly by lending institutions via the foreclosure process. As discussed in Chapter 2, when an entity accepts fee simple title to a contaminated property, that entity comes into the chain of parties responsible for cleanup of the site. Even if the lending institution had no fault in the contamination problem, if title is taken to the property, the responsibility for the contamination problem comes with it. The maintenance of only a security interest in a property does not place the institution in jeopardy.

To Take or Not to Take

The management of contaminated property prior to foreclosure may or may not be the simplest of the problems discussed in this chapter. The decision to foreclose seems to be based solely on the value of the asset versus the cost of cleanup, but in this general belief lenders can be mistaken. Evaluation of a contamination problem is truly far more complicated, with each site presenting different conditions to evaluate. The lingering dragon in the foreclosure scenario is the potential for third-party action claims and suits. Also, it is often difficult to actually evaluate the cost of contamination cleanup, particularly if the time frame of the project is long. In order to foreclose on property, the lending institution should have answers to key questions before initiating action, most importantly,

1. Has the contamination problem migrated off-site, and is there a possibility of a third-party action against the owner?
2. Is there some imminent health or safety problem that could cause the institution as an owner to face civil penalties or plaintiffs negligence litigation?
3. What is the estimated cost of the cleanup and the time frame in which it can be accomplished?

A lending institution can pursue different options to clean up the property without actually taking title. If the mortgagee still has a viable business and the contamination problem will force the mortgagee into a nonpayment status or into bankruptcy mode, the lending institution may wish to assist the owner in the cleanup process to work out the problem. In lieu of a write-down of the asset, the loan may be restructured to some degree. If this type of arrangement is used, the lender must be quite careful not to become defined as an operator or to become involved in management, because if the problem cannot be resolved, the institution could become a responsible party. Any proposed workout arrangement should be reviewed by appropriate legal counsel (see Fleet Factors case review in Chapter 2).

To acquire the information necessary to address the key questions, some on-site testing and analysis must be performed. The initial assessment process has been described earlier in this chapter. The question regarding off-site migration should be answered first to assess the third-party actions issue. Determining whether the problem poses an eminent health or safety hazard should be addressed next. Then, the cost of the cleanup should be estimated. A common error that lenders make in this process is asking for cleanup cost estimates based on insufficient information. When a consultant is asked to estimate cleanup costs without sufficient information, a reputable consultant will either refuse to make an estimate or will offer a high estimate, perhaps several times the real cost, in order to cover contingencies. The lender should request a proposal from the consultant that includes the specific determination of the cleanup cost. If this work is authorized, the consultant should be instructed to qualify the cleanup cost estimate carefully based on the facts and on what variables are included. The cost of the information collection necessary to determine the cleanup cost and duration may be substantial. If these costs are too high relative to the property value, the lender may wish to write down the asset at this time.

Cost Recovery Actions

During the initial assessment of the contamination problem by the lending institution, an attempt should be made to determine the entity responsible for the contamination problem. If the responsible party is financially viable, the lending institution may have the right to file a cost recovery action against the polluter. There are several types of potential action, including a CERCLA cost recovery action or a RCRA section 7002 citizens suit (discussed previously). Many state and local governments also have legal cost recovery remedies based on environmental laws and common law, depending on the specific circumstances. Before any cleanup measures are taken, the possibility of a cost recovery action should be researched. The type of cost recovery action considered may have an impact on the cleanup activities and the procedure under the law. The possibility of substantial recovery of cleanup costs bears greatly on the decision to foreclose on a property, but carries with it the possibility of loss in a court proceeding. This type of action should always be researched thoroughly.

Discussion

Foreclosure of contaminated property is truly a complex problem that requires sound advice from experienced legal counsel and some innovative thinking on the part of the lender. The primary issue of concern is the recovery of the security asset, which is considerably more complex than just subtracting the estimated cleanup cost from the property's market value. Issues such as potential third-party actions against the property must be carefully evaluated before the foreclosure is processed. If some type of workout deal is considered in lieu of foreclosure, the institution must protect itself from being considered as part of management of the entity having the problem. Also, the lending institution should research the possibility of a cost recovery action if a foreclosure is contemplated. Cost estimation for cleanup is far from an exact science, and the lender must evaluate all costs carefully, including legal fees, consulting fees, cleanup contractor costs, site restoration costs, and marketing fees to liquidate the property upon cleanup completion. The length of the cleanup process dictates when the property can be sold and has an effect on the asset value. In conclusion, whether or not to foreclose on contaminated property is a complex decision that requires considerable legal and technical input. The exact methodology to be used should be specified in the institution risk manual.

REFERENCES FOR FURTHER READING

Blakeslee, H. W. and Grabowski, T. M., *A Practical Guide to Plant Environmental Audits,* Van Nostrand Reinhold, New York, 1985, 299 pp.

Cahill, L. B. and Kane, R. W., Eds., *Environmental Audits,* 5th ed., Government Institutes, Inc., Rockville, MD, 1987, 656 pp.

7 THE LENDER IN TRUSTS AND IN MANAGEMENT INFLUENCE

The definition of "owner" in the Comprehensive Environmental Response, Compensation, and Liability Act is "a person owning a facility" (Bctcnsky, 1995). This rather nebulous and circular definition leads to many open questions regarding how individuals or entities with various relationships to a property could be classified as owners. It is obvious that the holder of the fee simple title to a property is an owner, but the courts have included additional parties in the owner classification, including lenders, lessees, parent corporations, and corporate stockholders and officers. Another party that may be classified as an owner is a trustee, who holds legal title to property held in a trust. Trustee CERCLA liability is an open question, depending upon many factors. Unfortunately, the courts have been inconsistent in this determination. A lender holding a security interest in a property or business may become an "operator" of a site by exerting influence over management decisions, as illustrated in the Fleet Factors decision (see Chapter 2). The purpose of this chapter is to explore the issues of trustee liability and management decision influence in more detail, to assist the lender dealing with CERCLA liabilities created by the courts.

TRUSTS

Because the question of trustee liability under CERCLA is somewhat debatable based on recent court rulings, every lender should be aware of potential liabilities and should comply with institution policies designed to limit liabilities. Trustees should become familiar with more detailed analyses of the legal basis for trustee liabilities under CERCLA, as provided in Betensky (1995), Bezdek (1995), and Holmes (1995).

Recent Court Decisions

A series of court decisions have led to a rather confused interpretation of the liabilities for trustees arising out of CERCLA. In *United States v. Burns*, a federal court ruled that a trustee holding only legal title to the property was liable for environmental cleanup costs. In this case, the defendant, Crowley, was both the trustee and the beneficiary of the trust. The court ruled that as trustee and beneficiary of the trust, Crowley exerted control over the property, and there was some evidence of property ownership (Betensky, 1995). "Since Crowley was found to be an owner of the facility, the court stated that there was no requirement for the plaintiff to show a causal relationship between the defendant's ownership and the disposal of the hazardous materials. A trustee's status as legal title holder was sufficient to hold the trustee personally liable" (Betensky, 1995).

In a decision conflicting with the Burns case, a federal court ruled in *United States v. Petersen Sand & Gravel* that a trustee was not an "owner" or "operator" under CERCLA. The defendant in this case, Petersen, claimed that several other parties should share cleanup liability, including the Northern Trust Bank, which had been trustee during the period of site contamination. The court issued a summary judgment containing the conclusion that "it is the beneficiary of an Illinois land trust and not the trustee who has full management and control over the property." The court ruled that a trustee holding bare title is deemed not to fall within the standards of "ownership" within CERCLA.

Another contradictory ruling occurred in the case of *City of Phoenix v. Garbage Services Company.* According to Brezek (1993) and Betensky (1995), a federal court ruled that a trustee is an owner under CERCLA and may be held personally liable beyond asset value in a trust. The facts in this case show that Wilbur Calvin Estes owned a landfill in Arizona, and when he died, his will placed the landfill into a trust managed by the Valley National Bank, which was also executor of the estate. About six years later, the city of Phoenix acquired the site via condemnation and brought suit against the Valley National Bank to recover the response costs it incurred in the cleanup of hazardous substances placed on the site while the bank was trustee. The city claimed the bank was an owner under CERCLA. The court ruled that a trustee holding legal title to a property is liable for obligations as an owner of the property. In this case a trustee with bare title to a property had liability despite having little control over the property. The bank attempted to limit liability, but the court ruled that the decision of the bank to exercise the trust option to purchase the landfill and its decision to continue the Garbage Services Company lease were sufficient to impose personal liability.

Based on the analysis of Betensky (1995), the Garbage Services Company case resulted in the court development of a threefold standard for determining the extent of trustee liability.

> First, where the trustee is determined liable as the current owner of property contaminated prior to the commencement of its trusteeship, its liability will be limited to the assets of the trust. Second, where the trustee is determined liable as owner of the property at the time that the hazardous substances were deposited there, but ... did not have the power to control the use of (the) trust property, its liability will again be limited to the extent of the trust assets available to indemnify it. Finally, (w)here a trustee had the power to control the use of trust

> property, and knowingly allowed the property to be used for the disposal of hazardous substances, then the trustee is liable (as an owner or operator at the time of disposal) to the same extent that he would be liable if he held the property free of trust.

Based on this analysis, a trustee should analyze exposure to the CERCLA liabilities in a trust to protect both institutional and personal assets.

These court decisions have made it apparent that there is no consistency in application of trustee liability under CERCLA. This confusion makes it necessary for each lending institution to treat trust agreements with great care and perform the necessary due diligence investigations. Properties held in a trust should be treated as if the institution is actually purchasing them, and in the case of operating companies, other considerations must be taken into account. The biggest pitfall to avoid is exposure to liabilities beyond the asset value of the trust. Legal counsel on construction of the trust agreement and management should be obtained.

Due Diligence Investigations Prior to Acceptance of Trusts

Because of the unsettled nature of trustee CERCLA liability, a lending institution or any other party acting as a trustee should employ similar due diligence procedures to those used by any party acquiring property. A due diligence investigation should be conducted on every property prior to acceptance into a trust. The lending institution environmental policy should include a matrix of property types with corresponding land uses that yield a risk profile for any given property. The environmental policy should also contain a classification of properties based on appraised or estimated market values to determine the type or degree of due diligence investigation that should be conducted. A combination of the risk and the property value should be used to determine the final scope of the due diligence investigation used.

The four basic types of due diligence investigations to be used in analysis of trusts are the checklist, the transactional screen process, the phase I environmental site assessment, and the full environmental audit. It is recommended that all proposed trust properties or businesses first be screened by trained institution personnel, using a checklist developed in the institution environmental policy manual (see Chapter 2). If the property is determined to pose a minimal risk based on the initial checklist assessment, it can be placed in the trust. Consideration in the checklist process should be given not only to the classification of the property, but also to its use. For example, a property may be a residential dwelling that carries an associated minimal environmental risk. However, if the dwelling is to be utilized as a rental property that the institution may manage at some point in time, it is necessary to protect the trustee from environmental tort actions arising out of potential tenant exposure to hazardous substances, such as asbestos, radon gas, lead paint, and perhaps lead leaching from old water pipes. In consideration of this use, a higher level of environmental due diligence investigation is merited.

If a property receives a possible environmental risk rating in the checklist process, the property should be examined by a qualified environmental professional, using the transaction screen process (see Chapter 5). The transaction screen process (TSP) should be employed only for potentially low to intermediate risk properties, because it is not a comprehensive investigation. The TSP not only provides a new assessment of a property conducted by a qualified professional, but also confirms the assessment made by the institution employee using the checklist analysis. Some institution environmental policies require that all trust properties valued over $100,000 have at least a TSP analysis.

A phase I environmental site assessment (ESA) should be conducted on all properties that are classified as high risk, based on the risk levels assigned within the institution environmental policy, and on all properties that may require active management in the future. The format of the phase I ESA should conform to ASTM Standard 1527 (see Chapter 5). The phase I ESA should be conducted by a qualified environmental professional who meets the qualifications of the institution environmental policy and has been prequalified. The scope of a phase I ESA conducted on properties to be leased by the trustee or in any way operated by the trustee should include all appropriate additional environmental investigations, so as to minimize operational risks. These ESAs may include one or all of the following: an asbestos survey, a radon gas survey, a lead paint survey, an indoor clean air assessment (with a possible pathogenic bacterial assessment), an electromagnetic field survey, and/or a plumbing inspection.

If an operating business is to be included in the trust and this business uses, stores, or transports hazardous or toxic substances, the trustee should very carefully assess environmental liabilities prior to acceptance. Acceptance of operating businesses into a trust creates exceptional liabilities for the trustee. The court decisions used as examples, and particularly the standards set in the Garbage Services case, show that the liability of a trustee may go above the value of the property or business held in the trust. When an operating business is accepted by the trust, the institution may be deemed the owner and operator, depending on the nature of the trust, the type of environmental problem that arises on the site, and the language contained in any exemptions within the trust. If the trust agreement states that the trustee will manage the property for the beneficiaries, the trustee is likely to be declared an owner and operator. In the case of a trustee that holds bare title to the property until the property is sold for distribution of proceeds, the trustee may or may not be deemed the owner and will probably not be deemed the operator. The personal liability potential declines if the trustee is solely the title holder and if there is no fault associated with the trustee in terms of hazardous waste disposal. The liability should then be limited to the asset value of the trust. Even when the language used in the trust agreement is legally constructed to minimize trustee liability, the trustee should still require a detailed environmental investigation of the facility before acceptance. Depending on the degree of risk, this environmental investigation usually should be a full environmental audit of the facility, including a phase I ESA scope to locate any potential contamination caused by the operation, and then a full environmental compliance audit. An environmental audit assesses the compliance of a facility to all federal, state, and local environmental rules and regulations. The issue of occupational health and safety should also be addressed in certain high-risk businesses. These types of investigations must be conducted only by highly qualified environmental specialists. The expertise required to conduct these assessments may not be covered in the institution's environmental policy manual, in which case the trustee should seek assistance from a qualified environmental attorney to help organize the investigation.

An example of a problem that could occur when an uninformed trustee accepts an operating business into trust is as follows. A lending institution, as both trustee and executor for the estate of a wealthy entrepreneur, accepts a chemical manufacturing company into a trust. His will leaves title to the property to his son, who is a sophisticated attorney. The son performs a due diligence investigation of the chemical company and property and determines that the environmental liabilities are severe and are in excess of the property value, with exposure to additional third-party liability claims. The son refuses to take title to the property, and the trustee suddenly becomes the owner with no reasonable means of disposal.

If a trustee must operate a facility for some period of time, perhaps because of a trust agreement executed many years ago, the trustee should protect itself by carefully monitoring the operating activities. Periodic environmental compliance audits should be conducted to assure continued compliance with environmental rules and regulations. All facilities should be required to obtain and maintain pollution liability insurance in limits that provide adequate coverage. Any lease agreements requiring the approval of the trustee should be preceded by a due diligence investigation, which in most cases entails a phase I ESA. The trustee should perform a phase I ESA on any property under a trust that is being vacated by a tenant, in order to assure that the tenant did not discharge hazardous or toxic substances on the site. All decisions by the trustee must consider the consequences of environmental liabilities and how they can be avoided or minimized.

Discussion

There will always be some exposure to environmental liabilities for trustees. Although due diligence must be performed in the trust acceptance process, the degree of environmental investigation cost must be weighed against the asset value in a cost-benefit analysis. Until the issue of trustee CERCLA liability is satisfactorily resolved by appropriate legislation, lending institutions and others acting as trustees should seriously evaluate the situation before accepting into trust any operating facilities that could pose high environmental risk.

There are some attempts being made to pass legislation in Congress to clearly define CERCLA liability for trustees. House Bill 2462, sponsored by Representative John LaFalce (D, NY), was introduced in June, 1993. This bill states that "a trustee...who acquires ownership or control of a property without having owned or participated in management of that property prior to assuming ownership or control as fiduciary, is not an owner under CERCLA." This bill does retain CERCLA liability for any trustee that "in a direct and active manner...willfully, knowingly, or recklessly causes a release of a hazardous substance." This bill ties trustee liability to the amount of actual management and control a trustee exerts over the property (Betensky, 1995). Another bill, House Bill 2718, was introduced by Representative Christopher Cox (R, CA) to limit trustee CERCLA liability. It is stated in this bill that "the term owner...does not include a fiduciary or trustee which acquires an interest in or control of a facility for the purposes of administering a trust." Although these two bills have been introduced, their basic lack of definitions may add to the confusion over trustee liability rather than solve the problem (Betensky, 1995). Neither bill has passed to date, and no clear resolution to trustee CERCLA liability is anticipated at this time.

There appears to be one common theme throughout the previously discussed court decisions and the currently proposed attempts to define trustee CERCLA liability, the issue of control. If the trustee truly exerts control by direct management and makes decisions about the disposition of hazardous or toxic substances, then CERCLA liability seems to be imposed in virtually all cases, using the definition of "operator." Those persons charged with the task of managing lending institution trust departments should carefully consider and address the control issue in the language of the trust agreement. An attempt should be made to minimize liability by shifting some control to beneficiaries or others, either to limit or spread the liability. All trust documents should be constructed to limit the maximum CERCLA exposure to the trust asset value. However, the only real trustee protection at this time depends on the quality of the due diligence investigation conducted prior to acceptance of properties and/or facilities into the trust and on avoidance of control.

DECISION INFLUENCE

Lender liability under CERCLA for influence on management or management decisions arises out of the Fleet Factors court decision. Although this decision appears to guide CERCLA liabilities in only one of the federal court districts, the threat of this decision pervades the lending industry. The question to be explored in consideration of the Fleet Factors decision is how can lenders protect themselves from becoming defined as an operator of a facility, while still exercising the necessary financial controls and monitoring security interests.

Influence of Financial Management on Environmental Decisions

When a lender extends credit to a business, there are many clauses in the loan agreement about financial conditions that must be maintained to assure the continued use of the credit vehicle. For example, when a company receives a credit extension secured by its accounts receivable assets (asset-based lending), stipulations include the percentage total of accounts receivable allowable to provide security, the maximum age of the assets used to secure the loan, the net tangible value of the company, and the maintenance of a whole variety of financial ratios used to assess the continued viability of the company. If the ratios are not maintained or the net tangible value of the company falls below the agreed value, credit extension can be or is withdrawn or modified. This financial monitoring and the influence the lending institution exerts on company finances may influence environmental decisions.

In one hypothetical situation, a company may be experiencing a cash flow crisis, and an environmental problem may arise that requires an immediate response. The response costs may cause a violation of the loan agreement, which may place the lender in the position of influencing management, triggering potential CERCLA liability. If the lender holds the position that the financial ratios must be maintained or credit is terminated and the company cannot respond to clean up the problem, the lender may be brought into some level of responsibility. However, this is an extreme example and may be a worst case possibility. If the lender is confronted with the problem and chooses to assist the company by requiring some additional collateral from the company to assure that the security interest remains viable, such as requesting liens on other company-owned property or equipment or personal loan guarantees by the company owners or operators, then it is unlikely that the lender would be held responsible under any future CERCLA action. A lender that becomes directly involved in some type of environmental cleanup activity may invoke direct CERCLA liability. This involvement may be the choice of a disposal site or the use of a qualified contractor. If the lender insists on disposal by the lowest bidder and the company becomes a Potentially Responsible Party at a later time over contamination at the disposal site, the lender could inherit some liability, because the influence on the decision was quite direct.

One possible method to avoid exerting undue influence on environmental issues is for the lender to add some language on environmental matters in the credit extension agreement. For example, when providing asset-based lending services to operating companies, a special condition of the loan could be that the company must be in compliance with all applicable environmental laws during the term of the loan. If the company or a regulatory agency claims that the financial controls placed on the company by the institution caused an environmental problem to be ignored, the environmental compliance stipulation could be used as evidence that the institution mandated environmental compliance and should not be held responsible for any environmental problems arising from day-to-day operations.

The issue of lender liability caused by providing "decision or management influence" under CERCLA remains unsettled after failure of the U.S. Environmental Protection Agency Lender Liability Rule (see Chapter 2). Potential liabilities created by the Fleet Factors decision must be considered by all lending institutions in transactions involving high-risk businesses and trusts. The exact wording of the Fleet Factors decision included the phrases "participating in management" and "by participating in the financial management of a facility to a degree indicating a capacity to influence the corporation's treatment of hazardous waste." This decision necessitates that a higher level of due diligence be mandated in lending institution environmental policies.

REFERENCES FOR FURTHER READING

Betensky, E., Trustee liability: an undefined standard, *UCLA J. Environ. Law Policy,* 1994–1995.

Bezdek, J. C., Trustee beware: toxic contamination on real estate under fiduciary management can bring forth personal liability for total cleanup costs, *South. Univ. Law Rev.,* 1993.

Holmes, W. J., The evolution of the trust: a creative solution to trustee liability under CERCLA, *Villanova Environ. Law J.,* 1995.

Spiotto, J. E., *Theories of Liability Which Have Been Raised Against the Indenture Trustee,* Practicing Law Institute, Real Estate Law and Practice Course Handbook Series, PLI Order No. N4-4591, 1995.

Court Case Citations

City of Phoenix v. Garbage Services Co., 816 F. Supp. 564 (D. Ariz. 1993).

U.S. v. Burns, No. C-88-94 L, 1988 U.S. LEXIS 17340 (D.N.H., 1988).

U.S. v. Petersen Sand & Gravel, 806 F. Supp. 1346 (N.D. Ill. 1992).

8 OTHER ENVIRONMENTAL ISSUES

This text has emphasized the issue of how to manage potential environmental liabilities caused by site contamination with hazardous or toxic substances. Although these liabilities are of great concern to all lenders, additional environmental problems can also threaten the ability of the borrower to repay loans or cause a lending institution considerable cost and inconvenience. Several of those issues are discussed in this chapter, and references are given for those unfortunate lenders who must deal with these other environmental issues. A phase I environmental site assessment may include an analysis of one or all of these problems, depending on the size and proposed use of a property. Most land developers carefully analyze all potential environmental issues prior to embarking on a large project because of the costs involved in possible loss of property use or delays in construction related to permitting. Smaller scale land users or unsophisticated purchasers may ignore these environmental issues and face the financial consequences.

WETLANDS

After the issue of contamination with toxic or hazardous substances, perhaps the most feared environmental issue facing lenders is the occurrence of wetlands on a property. Protection of wetlands became a national priority when the U.S. Army Corps of Engineers and the U.S. Environmental Protection Agency were given responsibility for protecting and maintaining the integrity of wetlands based on authority given in the Rivers and Harbors Act of 1899 and under Section 404 of the Clean Water Act (the 1977 amendments to the Federal Water Pollution Control Act of 1948). These laws require the designated agencies to evaluate (not necessarily issue) permits for a variety of activities in or adjacent to wetland areas. Federal, state, and local agencies have all enacted various additional wetland protection measures, requiring a permit to be obtained in order to conduct virtually any type of activity in a wetland area. This discussion centers on new activities to be conducted on properties with wetlands or activities conducted in the past on wetland areas. The issue of sovereign lands or past filling and use of tidal wetlands is covered in more detail in the succeeding section.

The key questions for a lender are what a wetland is, how much wetland area is located on a property, and how the occurrence of the wetland will affect the property value.

Wetlands are rather loosely defined on the basis of vegetation types, soil types, and the hydrology of the site (Lyon, 1993). From a scientific sense, all three factors must be satisfied for an area to be a truly functional wetland. The official definition of wetlands under the U.S. Army Corps of Engineers regulations (33 C.F.R. 328.3(b)) is

> ...those areas that are inundated or saturated by surface groundwater at a frequency and duration sufficient to support, and that under normal circumstances do support, a prevalence of vegetation typically adapted for life in saturated soil conditions. Wetlands generally include swamps, marshes, bogs, and similar areas.

However, wetlands delineation is not altogether based on pure science, because the environmental laws protecting wetlands also contain provisions to restore wetlands and to protect the transitional lands around wetlands as well as some of the upland basins feeding water to the wetlands. This rather broad protection scheme causes wetlands delineation to be based on negotiated lines rather than lines based on pure science. The very presence of wetlands vegetation on a property does not necessarily preclude use or diminish land value, because there are design options that allow the wetlands areas to be incorporated into the property surface-water management system; the wetlands may even be maintained for aesthetic or open space purposes. Also, if certain wetlands areas are no longer functional and cannot be restored, then sometimes a reviewing agency will allow some land uses to be permitted.

As part of a due diligence evaluation of a property, the wetlands should be mapped and a determination should be made with regard to agency jurisdiction. The jurisdiction determination can be extraordinarily complex, and construction activities within a given wetlands area can require as many as 25 different permits in states like California. The time and costs required to obtain the permits, if they can be obtained at all, are a prime consideration in the valuation of a property for a given use. Certain wetlands can be altered if they are mitigated by the creation of similar wetlands types on the site or at a designated area in the near vicinity. Some states have developed the concept of the mitigation bank, to be used by property developers to either make a cash payment or other contribution to ongoing wetlands restoration or wetlands development project in trade for development or use rights on some wetlands. It should be clearly understood by lenders that the national wetlands policy is "no net loss of habitat." Therefore, wetlands alteration will always be an issue on a given property at the federal, state, or local government level.

Financing of properties with past alteration of wetlands is not usually problematic, if the original land user met the provisions of the law at the time of development, although this issue is more complex with regard to tidal wetlands. As part of due diligence, it may be necessary to investigate whether all of the proper wetlands permits were obtained prior to construction and completion of the project. If wetlands protection laws were violated during construction of a project, regulatory agencies may have the right to seek penalties if an enforcement action is brought within the statute of limitations time frame for a given law. Projects developed on wetlands areas prior to enactment of the Clean Water Act usually are not scrutinized by environmental agencies unless a new violation of the rules occurs. However, if an area that was formerly wetlands has been left in an unused state, allowing wetlands vegetation to become reestablished, then that area may come under the jurisdiction of permitting agencies. This is a common occurrence on large agricultural properties.

Wetlands laws and rules are in constant flux, especially with the passage of state and local protection laws and rules. Therefore, a determination of wetlands jurisdiction and/or delineation on any undeveloped property must be considered part of the due diligence effort.

SOVEREIGN LANDS

Several states assert ownership of the navigable waters within the boundaries of the state. The exact legal terminology and how this ownership right is administered vary greatly from state to state. Perhaps the most structured administration of state-owned, submerged lands is in the state of Florida, where the submerged lands are termed *sovereign lands*. The definition of sovereign lands in the Florida Constitution is as follows:

> ...title to land under navigable waters within the boundaries of the state, which have not been alienated, including beaches below mean high water lines, is held by the state, by virtue of its sovereignty in trust for all the people. Sales of such lands may be authorized by law but only within the public interest. Private uses of portions of such land may be authorized by law but only when not contrary to the public interest,...
>
> Art. X § 11 F/A. Const.

The lender should be aware of the laws and rules that govern the use of submerged lands in each state of operation. Notwithstanding deed descriptions, actual private ownership may not include the submerged parts of the land within the boundary legally described. Also, there is no absolute guarantee that an owner adjacent to submerged land or navigable waters will be able to obtain the right to use or have access to the navigable waters. This is a very important issue in financing, because the viability of a project may depend on use of state-owned submerged lands, such as in the case of a marina as a primary or vital accessory land use. Whenever a lease or acquisition of state-owned submerged land is included in a financial deal, the borrower should demonstrate to the lender that the appropriate lease or permit has been obtained prior to release of construction loan funds. Since the use of sovereign lands or submerged lands may require a lease and compensation to obtain and maintain the lease, the lender should ask the borrower to reveal the financial terms of the lease to assess the impact on cash flow and the ability of the borrower to meet the terms of the loan. The lease fee can be significant; in the state of Florida for example, the standard annual lease fee for wetslip marina dockage is computed at a rate of 7% of the rental value of the wetslip area or the Department of Natural Resources base fee, whichever is greater (Conklin et al., 1992). There also may be provisions in the lease to demonstrate that the constructed facilities are not causing any harm to the environment. These provisions commonly require some type of environmental monitoring program, which adds a significant cost. A lease may be terminated by the state government if any provision is violated. A lender may require that copies of annual compliance reports be transmitted to the institution as part of the loan monitoring program.

In recent years, certain states have initiated retroactive legal actions against facilities that were built on sovereign or submerged lands without obtaining a land lease. Such actions were taken against some substantial facilities that encroached into tidal submerged lands either by accident or by design. In certain cases the claims for either damages or retroactive lease fees have been in the millions of dollars. Although these actions are generally rare, as part of due diligence, a lender considering a financing arrangement for a facility located adjacent to submerged lands or tidal wetlands should require a legal determination of liability for any retroactive assessments for use of the submerged lands.

Buildings adjacent to eroding beaches may be involved in issues of state ownership of submerged lands. When a beach is eroding, the state ownership of land advances onto private lands as the position of the mean high water line moves landward. If a structure is damaged during a storm and 50% of the value of the structure is lost, and the state government setback provisions from mean high water cannot be met, then the structure cannot be rebuilt. This can have a significant impact on the ability of a borrower to repay the loan, and it can eliminate the value of the security interest to the lender. The lender should carefully investigate the issue of beach erosion when financing properties and/or construction anywhere adjacent to the shoreline.

LISTED SPECIES AND CRITICAL AND UNIQUE HABITAT

Listed Species

The Federal Endangered Species Act of 1973 provided protection for specific listed species of animals and plants that are considered to be endangered or threatened. The original definition of an endangered species contained in the Act (16 U.S.C. 1532(6)) is

> any species which is in danger of extinction throughout all or a significant portion of its range other than a species of the Class Insecta determined by the Secretary to constitute a pest whose protection under the provisions of this chapter would present an overwhelming and overriding risk to man.

A threatened species as defined is any species likely to become an endangered species within the foreseeable future throughout all or a significant portion of its range. The U.S. Fish and Wildlife Service has the primary responsibility for managing and enforcing the Endangered Species Act. The species listed are not necessarily protected throughout the entire United States, with specific species listed in some regions and not in others. Also, individual states can list and protect various species under some primacy agreements with the U.S. Department of Interior. Some states, such as the state of Florida, have additional classifications for species protection, such as the "species of special concern," which has a unique list. If a lender needs to obtain information on a specific region of the country, a copy of the most current list can be obtained from the Department of the Interior, Fish and Wildlife Service, and from the appropriate state and local agencies.

Occurrence of a listed species on a property can significantly affect its value. In one example, a nesting bald eagle resides in a tree located in the middle of a 20-acre parcel of unused commercial property. A state and local environmental law requires a no-use buffer zone around the nest, with a radius of 750 ft. (This is a common zone in some states.) The buffer area covers about 40 acres of property, which renders the entire parcel unusable. This example is extreme, and the land owner may have some legal recourse with the government agency over the "taking" issue and force a purchase of the property. The example, however, illustrates the absolute necessity for research into this issue to avoid a financial loss. Local and state governments have avoided the taking issue by not allowing any construction during nesting season. The listed species issue applies mostly to the development of unused lands and new uses or activities on developed lands. A lender should have no significant concerns with listed species on properties that are developed unless it is agricultural development, which can be restricted based on various listed species issues.

Listed species can significantly interfere with the issuance of other environmental permits, such as dredge-and-fill permits and wetlands permits. The U.S. Fish and Wildlife Service (USFWS) conducts permit reviews as granted under the consultation part of the Act. If the USFWS believes that the issuance of a permit or proposed land use jeopardizes the continued existence of a species or could result in an adverse effect on a critical habitat, then a jeopardy biological opinion is issued. An issued opinion of this type must include a discussion of alternatives and possible project modifications to allow the requested activity to take place. A jeopardy opinion usually has some impact on property value in terms of both time delays and possible use restrictions. In areas known to harbor endangered species or supporting habitat, a survey of the property by a qualified biologist and a request for opinion letters from both the federal and state agencies would be prudent procedures as part of due diligence.

A sophisticated land purchaser will address the issue of listed species prior to closing. If a lender is involved in the process of financing a new use or development, endangered species assessment should be addressed and resolved as part of the due diligence process. A listed species survey should be conducted only by a qualified wildlife biologist, biologist, or ecologist who has proper expertise and experience. The lender must be aware that the willful destruction of listed species or of habitat containing or supporting listed species may be both a federal and state crime in much of the United States. In recent years, civil and criminal penalties have been assessed against persons seeking to rid their property of listed species. The lender should be aware that there are legal remedies to resolve the listed species and habitat issues, including dedication of wildlife easements and corridors, development of species management plans, and species relocation plans. These issues can be resolved through negotiation with the regulatory agencies.

Critical and Unique Habitat

The Federal Endangered Species Act of 1973 also provides for the protection of the listed species and, in addition, the habitat in which they live, feed, or forage. A property containing rare or unique habitat or listed plant species must be preserved in certain cases, with no viable use of the land possible. Habitat management for listed animal species commonly involves the development of a management plan and requires that some land be set aside to maintain the habitat. There is no question that critical and unique habitat issues affect the value of property and can preclude certain uses of specific properties. Therefore, the lender must again be aware of the issue and raise the question if the particular transaction will involve land development or other types of activities.

ASBESTOS

Billions of dollars have been spent in the United States over the past two decades on the abatement and management of asbestos used in buildings and building materials. Asbestos is a generic name for a series of naturally occurring, fibrous silicate minerals that were used to construct a wide variety of materials used in building beginning in the late 19th and early 20th centuries. There is a direct correlation between human exposure to the fibers and the incidence of a particular type of lung cancer, called mesothelioma. However, there is considerable scientific debate over the effects of "casual" exposure versus intense exposure, such as in mining and industrial operations. Despite the scientific debate over degrees of exposure, the occurrence of asbestos is a very serious regulatory issue that has a significant impact on property value. Federal regulations for asbestos are found in the National Emission Standards for Hazardous Air Pollutants (1985) (40 CFR Part 61, Subpart M) and in a number of other rules (29 CFR 1910 and 1926). Many states have adopted both the federal regulations and their own asbestos regulations.

Occurrence of Asbestos in Structures

Asbestos occurs in a wide variety of building materials, from floor tiles to acoustic ceiling materials to roofing materials. A list of the most common asbestos-containing construction materials and the approximate date of origin is given in Table 8.1 (from Hess, 1993). The occurrence of these asbestos-containing materials in existing buildings creates several technical issues that must be

Table 8.1 Date of Origin of Some Asbestos Products[a]

Roofing material	
1897	Sprayed-on acoustical insulation
1902	Pipe insulation
1909	Cement cladding
1910	Corrugated paper products
1910	Roofing felts
1920	Asphalt tiles
1926	Brake linings
1930	Cement
1930	Caulking putties
1935	High temperature, cement-like pipe elbows and joints
1935	Roofing shingles
1938	Transite board
1945	Theater curtains
1946	Drywall
1950	Vinyl floor tiles
1950	Asphalt
1951	Electrical insulation
1952	Paper laminate for electrical equipment
1953	Conduit
1965	Teflon
Unknown	Vinyl wallpaper

[a]From Hess, 1993.

resolved. First, is the asbestos present in the building friable, or does it have the ability to shed fibers into the air? *Friable* means that the asbestos can be easily broken and enter the atmosphere, which leads to potential human contact, a high-liability problem with potential third-party actions to a building owner. It also may involve federal and state regulations, depending upon the use of the building. Next, does the asbestos occurrence require remediation or total removal, or can it be sealed and left in place? The quantity, type, and location of asbestos-containing materials lead to an evaluation of which asbestos management strategy meets the provisions of any legal obligation and protects the safety of humans occupying the building at any given time.

Asbestos-containing materials also have been used in facilities that are not enclosed by structures. Cement-asbestos piping was commonly used by water utilities for distribution conveyance during the past several decades. The lender should be aware of this issue when either lending to a utility company or assisting in the underwriting of bonds. If piping must be replaced or if it must be removed from the ground, there can be some unexpected expense associated with the problem. During due diligence, the lender should simply ask what materials were used in the building and facility construction.

Impact of Asbestos on Property Values

Up until about 1986, the problem of asbestos in privately owned commercial buildings was not considered to be a problem involving public attention or financial liability (Harris, 1990). However, in 1988, the U.S. Environmental Protection Agency released a report to Congress with the conclusion that "friable asbestos containing materials — brittle and in danger of releasing asbestos dust

— are present in 20% of the nation's 3.6 million government and commercial buildings, and half of them contain asbestos that is already damaged." The estimate included 39% of the 14,000 federal buildings, 59% of the 350,000 apartments of ten or more units, and 16% of the 3.2 million private and nonresidential buildings (Harris, 1990). As a result of these findings, asbestos litigation exploded in the second half of 1986, and the issue was brought to the forefront of public attention by the media. Property damage litigations established that the mere presence of asbestos-containing materials in a structure constituted a type of structural damage, as well as endangerment to the health of building occupants.

In the present legal climate, it does not matter whether casual exposure to asbestos by humans is a real health hazard. The fact is, there is a real financial problem when a building contains significant quantities of asbestos. Harris (1990) reported that the 1989 issue of *ECON* stated the following economic impacts of asbestos on building values:

> The presence of asbestos automatically lowers the value of any given building by 20% or more. Mortgage companies and lending institutions often flatly refuse financing for the purchase of asbestos-containing structures. Mortgage companies and lending institutions that do provide financing are also requiring purchasers to put aside an amount of money equal to the cost of asbestos removal for the entire structure. Lending institutions are routinely requiring asbestos inspections and pre-purchase environmental audits before loan or mortgage applications are considered on commercial buildings. Insurance companies are declining to insure asbestos-containing buildings. Building owners are filing suit against previous owners, developers, and asbestos manufacturing companies seeking to recover the costs of removing asbestos from their structures. Purchasers are demanding special clauses in sales contracts that allow future tenants to sue the previous building owner instead of the current owner for asbestos-related diseases. Unions and other organizations representing building workers now routinely picket, invite in news reporters or otherwise take activist measures to emphasize demands that asbestos hazards be eliminated. Tenants can often break their leases if asbestos is discovered after they move into a building space. Brokers representing commercial buildings which do not contain asbestos are aggressively using that fact as a selling point against competing brokers representing buildings that do. Bankers are increasingly concerned about foreclosing on asbestos-containing buildings because they fear they may be held responsible for the structure's cleanup. Several law firms are now moving aggressively into the field of property-damage-related asbestos litigation. Large corporations and agencies, such as IBM, Xerox, and the U.S. General Services Administration, have recently established nationwide policies prohibiting their personnel from renting, leasing, or purchasing asbestos-containing building spaces. Many large investors are quietly assessing the long-term financial implications of asbestos on portfolios heavily weighed with urban real estate buildings.

These trends continue and may intensify, so it is imperative that a lender in a commercial building deal be aware of this problem and require the appropriate prefinancing inspection for asbestos-containing materials when it is merited.

The most common question asked by lenders is when an asbestos survey of an existing building should be required as part of due diligence. As a general rule, the older the building, the more likely that asbestos-containing materials were used in its construction. There are some consultants who use the year 1979 as the benchmark year, and if the building was constructed before that date, an inspection should be required. However, asbestos-containing materials, such as floor tiles, were commonly used in construction after that date. Many lending institutions require a prefinancing asbestos inspection for every large, existing structure. Perhaps a more economical approach would be to specify the level of detail for an inspection, because an intensely detailed inspection of a high-rise building can be quite costly, and if the building is relatively new, a detailed inspection may not be justified. Also, inspections performed according to AHERA specifications are very expensive because of the number of samples collected for analysis. This issue should be addressed in the institution environmental policy manual. Another issue often faced by a lender occurs when a building is to be demolished and replaced with a new structure. In this instance, an asbestos inspection should be required. If the building contains asbestos, the asbestos may have to be removed before a demolition permit is granted, based on possible human exposure to asbestos fibers during the demolition process. Also, asbestos-containing materials are classified as "special waste" by many solid waste disposal companies, and so landfills may not accept the waste or may require special disposal practices with higher disposal costs.

RADON GAS AND INDOOR CLEAN AIR

Radon Gas

Radon is a naturally occurring gas that exists in the atmosphere. Some of the isotopes of radon gas occur as daughter products in the breakdown of radioactive isotopes of uranium and other radioactive elements. One of these isotopes of radon is 222Rn, which is radioactive; when it decays, an alpha particle is emitted. The emission of the alpha particle creates a health problem, particularly in lung tissue, where critical alpha doses can cause cancer (Cross, Harley, and Hoffman, 1985; Jacobi, 1964). There is, however, considerable debate over the concentrations of radon and alpha particles dosage rates necessary to increase the risk of lung cancer in humans (Cliff, Davies, and Reissland, 1979; Stranden, 1980).

The most hazardous situation involving radon gas occurs within the interior of structures in which the radon concentration becomes high enough to create a human health risk. In order for the concentrations to become high, there must be a source of radioactive radon gas, and the air circulation within the structure must be insufficient to dilute or vent the gas. Areas most likely to have radon gas problems occur where buildings are located atop or adjacent to rock units that contain high concentrations of naturally occurring radon. The U.S. Geological Survey and state geological surveys have mapped many regions of the country to classify the land areas with potential radon problems (see Schumann, 1993). Although structures in areas of high naturally occurring radon gas concentrations are more likely to accumulate radon gas, there is no good correlation between the measured indoor radon gas concentrations and the local geology, because the design of the ventilation system within a structure is the controlling factor for radon gas accumulation. Soil surveys of radon gas concentrations prior to building construction are therefore not recommended because they often are not particularly useful. If a building is to be located in a high-risk area, the design of the ventilation system should include radon gas mitigation measures, as recommended by the U.S. Environmental Protection Agency.

A lender must be aware of the radon gas issue, particularly when financing an existing structure in an area where significant concentrations of radon gas are known to occur. The radon gas issue should be addressed as part of an overall indoor clean air survey. If the lender is the owner and operator of a building, either as part of the business or as a trustee, a radon gas survey of the structure should be included as part of an internal environmental audit procedure to comply with the institution environmental policy (see Chapter 6). Some references that provide additional information on radon gas are Kay, Keller, and Miller (1991), Godish (1989), and Brooks and Davis (1991).

Indoor Clean Air

Indoor clean air has become a significant consideration to the owners and operators of many structures. Liabilities have arisen from lawsuits filed by workers occupying "sick buildings," and airborne disease outbreaks have occurred, such as the Legionnaires' disease outbreak in Philadelphia. Clean indoor air should be considered as part of the due diligence effort prior to financing existing structures or in the operation of institution-owned facilities.

An indoor air quality survey should be triggered by the occurrence of certain structures included in a transaction and should be part of a phase I ESA. The types of structures most prone to problems are old, large buildings with old air-handling systems and limited external ventilation (no windows that open). However, the lender should also be aware that a significant number of rather new, modern buildings have been affected by the "sick building" syndrome. Once an air toxin has entered a building, a significant length of time may be required to remove the problem. One priority area of investigation is the air intake system, especially if it is located in an area containing known sources of air pollution. The air venting system in the structure must be able to remove radon gas, tobacco smoke, and other common air pollutants. Although compliance with indoor clean air guidelines can cause some financial hardship for the building owner, rarely does it cause default on loans to lending institutions. During the loan negotiation process, the lender should question the owner-operator or the purchaser about any monitoring or surveys of indoor air quality prior to closing the transaction. This can be a general checklist item or just a verbal inquiry. Some detailed information on the subject of indoor air quality assessment and management is available in Kay, Keller, and Miller (1991), Godish (1989), and Brooks and Davis (1991).

ELECTROMAGNETIC FIELDS

Over the past two decades, many questions have been raised about adverse effects of human exposure to electromagnetic fields. An electromagnetic field (EMF) is created when the conveyance of electricity creates a magnetic field in the area around it. Although we are always exposed to the earth's magnetic field, the magnetic fields created by the normal alternating current (AC) that passes through electric lines can create magnetic fields orders of magnitude greater in intensity than the earth's magnetic field. The intensity of the magnetic field is related to the intensity of the electric power source and the distance from the electrical conveyance. The most intense sources of magnetic fields that people come in contact with are electric lines and electrical appliances. A major power conveyance system (5 kV or higher electric lines) creates a rather large magnetic field so if people live directly below the lines, they are exposed to some rather intense magnetic fields. However, since the strength of magnetic fields is related both to the intensity of the electric power and the distance from the electricity, contact with a typical kitchen electrical appliance could cause greater human exposure to a magnetic field than that caused by electric lines.

Considerable research is currently being conducted to determine the long-term health effects of exposure to electromagnetic fields. Preliminary results have produced widely conflicting conclusions, ranging from statements that certain levels of exposure can cause cancer (Brodeur, 1989) to statements that there is no direct correlation between health issues and electromagnetic fields. The issue of power lines and public health has become controversial enough to prompt a statement by the Council of the American Physical Society, conveyed on April 22, 1995. The text of this statement is as follows:

> Physicists are frequently asked to comment on the potential dangers of cancer from electromagnetic fields that emanate from common power lines and electrical appliances. While recognizing that the connection between power lines and cancer is an area of continuing study by research workers in many disciplines in the United States and abroad, we believe that it is possible to make several observations based on the scientific evidence at this time. We also believe that, in the interest of making the best use of the finite resources available for environmental research and mitigation, it is important for professional organizations to comment on the issue.
>
> The scientific literature and the reports of reviews by other panels show no consistent, significant link between cancer and power line fields. This literature includes epidemiological studies, research on biological systems, and analyses of theoretical interaction mechanisms. No plausible biophysical mechanisms for the systematic initiation or promotion of cancer by these power line fields have been identified. Furthermore, the preponderance of the epidemiological and

> biophysical/biological research findings have failed to substantiate those studies which have reported specific adverse health effects from exposure to such fields. While it is impossible to prove that no deleterious health effects occur from exposure to any environmental factor, it is necessary to demonstrate a consistent, significant, and causal relationship before one can conclude that such effects do occur. From this standpoint, the conjectures relating cancer to power line fields have not been scientifically substantiated.
>
> These unsubstantiated claims, however, have generated fears of power lines in some communities, leading to expensive mitigation efforts, and, in some cases, to lengthy and divisive court proceedings. The costs of mitigation and litigation relating to the power line–cancer connection have risen to billions of dollars and threaten to go much higher. The diversion of these resources to eliminate a threat which has no persuasive scientific basis is disturbing to us. More serious environmental problems are neglected for lack of funding and public attention, and the burden of cost placed on the American public is incommensurate with the risk, if any.

Based on this statement and the large quantity of conflicting opinions in the literature, there may or may not be any threat to human health by power line fields, but because there is public concern, it affects lending institutions and, therefore, can affect the financial viability of many property transactions. An educated lender may ask a developer of a property to provide an analysis of the potential economic effects of a major power line on the proposed position of dwelling units in a new development. Although this issue is not currently of major concern to most lenders, public perceptions bear monitoring, particularly in regard to how they might affect the economics of a property transaction. The possible loss of property value based on its geographic position near a source of electromagnetic fields is an issue of concern to lenders. A list of articles on electromagnetic fields and possible health effects is provided in the references.

REFERENCES FOR FURTHER READING

Wetlands

Brinson, M. M., A Hydrogeomorphic Classification of Wetlands, Technical Report WRP-DE-4, U.S. Army Corps of Engineers Waterways Experiment Station, Vicksburg, MS, 1993, 79 pp.

Dressler, R., Hall, D., Perkins, K., and Williams, N., Identification Manual for Wetland Plant Species of Florida, IFAS Publication #SP-35, ISBN 0-916287-04-1, 1987.

Ewel, K. C. and Odum, H. T., *Cypress Swamps,* University of Florida Press, Gainesville, FL, 1984, 472 pp.

Lyon, J. G., *Practical Handbook of Wetland Identification and Delineation,* Lewis Publishers, Boca Raton, FL, 1993, 176 pp.

Resource Management Group, Inc., National List of Plant Species That Occur in Wetlands, a field guide, The Author, Grand Haven, MI, 1992.

U.S. Army Corps of Engineers, Wetlands Delineation Manual, Environmental Laboratory, Department of the Army, Waterways Experiment Station, Corps of Engineers, Vicksburg, MS, 1987.

Listed Species

School of Natural Resources and Environment, *Endangered Species Update,* The University of Michigan, Ann Arbor, MI.

Sovereign Lands

Conklin, E. J., Danser, R. K., Jr., Brookes, R., Crowley, K. X., and Lewis, T. E., State sovereign, aquatic preserves, outstanding Florida waters, in Sixth Annual Environmental Permitting Summer School Short Course Text, The Florida Chamber of Commerce, Tallahassee, FL, 1992, 821.

Asbestos

Benarde, M. A., Ed., *Asbestos: The Hazardous Fiber,* Lewis Publishers, Boca Raton, FL, 1989, 504 pp.

Cherry, K. F., *Asbestos: Engineering, Management and Control,* Lewis Publishers, Boca Raton, FL, 1989, 280 pp.

Harris, B., The impact of asbestos on a property's fair market value, in Solid and Hazardous Waste Management Short-Course Text, The Florida Chamber of Commerce, Tallahassee, FL, 1990, 232.

Hess, K., *Environmental Site Assessment: Phase I: A Basic Guide,* Lewis Publishers, Boca Raton, FL, 1993, 287 pp.

U. S. Environmental Protection Agency, Asbestos/NESHAP Regulated Asbestos Containing Materials Guidance, EPA 340/1-90-018, Office of Toxic Substances, The Author, Washington, D.C., 1990.

Radon Gas and Indoor Clean Air

Brooks, B. O. and Davis, W. F., *Understanding Indoor Air Quality,* Lewis Publishers, Boca Raton, FL, 1991, 208 pp.

Cliff, K. D., Davies, B. L., and Reissland, J. A., Little danger from radon, *Nature,* 279, 12, 1979.

Cross, F. T., Harley, N. H., and Hoffman, W., Health effects and risks from ^{222}Rn in drinking water, *Health Phys.,* 48, no. 5, 649, 1985.

Godish, T., *Indoor Air Pollution Control,* Lewis Publishers, Boca Raton, FL, 1989, 416 pp.

Jacobi, W., The dose to the human respiratory tract by inhalation of short-lived ^{222}Rn and ^{220}Rn-decay products, *Health Phys.,* 10, 1163, 1964.

Kay, J. G., Keller, G. E., and Miller, J. F., *Indoor Air Pollution,* Lewis Publishers, Boca Raton, FL, 1991, 264 pp.

Lao, K. Q., *Controlling Indoor Radon,* Van Nostrand Reinhold, New York, 1990.

Schumann, R. R., Ed., Geologic Radon Potential of EPA Region 4, U.S. Geological Survey Open-File Report 93-292-D, 1993.

Stranden, E., Radon in dwellings and lung cancer: a discussion, *Health Phys.*, 38, 301, 1980.

Electromagnetic Fields

Bennett, W. R., Jr., Cancer and power lines, *Phys. Today,* 1994.

Brodeur, P., *Currents of Death, Power Lines, Computer Terminals, and Attempts to Cover Up Their Threat to Your Health,* Simon and Schuster, New York, 1989.

Lee, J., Brunke, J. H., Lee, G. E., Reiner, G. L., and Shon, F. L., Electrical and Biological Effects of Transmission Lines: A Review, Bonneville Power Administration, U.S. Dept. of Energy, Portland, OR, 1989.

Nair, I., Morgan, M. G., and Florig, H. K., Biological Effects of Power Frequency, Electric, and Magnetic Fields — Background Paper, Report OTA-BP-53, Office of Technology Assessment, U.S. Congress, U.S. Government Printing Office, Washington, D.C., 1989.

National Institute of Environmental Health Sciences and U.S. Department of Energy, Questions and Answers About EMF, Electric and Magnetic Fields Associated with the Use of Electrical Power, The Author, January, 1995.

Pinsky, M. A., *The EMF Book, What You Should Know About Electromagnetic Fields, Electromagnetic Radiation, and Your Health,* Warner Books, New York, 1995.

U.S. Environmental Protection Agency, EMF In Your Environment: Magnetic Field Measurements of Everyday Electrical Devices, Rept. No. 402-R-92-008, Office of Radiation and Indoor Air, U.S. Environmental Protection Agency, 1992.

Appendix A SUBSTANCES KNOWN TO OCCUR IN GROUNDWATER*

CONTAMINANT	EXAMPLES OF USES
Aromatic hydrocarbons	
Acetanilide	Intermediate manufacturing, pharmaceuticals, dyestuffs
Alkyl benzene sulfonates	Detergents
Aniline	Dyestuffs, intermediate, photographic chemicals, pharmaceuticals, herbicides, fungicides, petroleum refining, explosives
Anthracene	Dyestuffs, intermediate, semiconductor research
Benzene	Detergents, intermediate, solvents, antiknock gasoline
Benzidine	Dyestuffs, reagent, stiffening agent in rubber compounding
Benzyl alcohol	Solvent, perfumes and flavors, photographic developer inks, dyestuffs, intermediate
Butoxymethylbenzene	NA°
Chrysene	Organic synthesis, coal tar byproduct
Creosote mixture	Wood preservatives, disinfectants
Dibenz[a.h.]anthracene	NA
Di-butyl-*p*-benzoquinone	NA
Dihydrotrimethylquinoline	Rubber antioxidant
4,4-Dinitrosodiphenylamine	NA

* From Fetter, C. W., *Contaminant Hydrology,* Macmillan, New York, 1992. With permission.)

CONTAMINANT	EXAMPLES OF USES
Ethylbenzene	Intermediate, solvent, gasoline
Fluoranthene	Coal tar byproduct
Fluorene	Resinous products, dyestuffs, insecticides, coal tar byproduct
Fluorescein	Dyestuffs
Isopropyl benzene	Solvent, chemical manufacturing
4,4-methylene-*bis*-2-chloroaniline (MOCA)	Curing agent for polyurethanes and epoxy resins
Methylthiobenzothiazole	NA
Naphthalene	Solvent, lubricant, explosives, preservatives, intermediate, fungicide, moth repellant
o-Nitroaniline	Dyestuffs, intermediate, interior paint pigments, chemical manufacturing
Nitrobenzene	Solvent, polishes, chemical manufacturing
4-Nitrophenol	Chemical manufacturing

AROMATIC HYDROCARBONS

n-Nitrosodiphenylamine	Pesticides, retarder of vulcanization of rubber
Phenanthrene	Dyestuffs, explosives, synthesis of drugs, biochemical research
n-Propylbenzene	Dyestuffs, solvent
Pyrene	Biochemical research, coal tar byproduct
Styrene (vinyl benzene)	Plastics, resins, protective coatings, intermediate
Toluene	Adhesive solvent in plastics, solvent, aviation and high-octane blending stock, diluent and thinner, chemicals, explosives, detergents
1,2,4-Trimethylbenzene	Manufacture of dyestuffs, pharmaceutical, chemical manufacturing
Xylenes (*m,o,p*)	Aviation gasoline, protective coatings, solvent, synthesis of organic chemicals, gasoline

CONTAMINANT	EXAMPLES OF USES
OXYGENATED HYDROCARBONS	
Acetic acid	Food additives, plastics, dyestuffs, pharmaceutical, photographic chemicals, insecticides
Acetone	Dyestuffs, solvent, chemical manufacturing, cleaning and drying of precision equipment
Benzophenone	Organic synthesis, odor fixative, flavoring, pharmaceutical
Butyl acetate	Solvent
n-Butyl-benzylphthalate	Plastics, intermediate
Di-*n*-butyl phthalate	Plasticizer, solvent, adhesives, insecticides, safety glass, inks, paper coatings
Diethyl ether	Chemical manufacturing, solvent, analytical chemistry, anesthetic, perfumes
Diethyl phthalate	Plastics, explosives, solvent, insecticides, perfumes
Diisopropyl ether	Solvent, rubber cements, paint and varnish removers
2,4-Dimethyl-3-hexanol	Intermediate, solvent, lubricant
2,4-Dimethyl phenol	Pharmaceutical, plastics, disinfectants, solvent, dyestuffs, insecticides, fungicides, additives to lubricants and gasolines
Di-*n*-octyl phthalate	Plasticizer for polyvinyl chloride and other vinyls
1,4-Dioxane	Solvent, lacquers, paints, varnishes, cleaning and detergent preparations, fumigants, paint and varnish removers, wetting agent, cosmetics
Ethyl acrylate	Polymers, acrylic paints, intermediate
Formic acid	Dyeing and finishing, chemicals, manufacture of fumigants, insecticides, solvents, plastics, refrigerants

CONTAMINANT	EXAMPLES OF USES
Methanol (methyl alcohol)	Chemical manufacturing, solvents, automotive antifreeze, fuels
Methylcyclohexanone	Solvent, lacquers
Methyl ethyl ketone	Solvent, paint removers, cements and adhesives, cleaning fluids, printing, acrylic coatings
Methylphenyl acetamide	NA
Phenols (e.g., *p-tert*-butylphenol)	Resins, solvent, pharmaceutical, reagent, dyestuffs and indicators, germicidal paints
Phthalic acid	Dyestuffs, medicine, perfumes, reagent
2-Propanol	Chemical manufacturing, solvent, deicing agent, pharmaceutical, perfumes, lacquers, dehydrating agent, preservatives
2-Propyl-1-heptanol	Solvent
Tetrahydrofuran	Solvent
Varsol	Paint and varnish thinner

HYDROCARBONS WITH SPECIFIC ELEMENTS (E.G., N, P.S.C., BR, I, F)

Acetyl chloride	Dyestuffs, pharmaceutical, organic preparations
Alachlor (Lasso)	Herbicides
Aldicarb (sulfoxide and sulfone; Temik)	Insecticide, nematocide
Aldrin	Insecticides
Atrazine	Herbicides, plant growth regulator, weed control agent
Benzoyl chloride	Medicine, intermediate
Bromacil	Herbicides
Bromobenzene	Solvent, motor oils, organic synthesis
Bromochloromethane	Fire extinguishers, organic synthesis
Bromodichloromethane	Solvent, fire extinguisher fluid, mineral and salt separations
Bromoform	Solvent, intermediate
Carbofuran	Insecticide, nematocide
Carbon tetrachloride	Degreasers, refrigerants and propellants, fumigants, chemical manufacturing

CONTAMINANT	EXAMPLES OF USES
Chlordane	Insecticides, oil emulsions
Chlorobenzene	Solvent, pesticides, chemical manufacturing
Chloroform	Plastics, fumigants, insecticides, refrigerants, and propellants
Chlorohexane	NA
Chloromethane (methyl chloride)	Refrigerants, medicine, propellants, herbicide, organic synthesis
Chloromethyl sulfide	NA
2-Chloronaphthalene	Oil: plasticizer, solvent for dyestuffs, varnish gums and resins, waxes wax: moisture-, flame-, acid-, and insect-proofing of fibrous materials; moisture- and flame-proofing of electrical cable; solvent (see oil)
Chlorpyrifos	NA
p-Chlorophenyl methylsulfone	Herbicide manufacture
Chlorophenylmethyl sulfide	Herbicide manufacture
Chlorophenylmethyl sulfoxide	Herbicide manufacture
o-Chlorotoluene	Solvent, intermediate
p-Chlorotoluene	Solvent, intermediate
Chlorthal-methyl (DCPA, or Dacthal)	Herbicide
Cyclopentadine	Insecticide manufacture
Dibromochloromethane	Organic synthesis
Dibromochloropropane (DBCP)	Fumigant, nematocide
Dibromodichloroethylene	NA
Dibromoethane (ethylene dibromide, EDB)	Fumigant, nematocide, solvent, waterproofing preparations, organic synthesis
Dibromomethane	Organic synthesis, solvent
Dichlofenthion (DCFT)	Pesticides
o-Dichlorobenzene	Solvent, fumigants, dyestuffs, insecticides, degreasers, polishes, industrial odor control
p-Dichlorobenzene	Insecticides, moth repellant, germicide, space odorant, intermediate, fumigants
Dichlorobenzidine	Intermediate, curing agent for resins
Dichlorocyclooctadiene	Pesticides

CONTAMINANT	EXAMPLES OF USES
Dichlorodiphenyl-dichloroethane (DDD, TDE)	Insecticides
Dichlorodiphenyl-dichloroethylene (DDE)	Degradation product of DDT, found as an impurity in DDT residues
Dichlorodiphenyl-trichloroethane (DDT)	Pesticides
1,1-Dichloroethane	Solvent, fumigants, medicine
1,2-Dichloroethane	Solvent, degreasers, soaps and scouring compounds, organic synthesis, additive in antiknock gasoline, paint and finish removers
1,1-Dichloroethylene (vinylidiene chloride)	Saran* used in screens, upholstery, fabrics, carpets, etc., adhesives, synthetic fibers
1,2-Dichloroethylene (*cis* and *trans*)	Solvent, perfumes, lacquers, thermoplastics, dye extraction, organic synthesis, medicine
Dichloroethyl ether	Solvent, organic synthesis, paints, varnishes, lacquers, finish removers, drycleaning, fumigants
Dichloroiodomethane	NA
Dichloroisopropylether (= *bis*-2-chloroiso-propylether)	Solvent, paint and varnish removers, cleaning solutions
Dichloromethane (methylene chloride)	Solvent, plastics, paint removers, propellants, blowing agent in foams
Dichloropentadiene	NA
2,4-Dichlorophenol	Organic synthesis
2,4-Dichlorophenoxyacetic acid (2,4-D)	Herbicides
1,2-Dichloropropane	Solvent, intermediate, scouring compounds, fumigant, nematocide, additive for antiknock fluids
Dicyclopentadiene (DCPD)	Insecticide manufacture
Dieldrin	Insecticides
Diiodomethane	Organic synthesis
Diisopropylmethyl phosphonate (DIMP)	Nerve gas manufacture
Dimethyl disulfide	NA

CONTAMINANT	EXAMPLES OF USES
Dimethylformamide	Solvent, organic synthesis
2,4-Dinotrophenol (Dinoseb, DNBP)	Herbicides
Dithiane	Mustard gas manufacture
Dioxins (e.g., TCDD)	Impurity in the herbicide 2,4,5-T
Dodecyl mercaptan (lauryl mercaptan)	Manufacture of synthetic rubber and plastics, pharmaceutical, insecticides, fungicides
Endosulfan	Insecticides
Endrin	Insecticides
Ethyl chloride	Chemical manufacturing, anesthetic, solvent, refrigerants, insecticides
Bis-2-ethylhexylphthalate	Plastics
Di-2-ethylexylphthalate	Plasticizers
Fluorobenzene	Insecticide and larvicide intermediate
Fluoroform	Refrigerants, intermediate, blowing agent for foams
Heptachlor	Insecticides
Heptachlorepoxide	Degradation product of heptachlor, also acts as an insecticide
Hexachlorobicycloheptadiene	NA
Hexachlorobutadiene	Solvent, transformer and hydraulic fluid, heat transfer liquid
x-Hexachlorocyclohexane (=Benzenehexachloride, or *x*-BHC)	Insecticides
B-Hexachlorocyclohexane (*B*-BHC)	Insecticides
y-Hexachlorocyclohexane (*y*-BHC, or Lindane)	Insecticides
Hexachlorocyclopentadiene	Intermediate for resins, dyestuffs, pesticides, fungicides, pharmaceutical
Hexachloroethane	Solvent, pyrotechnics and smoke devices, explosives, organic synthesis
Hexachloronorbornadiene	NA
Isodrin	Intermediate compound in manufacture of Endrin
Kepone	Pesticides
Malathion	Insecticides
Methoxychlor	Insecticides

CONTAMINANT	EXAMPLES OF USES
Methyl bromide	Fumigants, pesticides, organic synthesis
Methyl parathion	Insecticides
Oxathine	Mustard gas manufacture
Parathion	Insecticides
Pentachlorophenol (PCP)	Insecticides, fungicides, bactericides, algicides, herbicides, wood preservative
Phorate (Disulfoton)	Insecticides
Polybrominated biphenyls (PBBs)	Flame retardant for plastics, paper, and textiles
Polychlorinated biphenyls (PCBs)	Heat exchange and insulating fluids in closed systems
Prometon	Herbicides
RDX (Cyclonite)	Explosives
Simazine	Herbicides
Tetrachlorobenzene	NA°
Tetrachloroethanes (1,1,1,2 and 1,1,2,2)	Degreasers, paint removers, varnishes, lacquers, photographic film organic synthesis, solvent, insecticides, fumigants, weed killer
Tetrachloroethylene (or perchloroethylene, PCE)	Degreasers, drycleaning, solvent, drying agent, chemical manufacturing, heat transfer medium, vermifuge
Toxaphene	Insecticides
Triazine	Herbicides
1,2,4-Trichlorobenzene	Solvent, dyestuffs, insecticides, lubricants, heat transfer medium (e.g., coolant)
Trichloroethanes (1,1,1 and 1,1,2)	Pesticides, degreasers, solvent
1,1,2-Trichloroethylene (TCE)	Degreasers, paints, drycleaning, dyestuffs, textiles, solvent, refrigerant and heat exchange liquid, fumigant, intermediate, aerospace operations
Tricholorfluoromethane (Freon 11)	Solvent, refrigerants, fire extinguishers, intermediate
2,4,6-Trichlorophenol	Fungicides, herbicides, defoilant
2,4,5-Tricholoro-phenoxyacetic acid (2,4,5-T)	Herbicides, defoilant

CONTAMINANT	EXAMPLES OF USES
2,4,5-Trichlorophenoxy-propionic acid (2,4,5-TP or Silvex)	Herbicides and plant growth regulator
Trichlorotrifluoroethane	Drycleaning, fire extinguishers, refrigerants, intermediate, drying agent
Trinitotoluene (TNT)	Explosives, intermediate in dyestuffs and photographic chemicals
Tris-(2,3-dibromopropyl) phosphate	Flame retardant
Vinyl chloride	Organic synthesis, polyvinyl chloride and copolymers, adhesives

OTHER HYDROCARBONS

Alkyl sulfonates	Detergents
Cyclohexane	Organic synthesis, solvent, oil extraction
1,3,5,7-Cyclooctatetraene	Organic research
Dicyclopentadiene (DCPD)	Intermediate for insecticides, paints and varnishes, flame retardants
2,3-Dimethylhexane	NA
Fuel oil	Fuel, heating
Gasoline	Fuel
Jet fuels	Fuel
Kerosene	Fuel, heating solvent, insecticides
Lignin	Newsprint, ceramic binder, dyestuffs, drilling fuel additive, plastics
Methylene blue activated substances (MBAS)	Dyestuffs, analytical chemistry
Propane	Fuel, solvent, refrigerants, propellants, organic synthesis
Tannin	Chemical manufacturing, tanning, textiles, electroplating, inks, pharmaceutical, photography, paper
4,6,8-Trimethyl-1-nonene	NA
Undecane	Petroleum research, organic synthesis

CONTAMINANT	EXAMPLES OF USES
METALS AND CATIONS	
Aluminum	Alloys, foundry, paints, protective coatings, electrical industry, packaging, building and construction, machinery and equipment
Antimony	Hardening alloys, solders, sheet and pipe, pyrotechnics
Arsenic	Alloys, dyestuffs, medicine, solders, electronic devices, insecticides, rodenticies, herbicide, preservative
Barium	Alloys, lubricant
Beryllium	Structural material in space technology, inertial guidance systems, additive to rocket fuels, moderator and reflector of neutrons in nuclear reactors
Cadmium	Alloys, coatings, batteries, electrical equipment, fire protection systems, paints, fungicides, photography
Calcium	Alloys, fertilizers, reducing agent
Chromium	Alloys, protective coatings, paints, nuclear and high temperature research
Cobalt	Alloys, ceramics, drugs, paints, glass, printing, catalyst, electroplating, lamp filaments
Copper	Alloys, paints, electrical wiring, machinery, construction materials, electroplating, piping, insecticides
Iron	Alloys, machinery, magnets
Lead	Alloys, batteries, gasoline additive, sheet and pipe, paints, radiation shielding
Lithium	Alloys, pharmaceutical, coolant, batteries, solders, propellants
Magnesium	Alloys, batteries, pyrotechnics, precision instruments, optical mirrors
Manganese	Alloys, purifying agent

CONTAMINANT	EXAMPLES OF USES
Mercury	Alloys, electrical apparatus, instruments, fungicides, bactericides, mildew proofing, paper, pharmaceutical
Molybdenum	Alloys, pigments, lubricant
Nickel	Alloys, ceramics, batteries, electroplating, catalyst
Palladium	Alloys, catalyst, jewelry, protective coatings, electrical equipment
Potassium	Alloys, catalyst
Selenium	Alloys, electronics, ceramics, catalyst
Silver	Alloys, photography, chemical manufacturing, mirrors, electronic equipment, jewelry, equipment catalyst, pharmaceutical
Sodium	Chemical manufacturing, catalyst, coolant, nonglare lighting for highways, laboratory reagent
Thallium	Alloys, glass, pesticides, photoelectric applications
Titanium	Alloys, structural materials, abrasives, coatings
Vanadium	Alloys, catalysts, target material for X-rays
Zinc	Alloys, electroplating, electronics, automotive parts, fungicides, roofing, cable wrappings, nutrition

NONMETALS AND ANIONS

Ammonia	Fertilizers, chemical manufacturing, refrigerants, synthetic fibers, fuels, dyestuffs
Boron	Alloys, fibers and filaments, semiconductors, propellants
Chlorides	Chemical manufacturing, water purification, shrink-proofing, flame retardants, food processing

CONTAMINANT	EXAMPLES OF USES
Cyanides	Polymer production (heavy duty tires), coatings, metallurgy, pesticides
Fluorides	Toothpastes and other dentrifices, additive to drinking water
Nitrates	Fertilizers, food preservatives
Nitrites	Fertilizers, food preservatives
Phosphates	Detergents, fertilizers, food additives
Sulfates	Fertilizers, pesticides
Sulfites	Pulp production and processing, food preservatives
MICROORGANISMS	
Bacteria (coliform)	
Giardia	
Viruses	
RADIONUCLIDES	
Cesium 137	Gamma radiation source for certain foods
Chromium 51	Diagnosis of blood volume, blood cell life, cardiac output, etc.
Cobalt 60	Radiation therapy, irradiation, radiographic testing, research
Iodine 131	Medical diagnosis, therapy, leak detection, tracers (to study efficiency of mixing pulp fibers, chemical reactions, and thermal stability of additives to food products), measuring film thicknesses
Iron 59	Medicine, tracer
Lead 210	NA
Phosphorus 32	Tracer, medical treatment, industrial measurements, (e.g., tire tread wear and thickness of films and ink)
Plutonium 238, 243	Energy source, weaponry
Radium 226	Medical treatment, radiography

CONTAMINANT	EXAMPLES OF USES
Radium 228	Naturally occurring
Radon 222	Medicine, leak detection, radiography, flow rate measurement
Ruthenium 106	Catalyst
Scandium 46	Tracer studies, leak detection, semiconductors
Strontium 90	Medicine, industrial applications (e.g., measuring thicknesses, density control)
Thorium 232	Naturally occurring
Tritium	Tracer, luminous instrument dials
Uranium 238	Nuclear reactors
Zinc 65	Industrial tracers (to study wear in alloys, galvanizing, body metabolism, function of oil additives in lubricating oils)
Zirconium 95	NA

Appendix B ENVIRONMENTAL AGREEMENT*

BASIC ITEMS

<u>Item 1.</u> This AGREEMENT, which includes and incorporates by reference the attached GENERAL TERMS, DEFINITIONS ADDENDUM, and ADDENDA checked "yes" below, is made and entered into as of the date and by and between the parties set forth in Item 3. below, with the parties called BORROWER, LENDER and GUARANTOR(S) in this AGREEMENT (check "Yes" or "No" for each set of boxes below):

[__] YES	[__] NO	PROPERTY AND USE ADDENDUM
[__] YES	[__] NO	PRIOR USE ADDENDUM
[__] YES	[__] NO	TANK(S) ADDENDUM
[__] YES	[__] NO	HAZARDOUS SUBSTANCES ADDENDUM
[__] YES	[__] NO	DISCHARGE ADDENDUM
[__] YES	[__] NO	COMPLAINT ADDENDUM
[__] YES	[__] NO	MONITORING LETTER ADDENDUM
[__] YES	[__] NO	PERIODIC COMPLIANCE ADDENDUM
[__] YES	[__] NO	__________ ADDENDUM

<u>Item 2.</u> The parties entered into certain LOAN documents of even date herewith, for a LOAN in the amount set forth below, to be governed by the laws of the State set forth in the LOAN documents.

Principal Amount of LOAN: $____________

BORROWER and GUARANTOR(S), acknowledge that they will realize direct and indirect benefits from the making of the LOAN, and that LENDER would not make the LOAN in the event of HAZARDOUS SUBSTANCES or violations of ENVIRONMENTAL LAWS (both as defined in the DEFINITIONS

* (From Kammert, J. L., Lender liability/environmental contractual provisions in real estate transactions, *in* Enviornmental and Land Use Update, The Florida Bar, 1994. With permission.)

ADDENDUM) relating to the PROPERTY, except as specifically set forth in the ADDENDA hereto.

As a material inducement to LENDER making the LOAN, BORROWER and GUARANTOR(S) have agreed to jointly and severally make certain representations, warranties, covenants and indemnifications as detailed in the GENERAL TERMS and, except as specifically otherwise set forth in Paragraph 13 hereinafter, as a condition to making said LOAN, LENDER requires that the representations, warranties, covenants and indemnifications contained in this AGREEMENT shall survive the full satisfaction of the LOAN as the continuing, absolute and unconditional joint and several obligations of the BORROWER and GUARANTOR(S), as detailed hereinbelow.

BORROWER and GUARANTOR(S) have read this AGREEMENT in full, including all ADDENDA hereto and intend and agree to be legally bound, jointly and severally, by the terms of this AGREEMENT; BORROWER specifically acknowledges full and complete knowledge and understanding of and agreement to the representations, warranties, covenants, indemnifications and agreements in the GENERAL TERMS and the receipt and sufficiency of good and valuable consideration from LENDER relating to this AGREEMENT.

Item 3. IN WITNESS WHEREOF, BORROWER, LENDER and the GUARANTOR(S) have executed this AGREEMENT as of the ___ of ________, 19__.

BORROWER: ______________________________

____

By: ______________________________
Title: ______________________________

LENDER: ______________________________

____

By: ______________________________
Title: ______________________________

GUARANTOR: ______________________________

Print Name:______________________________

GUARANTOR: ______________________________

Print Name:_

GENERAL TERMS

(1) Condition of the PROPERTY. BORROWER has made all due inquiry and investigation into the present condition of the PROPERTY and the previous ownership and uses of the PROPERTY consistent with good commercial or customary practice in an effort to minimize liability with respect to HAZARDOUS SUBSTANCES.

(2) Use of the PROPERTY. The current use of the PROPERTY by BORROWER and BORROWER'S operations relating thereto are as detailed in the PROPERTY AND USE ADDENDUM. Neither BORROWER, nor any other person to the BORROWER'S and GUARANTOR(S)' knowledge, after due inquiry and investigation, has ever used the PROPERTY for the manufacture, processing, distribution, use, transport, handling, storage, treatment or disposal of any HAZARDOUS SUBSTANCES in violation of any ENVIRONMENTAL LAWS, nor has the PROPERTY ever been the subject of a contaminated site cleanup or remediation under any applicable ENVIRONMENTAL LAWS, except as described in the PRIOR USE ADDENDUM, if checked "YES" in the BASIC ITEMS.

(3) Compliance with ENVIRONMENTAL LAWS. The PROPERTY and BORROWER's use and operations relating thereto are and at all times hereafter will continue to be in full compliance with all ENVIRONMENTAL LAWS, except as otherwise specifically set forth in any ADDENDUM hereto.

(4) Storage Tanks. To the best of the BORROWER'S and GUARANTOR(S)' knowledge, after due inquiry and investigation, any aboveground or underground storage tanks on the PROPERTY have been properly registered with the appropriate governmental units and are in full compliance with all applicable STORAGE TANK STANDARDS, or have been properly removed in accordance with applicable laws, and there has never been a discharge, as that term is defined in any ENVIRONMENTAL LAWS of any HAZARDOUS SUBSTANCES from any aboveground or underground storage tanks, except as described in the TANK(S) ADDENDUM, if checked "YES" in the BASIC ITEMS.

(5) Disclosure of Past and Present HAZARDOUS SUBSTANCES; Compliance. To the best of BORROWER'S and GUARANTOR(S)' knowledge, after due inquiry and investigation, except as set forth in the HAZARDOUS SUBSTANCES ADDENDUM hereto, none of the real property owned, operated or occupied by the BORROWER, including, but not limited to the PROPERTY, has ever contained any HAZARDOUS SUBSTANCES, whether used in construction or operations or stored on the PROPERTY. BORROWER has fully disclosed to LENDER in writing in the HAZARDOUS SUBSTANCES ADDENDUM hereto, the existence, extent and nature of any HAZARDOUS SUBSTANCES which BORROWER is legally authorized and empowered to maintain on, in or under the PROPERTY or use in connection therewith, or which BORROWER will

remediate in full, in compliance with any applicable ENVIRONMENTAL LAWS. BORROWER has obtained and will maintain all licenses, permits, and approval required with respect to such HAZARDOUS SUBSTANCES, the remediation thereof, and the activities and operations of BORROWER, and BORROWER is in full compliance with all of the terms, conditions and requirements of such licenses, permits and approvals, except as otherwise specifically set forth.

(6) PROHIBITED DISCHARGES. BORROWER shall not cause or permit to exist, and, except as set forth in the DISCHARGE ADDENDUM, has not received any ENVIRONMENTAL COMPLAINT relating to any PROHIBITED DISCHARGES.

(7) No ENVIRONMENTAL COMPLAINTS or ACTIONS. To the best of BORROWER'S and GUARANTOR(S)' knowledge, there are and have been no ENVIRONMENTAL COMPLAINTS or ACTIONS, except as set forth in the COMPLAINT ADDENDUM, if checked "YES" in the BASIC ITEMS.

(8) ENVIRONMENTAL STUDY OR STUDIES, Periodic Certifications. BORROWER agrees to periodically (but not more frequently than annually unless an alleged violation of ENVIRONMENTAL LAWS or an ENVIRONMENTAL COMPLAINT is then outstanding) provide to LENDER (at BORROWER's expense) an ENVIRONMENTAL STUDY OR STUDIES of environmental matters as deemed necessary by LENDER, prepared by an environmental consultant satisfactory to LENDER and in form and content satisfactory to LENDER, of the PROPERTY, the remediation activities relating thereto, the hazardous waste management practices, activities and operations of BORROWER, and the hazardous waste disposal sites used by BORROWER. Should BORROWER fail to perform such ENVIRONMENTAL STUDY OR STUDIES within 30 days of LENDER'S written request, LENDER shall have the right, but not the obligation, to retain an environmental consultant to perform said ENVIRONMENTAL STUDY OR STUDIES. All costs and expenses incurred by LENDER in the exercise of such rights shall bear interest at the "Default Rate" set forth in the LOAN documents, shall be secured by the LOAN documents, and shall be payable by BORROWER upon demand or charged to BORROWER's LOAN balance at the discretion of LENDER. In addition, BORROWER agrees to provide to LENDER periodic monitoring letters at least every six (6) months during the term of this AGREEMENT, in substantially the form attached hereto as the MONITORING LETTER ADDENDUM, if checked "YES" in the BASIC ITEMS, and periodic certifications of compliance with all environmental matters, in substantially the form attached hereto as the PERIODIC COMPLIANCE ADDENDUM, if checked "YES" in the BASIC ITEMS.

(9) Notice of Change, HAZARDOUS SUBSTANCES or Environmental Problems. BORROWER shall immediately notify LENDER should BORROWER change the nature, extent or use of the PROPERTY or the activities or

operations of BORROWER, or should BORROWER become aware of (i) any HAZARDOUS SUBSTANCES or other environmental problem or LIABILITY with respect to BORROWER'S activities or operations, or the PROPERTY not disclosed herein, (ii) any ENVIRONMENTAL COMPLAINT or ACTION not disclosed herein; or (iii) environmental matters which could impair the value of BORROWER'S property, increase BORROWER'S expense, disrupt the activities or operations of BORROWER, or adversely affect the financial condition of BORROWER. BORROWER shall immediately transmit to LENDER copies of any ENVIRONMENTAL COMPLAINT or ACTION, where applicable. BORROWER shall, at its own cost and expense, take all actions as shall be necessary or advisable for the cleanup of the PROPERTY, including all removal, containment and remedial actions in accordance with all applicable ENVIRONMENTAL LAWS, and shall further pay or cause to be paid at no expense to LENDER all testing, investigation, cleanup, administrative, enforcement, and other costs of applicable governmental agencies or otherwise which may be asserted or assessed against BORROWER or the PROPERTY.

(10) Breach. Any breach of any warranty, representation or agreement contained in this AGREEMENT shall be a default, as that term is defined in the LOAN documents. In the event that any such breach is not cured within ten (10) days after written notice of the breach to BORROWER, or if a cure is not commenced within said ten (10) day period and diligently pursued to completion, LENDER shall be entitled to exercise any and all remedies provided in the LOAN documents, or otherwise permitted by law.

(11) Miscellaneous. Any one or more of the BORROWERS or GUARANTOR(S), or any other party liable upon or in respect of this AGREEMENT or the LOAN documents may be released without affecting the liability of any party not so released. This AGREEMENT may be executed in one or more counterparts, each of which shall be deemed an original. Said counterparts shall constitute but one and the same instrument and shall be binding upon each of the undersigned individually, as fully and completely as if all had signed but one instrument. If any provision of this AGREEMENT shall be contrary to any laws of the jurisdiction in which enforcement of this AGREEMENT is sought, then the illegality or unenforceability of any such provision shall not affect the other terms, covenants and conditions hereof, and the same shall be binding upon BORROWER and GUARANTOR(S) with the same force and effect as though such illegal or unenforceable provision were not contained herein. All of the terms of this AGREEMENT will apply to and be binding upon, and inure to the benefit of the heirs, devisees, personal representatives, successors and permitted assigns of BORROWER, GUARANTOR(S) and LENDER, respectively, and all persons claiming by, through or under them.

(12) Indemnification. BORROWER and GUARANTOR(S) hereby agree to indemnify, reimburse, defend and hold harmless LENDER and LENDER'S offic-

ers, directors, employees, agents, successors and assigns from and against any and all LIABILITIES which may at any time be imposed upon, incurred by or asserted or awarded against LENDER, directly or indirectly, related to or resulting from: (a) any alleged acts or omissions of BORROWER, its officers, directors, employees, agents or contractors, which contaminate air, soils, surface waters or groundwaters or violate any ENVIRONMENTAL LAWS on or about the PROPERTY or at any other site or locale whatsoever; (b) the breach of any representation or warranty under this AGREEMENT; (c) any ENVIRONMENTAL COMPLAINT or ACTION; (d) the application of any ENVIRONMENTAL LAWS to the acts or omissions of BORROWER, its officers, directors, employees, agents or contractors, and any environmental damage alleged to have been caused, in whole or in part, by the existence, manufacture, processing, distribution, use, handling, transportation, treatment, storage, or disposal of any HAZARDOUS SUBSTANCE; or (e) the presence, whether past, present or future, of any HAZARDOUS SUBSTANCES on, in or about the PROPERTY or any other failure to comply with ENVIRONMENTAL LAWS with respect to the PROPERTY or any operations or activities of BORROWER.

Without limiting the foregoing, this indemnification provision specifically protects LENDER against any ACTION from or relating to activities described in (a), (b), (c), (d), or (e) above, based in whole or in part upon any ENVIRONMENTAL LAWS, whether now in existence or enacted in the future.

BORROWER'S and GUARANTOR(S)' indemnification obligation hereunder shall be one of strict liability and shall be enforceable without regard to any fault or knowledge of LENDER with respect to any act, omission, condition or event which is the basis of the claim under such indemnification obligation. Except as set forth in Paragraph 13 hereinafter, BORROWER'S and GUARANTOR(S)' indemnification obligation hereunder shall not be limited to any extent by the term of the LOAN, and shall continue, survive and remain in full force and effect, notwithstanding payment in full or other satisfaction of the LOAN or any termination of this AGREEMENT.

Those LIABILITIES for which LENDER is indemnified under this Paragraph 12 shall be reimbursable to LENDER at LENDER'S option, without any requirement of waiting for the ultimate outcome of any litigation, claim or other proceeding, and BORROWER shall pay such LIABILITIES to LENDER as so incurred within thirty (30) days after notice from LENDER itemizing the amounts incurred to the date of such notice. In addition to any remedy available for failure to pay such amounts, such amounts shall thereafter bear interest at the "Default Rate" as defined in the LOAN documents. BORROWER and GUARANTOR(S) waive any acceptance of this indemnity by LENDER. The failure of LENDER to enforce any right or remedy hereunder, or to promptly enforce any such right or remedy, shall not constitute a waiver thereof, nor give rise to any estoppel against LENDER, nor excuse BORROWER and GUARANTOR(S) from their joint and several obligations hereunder. Any waiver of any such right or remedy must be in writing and signed by LENDER. This indemnity is subject to enforcement at law and/or in equity, including, without limitation, action(s) for damages and/or specific performance.

BORROWER'S and GUARANTOR(S)' obligations under this AGREEMENT are unconditional and shall not be subject to or limited by any nonrecourse or other limitation of liability provisions in the Promissory Note, or any of the other LOAN documents.

(13) Conditions for Releasing Indemnity. Notwithstanding anything herein to the contrary, the indemnity of the BORROWER and/or GUARANTOR(S) hereunder may be released by LENDER, at its sole option, upon payment in full of all amounts due under the LOAN documents, provided: (a) there has been no default or event of default during the term of the LOAN; (b) there have been no violations of any ENVIRONMENTAL LAWS, no ENVIRONMENTAL COMPLAINTS and no adverse developments in the ENVIRONMENTAL LAWS or case law pursuant to which LENDER could be held liable for environmental matters related to the LOAN; (c) if deemed necessary by LENDER, at LENDER'S option, an ENVIRONMENTAL STUDY OR STUDIES acceptable to LENDER have been prepared and provided to LENDER, at BORROWER's expense, ensuring that there are no environmental problems related to the PROPERTY; (d) if deemed necessary by LENDER, at LENDER'S option, an opinion letter relating to environmental matters has been obtained from an attorney acceptable to LENDER, at BORROWER'S expense, in form and content acceptable to LENDER; and (e) LENDER has not held title to the PROPERTY.

DEFINITIONS ADDENDUM

Definitions. The following words, terms and phrases when used in this ENVIRONMENTAL AGREEMENT shall have the following meanings and applications:

(a) "ACTION OR ACTIONS" shall mean any civil, criminal or administrative action, suit, demand, claim, hearing, demand letter, notice of violation, investigation or proceeding of any sort pending or threatened against the BORROWER or any GUARANTOR(S) relating in any way to any ENVIRONMENTAL LAWS or any plan, order, decree, judgement, injunction, notice or demand letter issued, entered, promulgated or approved thereunder.

(b) "ENVIRONMENTAL AUDIT" shall mean and include, without limitation, a systematic, documented and objective review of facility operations, processes and practices to verify compliance with ENVIRONMENTAL LAWS.

(c) "ENVIRONMENTAL COMPLAINT" shall mean and include, without limitation, any notice, summons, citation, order, directive, letter or other communication of any sort to BORROWER, or any of its subsidiaries, from any person, agency, or entity of any sort, of any past, present or future events, conditions, circumstances, activities, practices, incidents, actions or plans in violation of or which might interfere with or present compliance or continued compliance with any ENVIRONMENTAL LAWS or any regulation, code, plan, order, decree, judgement, injunction, notice, demand letter or other communication issued, entered, promulgated or approved thereunder, or which may give rise to any statutory or common law legal liability, or otherwise form the basis of any claim, action, demand, lien, suit, proceeding, hearing, study or investigation, based on or related to the existence, manufacture, processing, distribution, use, treatment, storage, disposal, transport or handling, or the emission, discharge, release or threatened release into the environment or onto the PROPERTY of any HAZARDOUS SUBSTANCES, whether with respect to its activities or operations, facility use or operations, the PROPERTY, or otherwise.

(d) "ENVIRONMENTAL LAWS" shall mean and include, without limitation, any federal, state, or local statutory or common law, ordinance, rule or regulation, whether now in existence or established or enacted in the future, relating to pollution or protection of the environment, including, without limitation, any common law of nuisance or trespass, and any law, rule or regulation relating to emissions, discharges, releases or threatened releases or pollutants, contaminants or chemicals, or industrial, toxic or HAZARDOUS SUBSTANCES or waste into the environment, including, without limitation, ambient air, surface water, groundwater, land surface or subsurface strata, or otherwise relating to the manufacture, processing, distribution, use, treatment, storage, disposal, transport or handling of pollutants, contaminants or chemicals or industrial, toxic of HAZARDOUS SUBSTANCES or wastes. ENVIRONMENTAL LAWS shall specifically include, without limitation, the Comprehensive Environmental Response Compensation and Liability Act of 1980 ("CERCLA"), 42 U.S.C. §9601, et seq., the Superfund Amendments and Reauthorization Act of 1986 ("SARA"), Public Law 99-499, 100 Stat. 1613, the Resource Conservation and Recovery Act ("RCRA"), 42 U.S.C. ˇ6901, et seq., if applicable, and any and all applicable federal, state or local environmental laws, statutes, ordinances, rules and regulations, whether now existing or in the future enacted, promulgated, adopted, entered or issued, both within and outside the present contemplation of BORROWER and LENDER.

(e) "ENVIRONMENTAL STUDY OR STUDIES" shall mean and include, without limitation, environmental audits, systematic, documented, and objective reviews of facility operations, processes and practices to verify compliance with ENVIRONMENTAL LAWS, and evaluations of the effectiveness of environmental management systems already in place and assessments of risks from regulated and unregulated materials.

(f) "HAZARDOUS SUBSTANCES" shall mean and include, without limitation, any substance or material (i) identified in Section 101(14) of CERCLA,

42 U.S.C. §9601(14) and as set forth in Title 40, Code of Federal Regulations, Part 302, as the same may be amended from time to time, or (ii) determined to be toxic, a pollutant or contaminant, under or any applicable federal, state or local statute, law, ordinance, rule, or regulation or judicial or administrative order or decision, as the same may be amended from time to time, including, but not limited to, petroleum and petroleum products as defined in state statutes, as the same may be amended from time to time, or the applicable provisions of the laws of any other state, (iii) asbestos, (iv) radon, (v) polychlorinated biphenyls, and (vi) such other materials, substances or waste which are otherwise dangerous, hazardous, harmful or deleterious to human health or the environment.

(g) "LIABILITY OR LIABILITIES" shall mean and include, without limitation, any and all demands, claims, civil, criminal or other actions or causes of action, liens, assessments, civil, criminal or other judgements, penalties or fines, losses, liabilities, damages, costs, disbursements, expenses, fees or obligations of any kind or nature (including, without limitation, cleanup costs, attorneys', paralegals', consultants' or experts' fees and disbursements and costs of litigation).

(h) "PROHIBITED DISCHARGES" shall mean and include, without limitation, any discharge as the result of an intended or unintended act or omission on BORROWER'S part, relating to a releasing, discharging, spilling, leaking, pumping, emitting, pouring, emptying or dumping of a "HAZARDOUS SUBSTANCE" into waters or onto lands of the State of ____________ or the waters of the United States (or into waters outside the jurisdiction of the State of [Florida]) where damage may result to the lands, waters, fish, shellfish, wildlife, biota, air and other resources owned, managed, held in trust or otherwise controlled by the State of ____________ any other state or the United States, unless said release, spill, leak, etc. is pursuant to and in compliance with the conditions of a permit or other approval issued by the appropriate federal, state or local governmental authorities.

(i) "STORAGE TANK STANDARDS" shall mean and include, without limitation, all applicable federal, state and local standards for stationary tanks, including, without limitation, the standards for stationary tanks contained in the applicable provisions of the laws of any other state, and regulations for underground storage tanks promulgated by the U.S. Environmental Protection Agency in 40 CFR Part 280.

Gentlemen:

In connection with the credit facilities we are extending to you, we have requested certain environmental reports to evidence your compliance with various environmental laws and regulations, or the carrying out of ongoing cleanup projects, as and if applicable.

While we believe these reports which we have requested will suffice for our purposes, we are not environmental experts and do not have the knowledge which you and your consultants have about these matters, especially in relation to your business activities. Accordingly, the requests that we have made should in no way be construed as indicating that compliance with the steps detailed will suffice for your purposes. In fact, we are looking entirely to you to do what is necessary to comply with appropriate laws and regulations and clean up past problems, if applicable, including best management practices.

Should you feel it necessary to modify any of these reports to convey to us the proper scope of the actions you are taking for compliance and/or cleanup, we would expect you to advise us promptly. In short, we are in no way attempting to manage your affairs, but rather wish to be kept informed by you of environmental matters, because unnecessary costs in this area could reduce resources available for your ongoing business and could under some circumstances impact the credit facilities we are making available.

We appreciate this opportunity to extend credit to your firm and your cooperative attitude and willingness to keep us informed concerning environmental matters.

Kindly sign and return to us the enclosed copy of this letter to acknowledge your receipt and acceptance of its contents.

____

Appendix C ENVIRONMENTAL CONSULTING SERVICES AGREEMENT*

PHASE I
BASIC ITEMS

Item 1. This AGREEMENT, which includes and incorporates by reference the attached GENERAL TERMS ADDENDUM, MEDIATION RULES ADDENDUM, and SCOPE OF SERVICES ADDENDUM, as well as any other attached ADDENDA indicated "Yes" as follows, is made and entered into as of the date and by and between the parties set forth in Item 8. below, with the parties called USER and CONSULTANT in this AGREEMENT (check "Yes" or "No" for each set of boxes below):

[__] YES	[__] NO	ASBESTOS ASSESSMENT ADDENDUM
[__] YES	[__] NO	ASBESTOS TESTING ADDENDUM
[__] YES	[__] NO	RATES AND EXPENSES ADDENDUM
[__] YES	[__] NO	LEGAL DESCRIPTION ADDENDUM
[__] YES	[__] NO	CHAIN OF TITLE ADDENDUM
[__] YES	[__] NO	______________________}
[__] YES	[__] NO	______________________}*

* Use space preceding asterisk to describe any additional ADDENDA relating to other requirements, if "Yes".

Item 2. FACILITY Description. (See LEGAL DESCRIPTION ADDENDUM, if checked "Yes" in Item 1. above, and first WHEREAS of GENERAL TERMS ADDENDUM.)

[__] YES	[__] NO	Includes real estate (land or land and improvements)

* From Kammert, J. L., Lender liability/environmental contractual provisions in real estate transactions, *in* Environmental and Land Use Update, The Florida Bar, 1994. With Permissiion

Site/File Name:___________________________
Street Address:___________________________
City:_________________________________
County:_______________________________
State: ______________________________
Contact Person Telephone Number:________________

[__] YES [__] NO Other information attached, briefly described as: ___________________________

Item 3. Title Chain Review Period Other Than 50 Years (See CHAIN OF TITLE ADDENDUM, if checked "Yes" in Item 1. above, and Paragraph 3 of SCOPE OF SERVICES ADDENDUM.)

[__] YES [__] NO If other than 50 years, answer "Yes" and provide years: _________ (if 50 years, answer "No").

[__] N/A If title review already conducted in Phase I Assessment.

Item 4. Asbestos Assessment/Testing (if indicated "Yes")

[__] YES [__] NO Assessment for asbestos (if "Yes", also answer "Yes" for Item 1., ASBESTOS ASSESSMENT ADDENDUM, and attach).

[__] YES [__] NO Testing for asbestos (if "Yes", also answer "Yes" for Item 1., ASBESTOS TESTING ADDENDUM, and attach).

Item 5. Term and CONSULTANT'S Report Due Date. (See Paragraph 10 of SCOPE OF SERVICES ADDENDUM.)

CONSULTANT'S Report is due no later than:____________________
(month) (day) (year)

CONSULTANT'S services hereunder shall commence on __________ and shall be completed no later than the CONSULTANT'S Report due date set forth above, subject to force majeure or other uncontrollable circumstances not caused by CONSULTANT. Time is of the essence of this AGREEMENT.

Item 6. CONSULTANT'S Compensation (answer "Yes" for only one box)

[__] YES [__] NO Total fee of $___________, for work set forth in the GENERAL TERMS ADDENDUM, SCOPE OF SERVICES ADDENDUM, and other ADDENDA per Item 1. hereof, as applicable and attached, which total fee shall include, without limitation, all labor, materials, equipment, transportation and other costs, expenses, facilities, services or items of any sort necessary to perform the work under this Agreement.

[__] YES [__] NO Compensation for Time and Expenses not to exceed $________________, for or set forth in the GENERAL TERMS ADDENDUM, SCOPE OF SERVICES ADDENDUM, and other ADDENDA per Item 1. hereof, as applicable and attached, at rates set forth in the RATES AND EXPENSES ADDENDUM attached, if applicable (if applicable, also answer "Yes" in Item 1. above for RATES AND EXPENSES ADDENDUM, and attach).

[__]YES [__] NO Compensation as detailed in the additional ADDENDUM indicated in Item 1.

Item 7. Notice Provision Addresses *

USER: ________________________________

____

____

with a copy to:

____

____

CONSULTANT: ________________________________

____

____

with a copy to:

____

____

*See Article 12, Section 12.1 of GENERAL TERMS ADDENDUM

Item 8. Date, Parties and Signatures

The date of this AGREEMENT is as of:____________________
(month) (day) (year)

USER:
By: ________________________________
Title:________________________________
CONSULTANT:
By: ________________________________
Title:________________________________

GENERAL TERMS ADDENDUM
WITNESSETH THAT:

WHEREAS, USER requires the assistance of an expert environmental consultant concerning assessment of environmental conditions at the address set forth or otherwise described in Item 2. of the BASIC ITEMS and the LEGAL DESCRIPTION ADDENDUM, if applicable and attached, including, without limitation, any improvements and/or operations thereon (the land, improvements and operations collectively or separately, as applicable, herein called the "FACILITY");

WHEREAS, CONSULTANT is an expert environmental consultant and desires to render such assistance to USER;

WHEREAS, CONSULTANT represents that it is a qualified, professional, independent contractor and is willing and able to perform such work and incidental services upon the terms and conditions hereinafter set forth; and

WHEREAS, USER desires to engage CONSULTANT to perform the necessary environmental consulting work in accordance with the terms and conditions hereinafter set forth.

NOW THEREFORE, in consideration of these premises and other good and valuable consideration, the receipt and sufficiency of which are hereby acknowledged, the parties hereto hereby covenant and agree as follows:

ARTICLE 1. Engagement; Scope of Services

1.1 USER hereby engages and contracts with CONSULTANT to have CONSULTANT provide certain specified services as set forth in this AGREEMENT, and CONSULTANT accepts such engagement as an independent contractor, subject to and in accordance with the terms, provisions, conditions and limitations of this AGREEMENT.

1.2 USER shall undertake to obtain the necessary permission for CONSULTANT to enter the FACILITY for the performance of the work hereunder, and to provide the LEGAL DESCRIPTION ADDENDUM and CHAIN OF TITLE ADDENDUM relating to the FACILITY, unless otherwise set forth in the BASIC ITEMS.

1.3 CONSULTANT shall provide and direct the necessary qualified personnel to perform the work required of and from it pursuant to the express and implied terms of this AGREEMENT, specifically including, without limitation, the SCOPE OF SERVICES ADDENDUM.

ARTICLE 2. CONSULTANT'S Responsibilities

2.1 CONSULTANT shall perform all obligations, duties, requirements and responsibilities required for the successful and timely completion of the work in accordance with the terms of this AGREEMENT.

2.2 CONSULTANT shall give all notices and perform all work in compliance with the provisions of all applicable federal, state and local laws, rules, ordinances and regulations, including, without limitation, occupational safety and environmental protection statutes and regulations, and with any directive or order issued by any governmental agency relating to the FACILITY and affecting any of the work to be performed by CONSULTANT hereunder. CONSULTANT shall take all reasonable and commercially standard safety precautions and shall provide all reasonable protection against damage, injury or loss of any sort relating to or resulting from the work.

2.3 CONSULTANT shall perform the work or cause the work to be performed to the reasonable satisfaction of USER in accordance with the degree of care, skill, and judgement normally exercised by recognized members and experts of the environmental consulting profession performing services of a similar nature under similar conditions.

2.4 CONSULTANT may employ subcontractors to perform certain services customarily performed by subcontractors as provided in Article 4. CONSULTANT shall furnish to USER in writing the names of the subcontractors which CONSULTANT desires to engage for any portion of the work and shall not employ any subcontractor to which USER expresses a reasonable objection.

2.5 CONSULTANT assumes all responsibility for and risk in connection with the work, unless due to the negligence of USER. CONSULTANT shall be responsible for the acts and omissions of all of its employees and agents, all subcontractors, their agents and employees, and all persons performing any of the work on CONSULTANT'S behalf. CONSULTANT shall at all times be solely responsible for the safety of its own employees, agents, subcontractors, their employees and agents.

2.6 CONSULTANT shall keep accurate and detailed records and books of account as reasonably necessary to document all charges, fees, disbursements or expenses made or incurred by CONSULTANT in the performance of the work and documenting the accuracy of all testing, sampling, drilling and other services performed by CONSULTANT and its agents and subcontractors. USER shall at all times have the right, but not the obligation, to inspect the progress, quality and results of the work.

2.7 CONSULTANT, if specifically and reasonably requested in writing, shall provide USER with written reports in a manner directed by USER, describing work progress, status of cost data, and other matters pertaining to the services rendered, at no additional cost to USER, in addition to the report required under Item 5. of the BASIC ITEMS.

2.8 CONSULTANT will appoint an experienced and competent Project Manager who will represent CONSULTANT during the performance of the work. The Project Manager shall be familiar with and supervise all phases of the work. CONSULTANT'S Project Manager shall keep USER informed about the progress of the work and shall be CONSULTANT'S primary communication link with USER.

ARTICLE 3. Compensation

So long as CONSULTANT is discharging its obligations hereunder to USER'S reasonable satisfaction, CONSULTANT shall be paid as provided in Item 6. of the BASIC ITEMS or an attached ADDENDUM, as applicable. Payments shall be due and payable on the last business day of the calendar month which follows the month of receipt by USER of the CONSULTANT'S Report and an invoice for services rendered.

ARTICLE 4. Subcontracting

When and if CONSULTANT hires or retains any person, firm or corporation to perform services under this AGREEMENT, CONSULTANT shall assure that such subcontractors have adequate insurance appropriate for their type of work, have all necessary licenses and permits, and agree to be bound by the provisions of Section 2.2 and Articles 5, 6, 7, 9, 10, 12, 14 and 15 of this AGREEMENT and Article 8 as appropriate for the type of work performed. Nothing contained in this AGREEMENT shall create any contractual relationship between USER and any subcontractor.

ARTICLE 5. Independent Contractor

CONSULTANT is and shall perform its services under this AGREEMENT as an independent contractor and shall not be deemed to be an agent, employee or legal representative of USER. CONSULTANT has no authority to assume or create any commitment or obligation on behalf of or to bind USER in any respect whatsoever, without its prior written consent.

ARTICLE 6. Licenses and Permits

CONSULTANT shall obtain and keep in effect during the term hereof, at its expense, any and all licenses and permits required by federal, state or local laws, statutes, regulations or ordinances necessary for the performance of its services pursuant to this AGREEMENT, provided, however, that USER shall not hereby be relieved of or from any duties it may otherwise have by law.

ARTICLE 7. Indemnity

7.1 Subject to the provisions contained in this Article 7, CONSULTANT shall indemnify and hold harmless USER from and against losses, damages, costs and expenses, including, without limitation, attorneys' fees, claims, demands and causes of action (hereinafter collectively called the "DAMAGES") arising out of or relating to this AGREEMENT or the service performed hereunder, including, without limitation, DAMAGES on account of injury to or death of persons (including, but not limited to, employees of CONSULTANT or USER), or loss of or damage to property (including, but not limited to, the FACILITY or any property of CONSULTANT or USER), to the extent caused by or resulting in any manner from any negligent, intentional or bad faith acts or omissions of CONSULTANT or any of CONSULTANT'S subcontractors, agents or employees, in performing or failing to perform any of the services or duties on the part of CONSULTANT to be performed under this AGREEMENT.

7.2 CONSULTANT'S indemnify and hold harmless obligations undertaken pursuant to this AGREEMENT shall specifically exclude: (a) that portion of such obligations which could require CONSULTANT to indemnify or hold harmless USER, its agents or employees, for their own negligence or for matters occurring as the result of USER's failure to provide CONSULTANT with the information or documents required by this AGREEMENT, or providing CONSULTANT with incorrect information, including without limitation, the wrong legal description or chain of title relating to the FACILITY; and (b) any obligations resulting from claims against USER based upon pre-existing pollution, toxic substances, asbestos or hazardous wastes at the FACILITY and not in any manner relating to or resulting from CONSULTANT'S negligent, intentional or bad faith acts or omissions with respect to the FACILITY, the remediation thereof, or CONSULTANT'S obligations or performance under this AGREEMENT.

7.3 Any issues, disputes, claims or controversies arising under this Article, or relating to the liability of CONSULTANT for any DAMAGES shall be subject to and settled in accordance with the provisions of Article 14 hereof. Although this AGREEMENT contains no specific limitation on DAMAGES, the parties agree that in negotiating with each other, or in the event of any mediation or arbitration to settle disputes under this Agreement, and in determining the amount of any settlement or award of DAMAGES relating hereto, the parties shall, and mediator or arbitrator is hereby instructed by the parties to consider and take into account the role of CONSULTANT as the provider of services under this AGREEMENT and the benefits to CONSULTANT resulting therefrom, in relation to the value of the FACILITY and its potential benefit to USER, specifically including consideration of the following:

a. that the scope and duration of CONSULTANT'S services may be limited, with correspondingly modest fees or other benefits, including profits, for dealing with a broad range of technical and related subject matters, relative to the USER'S anticipated benefits from the Property, especially relating to the value of the FACILITY to USER; and

b. a reasonable balance between the risks undertaken and the benefits received under this AGREEMENT.

ARTICLE 8. Insurance

CONSULTANT shall obtain and maintain the following policies of insurance:

(1) Workman's compensation and employer's liability, including occupational disease insurance, with an insurance carrier authorized by and operating under the laws of the State of ____________, with the limit of employer's liability insurance not less than ____________ Dollars and no/100 ($______).

(2) Comprehensive general liability or commercial general liability insurance for bodily injury, death or loss of or damage to property of third persons, including coverage for liability assumed by CONSULTANT under this AGREEMENT, in a minimum amount of ____________ Dollars and no/100 ($__________) per occurrence and annual aggregate.

(3) Errors and omissions liability insurance covering professional liability assumed by CONSULTANT under this AGREEMENT, with a combined single limit and annual aggregate of not less than ____________ Dollars and no/100 ($_________), which insurance required may be a "claims made" type policy and shall be continued for a minimum period of one (1) year after all of CONSULTANT'S responsibilities have been executed.

(4) All policies required in (2) above to be carried by CONSULTANT as listed in this Article shall name USER as an additional insured and provide USER with a minimum of thirty (30) days notice of policy cancellation, non-renewal or any major change within the coverage.

ARTICLE 9. Confidentiality

9.1 CONSULTANT, its employees, agents, officers and directors shall treat as confidential and proprietary and not disclose to others during or subsequent to the term of this AGREEMENT, except as is necessary to perform under this

AGREEMENT and with prior notice to and consent by USER, any information, whether verbal or written, of any description whatsoever (including, without limitation, any technical information, study, finding, result, report, document, material, experience or data) regarding USER'S of the FACILITY'S plans, programs, plants property, processes, products, costs, equipment, operations or the work which may come within the knowledge of CONSULTANT, its officers or its employees in the performance of this AGREEMENT, without in each instance securing the prior written consent of USER.

9.2 CONSULTANT shall maintain as confidential and not disclose to others, including, without limitation, individuals, corporations, governmental agencies, or other entities, either before or after the termination of this AGREEMENT, any data, documents, materials, studies, findings, results, reports, experiences, or other information of any sort provided to USER or any employees, agents or consultants of USER, or any data, documents, materials, studies, findings, results, reports, experiences or other information of any sort learned, developed, obtained, prepared or produced by CONSULTANT during its performance hereunder, except as expressly authorized in writing by USER.

9.3 CONSULTANT'S obligation of confidentiality shall not apply to disclosures compelled by law, any order or subpoena of a court of competent jurisdiction, matters of eminent danger to the public health, safety or welfare, or disclosures required to establish a sound defense on behalf of CONSULTANT in a legal dispute or proceeding between USER and CONSULTANT or in a criminal or civil proceeding against CONSULTANT based upon conduct in which CONSULTANT was involved pursuant to this AGREEMENT, in which event(s), CONSULTANT shall promptly notify USER of the circumstances requiring such a disclosure.

9.4 Nothing in this Article shall preclude CONSULTANT from using USER'S name or the projects performed for USER in CONSULTANT'S promotional materials, provided that CONSULTANT has obtained prior written permission from USER'S officer for environmental policy matters at [ ].

<u>ARTICLE 10.</u> Assignment

Neither this AGREEMENT nor any of the rights or obligations hereunder may be assigned or otherwise transferred by CONSULTANT, nor shall the benefits of this AGREEMENT inure to the benefit of any trustee in bankruptcy, receiver or creditor of CONSULTANT, whether by operation of law or otherwise, without the prior written consent of USER. Any attempt to assign or transfer this AGREEMENT or any rights hereunder without such consent shall be null and void and of no force and effect.

<u>ARTICLE 11.</u> Termination

USER may terminate this AGREEMENT without cause upon seven (7) days written notice to CONSULTANT. CONSULTANT shall, upon such early termination by USER, be entitled to all compensation payable to CONSULTANT hereunder up to the date of termination of such work.

ARTICLE 12. General Provisions

12.1 Notice. Any notice, communication or statement required or permitted to be given hereunder shall be in writing and deemed to have been sufficiently given when delivered in person or when sent by registered or certified mail, postage prepaid, return receipt requested, to the address of the respective party as provided in Item 7. of the BASIC ITEMS.

12.2 Definition of AGREEMENT; Entire Agreement. When used herein, the term "AGREEMENT" shall mean and include the BASIC ITEMS, this GENERAL TERMS ADDENDUM, the MEDIATION RULES ADDENDUM, the SCOPE OF SERVICES ADDENDUM, and any other ADDENDA or amendments executed by the parties hereto in connection herewith. The documents which are part of this AGREEMENT are complementary, and any item, provision, or condition in any one shall be as binding as set forth in all. This AGREEMENT represents the entire understanding and agreement between the parties hereto and supersedes any and all prior agreements, whether written or oral, that may exist between the parties regarding the subject matter of this AGREEMENT.

12.3 No Waiver. Any waiver by either party of any provision or condition of this AGREEMENT shall not be construed or deemed to be a waiver of any other provision or condition of this AGREEMENT, nor a waiver of a subsequent breach of the same provision or condition, unless such waiver be so expressed in writing and signed by the party to be bound.

12.4 Governing Law. Except as otherwise specifically set forth herein, the validity, performance and construction of this AGREEMENT shall be governed by and interpreted in accordance with the laws of the State of ____________.

12.5 Severability. If any provision of this AGREEMENT, or the application thereof to any person or circumstance, shall to any extent be invalid, the remainder of this AGREEMENT and the application of such provision to persons or circumstances other than those as to which it is held invalid, shall not be affected thereby, and each provision of this AGREEMENT, shall be valid and enforced to the fullest extent permitted by law.

ARTICLE 13. Successors and Assigns

The covenants and agreements contained in this AGREEMENT shall apply to, inure to the benefit of and be binding upon the parties hereto, and their respective successors and permitted assigns, if any. This AGREEMENT, and the rights, obligations and duties of the parties hereunder may not be assigned without the prior written consent of the other party hereto.

ARTICLE 14. Dispute Settlement

14.1 The parties agree that all disputes, claims, or controversies of any sort arising under, out of, in connection with, or in relationship to this AGREEMENT, including any amendment, or any breach of this AGREEMENT, shall, upon written notice by one party to the other party of such dispute given in accordance with the terms of this AGREEMENT and any applicable law, first be submitted to non-binding voluntary mediation in accordance with the MEDIATION RULES AND PROCEDURES ADDENDUM hereto. In the event that the parties do not reach an agreement with respect to the dispute as a result of mediation within sixty (60) days from the notice of dispute given as set forth above, the matter shall be submitted to and settled by binding arbitration in _______________. The arbitration shall be before one (1) disinterested arbitrator, if the parties can agree upon one; otherwise, it shall be before three (3) disinterested arbitrators, with one arbitrator appointed by each party and a third arbitrator appointed by the two other arbitrators, provided, however, that at least one of the three arbitrators, who shall serve as the chief arbitrator, shall meet the qualifications described in the appropriate state statute, as amended from time to time. In the event of any failure of any party to make an appointment within ten (10) days after written request by the other party to do so, the two (2) remaining arbitrators shall be appointed by the one (1) arbitrator already appointed.

14.2 The parties have chosen mediation and arbitration as a means of alternative dispute resolution and in the interest of providing a more efficient, cost-effective option to court litigation, and as part of this effort, when selecting any mediator or arbitrator, the parties will consider members of the Environmental and Land Use Law Section of the ____________ Bar for these roles.

14.3 The laws of the State of ____________ shall apply to and govern this AGREEMENT, its interpretation and performance with regard to commercial, technical and scientific matters. However, the parties and the mediator or arbitrator(s) are encouraged to use laws, regulations, and similar materials from other states or the federal government of the United States of America, or even foreign nations and their governmental subdivisions, for dealing with commercial, scientific or technical matters when this would help resolve disputes, especially where technical standards and scientific matters are not developed under the laws of the State of ____________. With regard to process, mediation shall be conducted in accordance with the rules and procedures set forth in the MEDIATION RULES AND PROCEDURES ADDENDUM and any laws, statutes, rules, or regulations of the State of ____________ applicable to mediation; arbitration shall be conducted in accordance with the appropriate state statutes, as amended from time to time, and the then current rules of the American Arbitration Association, to the extent that such provisions are not in conflict with or superseded by the provisions of the above-referenced statutes.

14.4 The award of the arbitrator(s) shall be final and binding upon each of the parties. Judgement upon the award rendered may be entered in accordance with applicable law, in any court having jurisdiction thereof. The parties agree that the provisions herein for mediation and arbitration shall be the sole and exclusive options of the parties for the resolution of disputes hereunder, and the parties expressly waive any right to court litigation, provided that no constitutional issue is involved. The parties further agree that voluntary non-binding mediation hereunder shall be a condition precedent to the initiation of arbitration proceedings in accordance with the provisions hereof. Notice of any matter to be mediated hereunder shall be given within the applicable statute of limitations for that matter, and the giving of said notice shall toll the running of said statute of limitations.

ARTICLE 15. Attorney's Fees and Costs

In the event of arbitration as described in Article 14 to resolve a dispute under this AGREEMENT, the prevailing party shall be entitled to all costs and expenses, including, without limitation, reasonable attorneys' fees, incurred in such proceedings, unless the parties agree otherwise, or unless the arbitrator(s) decide(s) otherwise.

SCOPE OF SERVICES ADDENDUM AND INSTRUCTIONS FOR PHASE I ESAS

1. Lender requires, unless otherwise specifically indicated in writing, that all Phase I Environmental Site Assessments, abbreviated as Phase I ESAs or Phase Is, whether performed for the Consultant's clients, which will be using the Phase I results, to satisfy USER'S business requirements (for loans or trust relationships, for example) or performed directly for User use (for example, for User's own facilities or for problem loans) follow the ASTM Designation E 1527 Standard Practice for Environmental Site Assessments: Phase I Environmental Site Assessment Process (ASTM Practice E 1527), as modified by these instructions.

2. User feels that Consultants on User's prequalified list should be able to use professional judgement case-by-case with regard to some items on the ASTM Phase I Practice and that generally the law does not require someone to do a useless thing. Therefore, when Consultant reasonably believes in an area of professional judgement and expertise that some ASTM item is unnecessary, typically based on satisfactorily resolving the item by work or results from steps taken to accomplish other ASTM items, then Consultant need not perform the item, provided Consultant (1) follows the ASTM outline in the written report and explains by the title of that item why (briefly in a sentence or two) Consultant did not

perform the item and (2) indicates in the conclusion that Consultant did not follow the item. See sample conclusion wording in item 3. below.

3. Consultant must follow ASTM Practice E 1527 as modified by this letter, and must also state in the written report that they did so. Accordingly, as provided in sections 11.6.1, 11.6.2 and 11.7 of ASTM Practice E 1527, reports of Phase Is shall conclude as follows:

   A. "We have performed a Phase I Environmental Site Assessment in compliance with the scope and instructions of ASTM Practice E 1527 of (insert address or legal description), the property. Any exceptions to, or deletions from, this practice are described in Section ( ) of this report. This assessment has revealed no evidence of recognized environmental conditions in connection with the property."

   or

   B. "We have performed a Phase I Environmental Site Assessment in conformance with the scope and limitations of ASTM Practice E 1527 of (insert address or legal description), the property. Any exceptions to, or deletions from, this practice are described in Section ( ) of this report. This assessment revealed no evidence of recognized environmental conditions in connection with the property except for the following: (list)."

4. Matters outside the scope of ASTM Practice E 1527, including but not limited to:

   Permits, including, for example, air emission permits, sewage and pollutant discharge permits, water consumptive use permits, well-field permits, stormwater permits, asbestos containing materials, radon, lead-based paint, lead in drinking water, and sovereign/submerged lands issues, and wetlands, including, for example, the need for dredge and fill permits, shall not be included in the body of the report, but shall be included as appendices to the report (one appendix for each of any of the above topics), as Consultant determined such matters to be present or potentially present.

5. If Consultant believes from work or other experience, that any of these issues may be present and adversely impact the property or a facility at the site, or if Consultant has other recommendations for further environmental investigations, then Consultant shall put recommendations on these matters in a separate letter to Consultant's primary client and User. User may then decide that further work outside the scope of the original Phase I is required in connection with such recommendations.

INDEX

D

E

F

G

P

Q

R

S

T

U

W